DAVID O. MCKAY LIBRARY

3 1404 00876 3994

JUN 10 2001

D0769085

CO-OPPORTUNITY

This book has been manufactured using materials and processes that cause as little environmental impact as possible for a product of this kind. It is printed in vegetable ink on acid-free paper, responsibly manufactured from sustainable forestry in which at least two trees are planted for each one used for paper production.

Printed and bound in Great Britain by TJ International Ltd, Padstow, Cornwall, an ISO14001 Environmental Management System accredited company; winner of the 2008 British Book Design & Production Awards Environmental category for its production of *The Green Marketing Manifesto* by John Grant.

FSC
Mixed Sources
Product group from well-managed
forests and other controlled sources
Cert no. SGS-COC-2482
www.fsc.org
© 1996 Forest Stewardship Council

CO-OPPORTUNITY

JOIN UP FOR A SUSTAINABLE, RESILIENT, PROSPEROUS WORLD

JOHN GRANT

A John Wiley & Sons, Ltd., Publication

This edition first published in 2010
Copyright © 2010 John Wiley & Sons Ltd

Registered office
John Wiley & Sons Ltd, The Atrium, Southern Gate, Chichester, West Sussex, PO19 8SQ, United Kingdom

For details of our global editorial offices, for customer services and for information about how to apply for permission to reuse the copyright material in this book please see our website at www.wiley.com

The right of the author to be identified as the author of this work has been asserted in accordance with the Copyright, Designs and Patents Act 1988.

All rights reserved. No part of this publication may be reproduced, stored in a retrieval system, or transmitted, in any form or by any means, electronic, mechanical, photo-copying, recording or otherwise, except as permitted by the UK Copyright, Designs and Patents Act 1988, without the prior permission of the publisher.

Wiley also publishes its books in a variety of electronic formats. Some content that appears in print may not be available in electronic books.

Designations used by companies to distinguish their products are often claimed as trademarks. All brand names and product names used in this book are trade names, service marks, trademarks or registered trademarks of their respective owners. The publisher is not associated with any product or vendor mentioned in this book. This publication is designed to provide accurate and authoritative information in regard to the subject matter covered. It is sold on the understanding that the publisher is not engaged in rendering professional services. If professional advice or other expert assist-ance is required, the services of a competent professional should be sought.

A catalogue record for this book is available from the British Library.

ISBN 978-0-470-68436-8

Typeset in 11/15.5pt Sabon by Toppan Best-set Premedia Limited
Printed in Great Britain by TJ International Ltd, Padstow, Cornwall, UK

For Cosmo, Yong and the rest of the living world

CONTENTS

PART 4: ECONOMIC RESILIENCE 191

PART 5: ABUNDANCE 251

FOREWORD

JOHN GRANT IS YOUR ARCHETYPAL GLASS-HALF-FULL MAN. Not in some spuriously cornucopian way, ignoring the reality of environmental limits and cruelly persistent injustice across the planet, but because that's just the way he is. Genetically predisposed to the upside.

Which makes for a pretty positive read, despite all the latest data on the science of accelerating climate change, and the shrivelling dysfunctionality of contemporary political and economic orthodoxies. Each chapter abounds with specific examples and case studies of people and organisations out there adding to today's extraordinarily innovative solutions agenda.

John lives and breathes the world of Web 2.0. I have to be honest about this: I don't. So my untutored mind has been constantly boggled by its introduction to Twitter trends, Tweehive and Trashon, Joycotting, Crowdfunding and Pledge-Banking, BoGos and Whuffie Banks, Generativity and Us-tainability!

(John is no fan of the geeky language of sustainability; for him, Us-tainability better captures the notion of more and more people getting better and better at co-operating for the common good. Activism 2.0)

If the name of the game is indeed 'relocating our dreams' (as per David Puttnam's challenge to the marketing profession),

especially for young people, then the seeds for that process are
scattered throughout the pages of this text. John showcases that
world with a lot of verve and empathy, drawing people in to
his own excitement at what it means to work through 'a village-
scale democracy operating at the global level'.

Framing it that way is really important. Democracy is primarily about citizens rather than consumers. There's currently
a big buzz around mobilising people as consumers rather than
people as citizens. Same people, of course, but swayed by different motivations. At a time when most progressive company
strategies are geared (understandably) to people as consumers,
and most of the government's (and even some NGOs') engagement strategies are also geared to people as consumers rather
than people as citizens, it's really good to see that orthodoxy
challenged.

Take the issue of lighting and super-efficient LEDs – as John
does on page 172. The faster we move from incandescent light
bulbs to compact fluorescents to LEDs, at scale, in every possible area of the built environment, the bigger the win from a
CO_2 point of view. (And I mean big!) But LEDs cost an arm
and a leg, relative to the price of compact fluorescents, let alone
incandescents. So pitching it from a consumer's perspective
(LEDs may be expensive, but you'll get a good return on your
investment in terms of the substantial reduction in your energy
bills over time) is painfully laborious. Why not look at it instead
as a civic responsibility, without a 'business case' as such. You
know this is the right thing to do, so do it.

John's route into all the stuff here about economics is from
the bottom up, via the innovation of small companies,
social enterprises, co-operatives, community initiatives and
so on. A positive pluriverse of value-creating organisations.
And that's such a refreshing perspective. Just check out the

splendidly provocative comparison between the central precepts of Adam Smith and the analysis of the craft guilds in Chapter 14.

If there is indeed a 'better world in the making', it will emerge in large part from this kind of ideas laboratory, where the cost of failure is relatively low, and where it matters more to change what people do, letting their thoughts and attitudes catch up with their actions. No better way to counter today's ubiquitous bystander apathy.

There is a generosity of spirit about all this which is highly stimulating – especially at a time of such prevailing doom and gloom. Those who favour the school of eco-asceticism, characterised by hairshirts, horror stories and self-denial won't get much joy out of this particular text. No spurious cornucopianism, as I said, but a paean of praise for the whole idea of abundance, with ingenuity and the genius of the human spirit substituting for today's suicidal abundance of material flows and cretinous consumption.

And in that respect, beneath all the exuberant bubbles, the campaigning message is clear: do whatever it is you can do today, not tomorrow. Be part of a movement based on 'the division of brilliance', whilst there's still time, rather than waiting around to pick up your very own division of misery.

Jonathon Porritt
November 2009

Jonathon Porritt is Founder Director of Forum for the Future and author of *Living Within Our Means*, 2009 – available at www.forumforthefuture.org.uk.

INTRODUCTION

THERE IS AN OLD CHINESE PROVERB: 'One monk will shoulder two buckets of water, two monks will share the load, but add a third and no one will want to fetch water.'[1] A 1980 animated short film called *Three Monks, No Water* by A. Da spun this out into a story; one with a more hopeful resolution.

At the start of the film we see a young monk living alone in a temple. A sprig in a vase placed before the statue of Buddha is wilting. He goes to the water jar and finds it empty. So he takes the two heavy buckets on their pole down to the lake, fills them and staggers back up the steep hill with the water. He puts water in the vase, the sprig revives and the statue smiles. We then see him fetching water every day and concentrating on his meditation.

A mouse arrives at the temple. The young monk shoos him away.

A second monk arrives. He is thirsty and drinks all the remaining water. The first monk gives him the water pole and buckets. Obligingly the second monk goes to fetch the water. But after several trips he becomes resentful of the first monk being so carefree. As a compromise they both carry the water together. This means each of them carrying one end of the pole, with only one bucket carried in the middle. At first they struggle with this arrangement, but then the young monk measures the pole and marks a spot exactly half way. Hanging the bucket there makes it easier to carry at least.

A third monk arrives. He looks like a big round fish. And he certainly drinks like a fish. After he drinks all the water the other two monks send him down the hill to fetch more. But when he gets back he is so thirsty he drinks nearly all of it again. The three monks fight over the remaining water. And after that there is a sulky impasse. No one monk will go and get water. They even resort to drinking the water from the vase by the statue, which looks sad.

A lightning storm comes and they all rush out with the water buckets. But no rain falls.

The mouse is running around the temple, while the three monks sulk with their backs to each other. The mouse nibbles through a candle. It falls by a curtain and a fire breaks out. Now we see the monks running to get water and working together. With a great effort they manage to put out the fire.

The film ends showing the temple fixed after the fire, and the three monks working together to fetch water. One fills a bucket by the lake. One pulls this straight up the side of a cliff to the top, using a long rope and pulley. The third takes the water from the top and fills the water jar.

This story touches on many themes in this book. Like the monks at the second stage of this story, our production systems have indeed been based on self-interest and precise measurement. And yet when you add up the good that they do, they are often less effective. We ship fruit and vegetables half way around the world, making them stale and tasteless compared to what we can grow in our own back yard. As Nobel economist Amartya Sen discovered and numerous subsequent studies have confirmed, small traditional farms are more productive (of food, as opposed to profit) than big industrial farms. 'Three monks, no water' also rings true. 'What about China?' people say in response to climate change. 'What's the point of our little country making an effort to reduce emissions, if theirs keep growing?'

But as with running out of water, there is no ignoring these problems. Sooner or later we will recognise that climate change, food, energy, biodiversity, poverty ... represent a crisis that is a threat to everyone. And then we will have to work together; not only to deal with the crisis; but also to redesign society around more co-operative systems, to serve the common good.

Many of the challenges we face today require co-operation. As Games Theory points out, competition and co-operation are not simple opposites. Rather competition focuses on the immediate needs of individual participants, while co-operation focuses upon global or group needs – i.e. the common good. That may of course end up being better for the individuals too. But pursuing their own selfish interests will never get people to that realisation. It's the difference between an 'everyone for themselves' stampede for exits and an orderly fire drill-style evacuation. The second is more likely to get everyone out alive. Yet it paradoxically requires a suspension of pushing your own interests. Something that only happens when each participant is thinking about – and taking some responsibility for – the bigger picture.

The Co-opportunity title of this book refers to the possibility that being forced to co-operate may lead to a better human society; one which is 'nicer' (fairer and more inclusive) and capable of greater progress in politics, knowledge, communities and so on. Many phases of human progress were driven forward by climate. It's likely that our ancestors left Africa and spread across the world 55 000 years ago, partly in response to climate change.

Climate change is only one of a number of crises – all of which have to do with running out of world and running out of time. Climate change is one of the most immediate large-scale threats to human life though. At the very least climate change could make some densely populated parts of the world uninhabitable, resulting in unimaginable levels of dislocation and conflict. 600 million live at or near sea level and will be at some risk of flooding. That's over 70 times more than the global refugee population today. And so governments have tried to get our individualised societies behind solutions; either through a 'leave it to us' overhaul of energy and other infrastructure ('carry on driving and flying while we switch to biofuels'); or through encouraging individuals to fall into line with new social norms, positive (hybrid cars as the choice of Hollywood stars) and negative (supermarket plastic bags being antisocial – a bit like litter); or through simple changes in pricing and incentives (green taxes or carbon pricing).

If the changes we needed to make were small then working within current systems and prevailing individualist attitudes would be the right choice. They aren't though. The changes we need to make are huge. For instance, according to Nicholas Stern[2] the global average household carbon footprint needs to fall by 60% to 2 tonnes per year – whereas today the average footprint per household is 6 tonnes in China, 12 in Europe, 25 in America.

The good news on climate change, poverty, energy, food, water, social justice, biodiversity … is that solutions to all are possible. There are no physical limits caused by the size or basic needs of the human population, whose numbers are large in mammal terms, miniscule in ant terms. We have plentiful new energy from the sun every day and more than enough water, food, minerals and materials to go around and – used wisely – to last indefinitely. The difference is that we are tearing up and trashing our environment, whereas ants perform numerous regenerative services for their ecosystems; globally ants process more earth than earthworms.

The 'catch' is that to solve these issues we need to shift the way that society is organised. We are like the addict who 'only has to give up' to restore a healthy, connected and fulfilling life. We need a different kind of economy, different kinds of government, business and community. In each case we need to find a configuration whereby resources are used for the maximum common good, and the net effect on ecosystems is positive. In each case this means moving towards greater co-operation.

It's easy to see the sort of shift that would be needed. Making the shift is another matter – there is fierce resistance to change built into the current economic, political and social systems. No individual or pressure group could hope to change these. Fortunately all these current systems are still subordinate to the general will. There is no organisation in the free world that can stand against its citizens, shareholders, employees, viewers or customers. Hence there is openness to radical change, if everyone wishes it. That would have seemed an impossibility a few decades back. Nowadays the internet has started to function as a lightning rod for joined up social change. Even before the use of information networks, we saw political systems like Apartheid and Soviet communism brought down, corporate policies changed, social movements started by word of mouth. It's far from a foregone conclusion though. In times of social stress, central powers can retreat into using force to 'keep order' and hence thwart change. It's up to all of us. Given recent history there are at least some grounds for hope.

For these new velvet revolutions to bring mass change, we would need a general public who were engaged in and restlessly pursuing change – pushing business, governments and communities to go faster and further. Nothing could be further from the truth today. The general public does not yet perceive there to be much real risk. For the examples in this book to coalesce and create critical mass, we need the public to wake up and smell the planet burning. And we need to move to a public consciousness that it is not 'China' or 'America' which will solve these issues, it is *all of us*. The true impact of examples in the book may not be in their specific causes and effects, but their general role in waking up a new generation to an active, participative role and worldview. Once people are in the debate, they will likely at least come to similar conclusions to world leaders about how much urgently needs to be done – as Obama says 'make me do this'.

The shift from competition to co-operation is not as some have portrayed it (the better to resist it) a shift from capitalism to communism. Both those twentieth century ideologies were hierarchical, centralised and massively damaging from an eco-systems perspective. The shift is to a system of parallel co-operation, where most of the real action happens at a local community level.

Co-operation not only works, it also undoes resistance. I was talking to an architect the other day, who used to work in Arup's San Francisco practice. They had a city project to redevelop an old military base. If you ask people what they want in redeveloping a city area they come up with an impossible list. If you involve them in the planning process then they will compromise and come up with a good mix of balanced solutions. In this case Arup gave locals a map with a 100-square grid on it, representing the 100 acres for development. They had coloured squares they could place on the map representing different uses. At first there was a tendency to focus on green squares – leisure and community uses only. But then they would discover that these wouldn't create many local jobs. So they started including some more red squares – commercial uses. And so on. It sounds like a great project. Even more so given that the norm at that time in many cities would have been to build gleaming dockside residential properties and simply displace the locals.

A good co-operative system preserves individual initiative, within a shared goal. We can see the same patterns of co-operation in social media. The big gain in my view is not an average 'wisdom of crowds' it's the distribution of individual brilliance – millions of newspaper editors and columnists (bloggers) digesting and disseminating their take on the news. The breadth of talent and mutual quality control that such open source systems call upon outstrips anything within the corporate model. The decrying of the 'cult of the amateur' misses a vital point. It's the cult that is smart, just as it always had been in systems like academia. It's not that such systems exclude mediocrity – rather they filter it. And the participants learn more from writing their own version of the news than they ever did when the elite few covered it. The result is a more flexible, progressive and intelligent global information system.

This book is an attempt to outline what co-operative solutions to sustainability challenges could look like. There have already been some big shifts in this direction; either driven by desperation and lack of alternatives (like microcredit, banking for the world's poor) or through the new opportunities afforded by media to take part in politics and society as an active contributor, rather than passive consumer (as in Web 2.0). It's hopefully more than just a commentary; this book is also intended as a sourcebook for social innovators; whether in policy, innovation, business or community. By absorbing examples from disparate fields you can go further in your own schemes. It's not a matter of 'copying'. It's about being closer to 'the adjacent possible'. And also feeling confirmed – despite being told your plans are 'unrealistic' by those defending existing habits of thoughts – by the fact that others are pursuing similar ideas and ideals.

While change could hardly be radical enough to keep pace with the challenges, this book also tends to the view that the greatest change will come from evolving the systems we have, rather than starting again – whether in a 'back to nature' or 'techno-futurist' sense. The future is not to be found in eco villages, nor in new build carbon neutral cities. It will be found in adapting the way we live in London, Mumbai, Sao Paulo. It won't be neat, utopian, or perfect either. It will be what we humans do best: muddling through.

There was a moment in late 2008, after the Credit Crunch truly crunched, when anything seemed possible. The systems came crashing down. So did the old certainties. The arrogant elites started making humble, almost apologetic, noises. Everyone seemed open to new ideas. The theme for the World Economic Forum meeting at Davos that year was 'building a post crisis world'. Although many attending commented that they could actually see no end to that crisis. Some thought it could be the end for Western capitalism.

In sustainability circles at that time, it became common for people to say (in their introduction at a workshop or similar public event):

I see my work now as building the new world.

Not bringing down the old world, patching it up, reforming it, arguing over where it went wrong, untangling the unholy mess of nation state politics, unaccountable transnational corporations, free market economics, market failures, perverse subsidies, media myopia ...

... rather building a new world, based on fundamentally different organizing principles. The first principle being mass co-operation for the common good.

Sadly during 2009 some of that sense of possibility seemed to close over again, at least for now. The stock markets bounced back. Corporate results were not as bad as expected. Forecasters are predicting a return to growth next year. Time will tell. More cautious economists still point to similar 'false starts' early in the 1930s Great Depression. Meanwhile we – the new world builders – have mixed feelings about a resumption of economic growth and business as usual. It seems a chance for radical change might have been lost. But maybe we weren't ready either.

A key word for many who have this mindset is transition.

There are many different stories about what the transition involves: from climate change to restoring a natural balance: from oil addiction to renewables: from the wealth gap to global equity: from economic growth to steady state: from lean and mean to resilient: from global to relocalised. We'll meet all of these shifts in the pages that follow. As well as the view (from the Transition Town movement) that we can't know what the end point is; our job is to get into the transition stage itself. Only when we have started to leave behind some of the current systems, and their accompanying mental habits, can we start to design new ones that actually work.

> If a factory is torn down but the rationality which produced it is left standing, then that rationality will simply produce another factory. If a revolution destroys the government, and the systematic patterns of thought that produced that government left intact, then those patterns will repeat themselves ... There's so much talk about the system. And so little understanding.
>
> > *Robert Pirsig, Zen and the Art of*
> > *Motorcycle Maintenance (1974)*

Systems tend to replicate themselves through their tenacious hold on what people think 'normal'. However systems are also the result of simple rules and conventions. When you tinker with these rules the ballooning change that results can create a kind of runaway train. It's not what people would have expected, but they do tend to get on board. That was the case with Luther's 22 propositions (originally intended as sensible reforms within the Catholic Church). It was also the case with the mainly economic liberalisation (*perestroika*) introduced by Gorbachev in 1986. Frustrated by the bureaucratic old guard, Gorbachev appealed over their heads to the people in 1987. And a process of change was set in motion by 1989 that culminated in the fall of the Berlin Wall. Several decades on we're also only just starting to appreciate how true it could be that 'the internet changes everything'.

All of which is to say that small adjustments going on right now, within government targets, corporate regulation, public disclosure of information ... may have untold consequences – it could become another runaway train. Although for this to happen it does have to follow Gorbachev's *demokratizatsiya* and appeal directly to the people too.

Why is a great transition needed? If it were only climate change we had to solve we might 'fix it' without moving to a different model of society? I know quite a number in the clean-tech camp who think exactly that. They see this as an engineering problem and point to plenty of viable engineering solutions.

Unfortunately the evidence (historically) says that we can't 'fix it' by converting to cleaner energy and efficient technologies alone. Studies such as Tim Jackson's *Prosperity Without Growth?* for the Sustainable Development Commission found – counter to what is claimed for 'green growth' – that we have failed in 'angelising' our economy. However, cleantech is only one solution. Combine this with programmes aiming to promote the natural absorption of atmospheric carbon, like soil sequestration. Add radical moves to halt the decline in forest cover. Add equally radical moves to limit fossil fuel use, probably through carbon pricing and taxation. Then maybe we do have the existing solutions to tackle climate change. Although these radical solutions would require huge economic, political and social changes.

If only we could find a breakthrough 'technofix'. I had some meetings last year with a group who are convinced that the world's oceans can be stimulated to absorb 25–35% of all atmospheric carbon. They would do this by seeding the oceans south of Argentina with iron. This would cause the algae to bloom. The algae then sink to the bottom of the ocean taking the carbon with them, destined to become limestone. It's happened a number of times in the geological record; when unusual quantities of iron rich dust have apparently led to substantial global temperature falls. And the process has been shown to work in smaller scale tests over the last 20 years. The problem they faced was in convincing regulators that this wasn't what some environmentalists labelled 'toxic dumping'. The idea of tinkering with nature (like Dr Frankenstein) evokes cultural horror; coupled with reasonable concerns about unintended consequences. Another block was that the team's plan was to do this financed by carbon credits – i.e. for profit. Assume those resistances were overcome. What would happen if it worked? Would that buy us the time to transition to a safer economy? Or would we just breathe a sigh of relief and put our foot down on the energy guzzling global economy? If we did so we would run straight back up against climate change.

I liken all of this to the human problem of having a close friend with a gambling habit. Should you solve their debt problem by giving them a fully loaded credit card? Or is the only real solution to tackle the actual habit? The answer to that dilemma would probably change if your friend's gambling debts were about to get them killed by the mafia. There is a view within climate science that we may be so perilously close to triggering runaway climate change – a chain reaction of positive feedback mechanisms – that we probably should consider anything that could pull us back from that brink.

Even so, from a human social point of view no one 'fix' can work. We are running out of planet and running out of time. Looming next on the horizon after climate is energy. We are running out of affordable oil. Something we also depend upon for our food supply in its current form. If we fix the energy crisis and the climate crisis and the food crisis ... there are many others queuing. Most people in the world already live with the insecurity and constraints of poverty. In the food crisis of 2008 the UN reported that the number of households who could only afford one meal a day (rather than three) doubled. Our monoculture food system is prone to collapse. Human populations are vulnerable to pandemics. We are losing species, mainly through deforestation, at a rate equivalent to a mass extinction. Biodiversity is vital to how adaptable ecosystems are, so this is not just a 'save the panda' issue. It's yet another example of systems brittleness. Our economies seem set to self-destruct. If they do not grow at an accelerating (compound) rate they crash. This used to be a local matter. Even in the 1990s in the Asian financial crisis China acted as a firebreak, being uncoupled from the world economy at that point. Now everything is connected.

This is not to retreat into doom and gloom. It's simply to say transition is inevitable. Something has to give. The current systems cannot hold. That's why those that are convinced of the transition view think that more change could happen in the next 20 years than was experienced over the last 200.

My tentative view on the impending transition itself is as follows.

Firstly it will be a *new* world. Not a collapse into any old agenda, be it 'back to nature' eco villages, nor science fiction futurism in its latest 'cleantech' guise. Both of these are likely to be components of a world we don't yet know. Even the familiar ingredients will find an unfamiliar configuration. We can't predict where it will all land, we can only set out and see.

Secondly it could be quite *sudden*, as previously isolated and unconnected developments join up into a bigger whole. That's just how big change in complex systems happens. It's called a phase transition. It's how a gas liquefies. It's how evolution seems to work ('punctuated equilibria'). It's also how human innovation seems to be patterned. Big change is sudden change, a kind of buckling or tipping point. Sometimes precipitated by an event, like a financial market meltdown. But 'caused' by many mutually reinforcing factors. All the types of mammal (phyla) present today were already evolved 20 million years before the collapse of the dinosaurs. It took a meteor impact to trigger the actual transition. But it was already on the cards. Similarly it may take a singular crisis to shake up the current system. Yet this will not be the 'cause' of the change, rather just a trigger for change.

Thirdly I see the transition as involving a shift from hierarchies to what Bill Drayton (founder of Ashoka) calls *parallel co-operation*:

> Since the agriculture revolution, our society has been organized through hierarchy. The new paradigm would be more equitable, organized through parallel cooperation.[3]

I'm something of a veteran of parallel co-operative systems. I feel at home with them, in the same way that I feel out of sorts with dominant hierarchies. I attended a school organised on these self-managing lines in the 1970s. I was a co-founder of St Luke's in the 1990s – a radical experiment in workplace democracy, employee shareholding and other such themes. Many of the projects and organisations I work with today have this 'shape'.

When you recognise this pattern you start to see it everywhere. In social movements like Transition Towns. In the design of public events like BarCamp. In NGO campaigning like 'Green My Apple' from Greenpeace. In political processes like MyObama.com. In the reorganisation of companies and their dealings with networks of suppliers, customers or other partners (as in open innovation). In media, particularly Web 2.0 and the developments in peer-to-peer, social production, social networks and so on. The distributed network for parallel co-operation seems to be the organising idea of our age. And while this is partly due to the phenomenal influence of the internet, it is also present in a broader range of examples. It's possible to see the internet itself as a prominent product of a mindset that has been taking hold for at least half a century. Many of these ideas hark back to the counter-culture of the 1960s, to postcolonial developments in India and elsewhere, to long-standing theories about the direction of social change such as McLuhan's Global Village or Toffler's Prosumer.

It is clear that we are still at the early stages of this transition; it is far from reaching critical mass yet. Although there is a lot already happening and it is starting to gather pace. A 'joined up' picture is slowly emerging too and this book is an attempted contribution to that.

Drayton describes 'parallel co-operation' as an alternative to the hierarchy. It is self-organising, consensual, self-regulating. I agree with all that. What I don't necessarily agree with is the idea that society has been (only) hierarchical since the invention of farming. I am more inclined to agree with historian Lewis Mumford who viewed human history as a struggle between two key ideas about organisation. One Mumford called the mega-machine – society itself operating like a machine, with any human individuals as only an interchangeable 'moving part'. That pattern is familiar since the industrial revolution, never more so than in the mechanised world wars. It was also the worldview that gave rise to the Egyptian pyramids, to the Roman Empire, to the Medieval Church. The other view Mumford called the village democracy. Exemplified by the village council of elders, by the co-operation at harvest time, by systems of gifting, barter and mutual support. This Mumford pointed out is probably the older structure, perhaps typifying matriarchal hunter-gatherer tribes. It has been dominant at other points – in Athenian or Icelandic assembly democracy.

The problem village democracy always had was scale. It works well with hundreds or even thousands of people. Not so well with millions. The significant new development today – with patterns of collaboration and information-sharing (like those enabled by the internet) – is the emergence of a multicellular format. One where we can have both village-style democracy and scale. Mumford's view, writing in the 1970s, was that the village democracy form was in danger of extinction. Recent decades have seen its resurgence, in Web 2.0 and the open source movement and also in social ventures (such as microcredit) and social change movements.

Except in the hands of Yuri Geller, metal does not buckle without considerable stress. For sudden and complete change – a phase transition – you need not only a more adaptive structure to 'collapse' into, nor only triggering events. You also need an unbearable pressure building in the old system. Not to be gloomy. This book is about solutions not problems; specifically about parallel co-operative systems as an answer to key questions being posed by sustainability. Questions the current systems cannot answer.

Hence the book is structured around five of the key sustainability challenges. That's the only way to understand human systems, I'd argue, not just as abstract configurations, but as having a meaning. Under enough pressure a gas cannot but become a liquid. Yet physicists speak of the molecules having a 'memory' of how to achieve this. A reminder that human phase shifts are not just mechanical patterns, they are also about consciousness.

I have found it clarifying to ask: if co-operation is the answer, what are the key questions? In self-regulating systems (where there are no central 'commands') one way to express challenges is as bottlenecks. Co-operative solutions are about opening these out to broader collaboration. The structure of this book is based around five key bottlenecks; topics that come up repeatedly in many of the discussions on sustainability:

Creating a climate for change. The bottleneck is that representative democracy said 'leave it to us' (a few politicians) and now all of us need to be involved. Centralised information campaigns won't on their own create a 'climate for change'. We need to create forums where people can take it all in, reflect on it and come up with their own plans, trade offs and ideas. And we also need ways for people to see each other responding as if there actually is a crisis, so they can take their cue from that. You could read this section to get ideas about new forms of social organisation and campaigning, beyond passive media audiences.

Relocating the dreams. The bottleneck is a narrow definition of the good life. We have come to think of this as individual consumer lifestyle choice-based. By opening out this definition and exploring the many alternatives we can start to create a widely shared dream of a better future; one that is more elegant, wise and enjoyable. People are yearning to reconnect with community and nature. People are curious, playful, restless. There are so many other things they could do than own stuff; so many other services companies could offer to meet their needs too. You could read this section to get ideas about creating desire for brands, campaigns, movements that heal the world.

Making organisations accountable (and hence responsible for wellbeing). The bottleneck is a narrow pass (bristling with banditry) between buyers and sellers. Two billion farmers grow our food, and all we know of what is really involved is glimpses. Even these glimpses (such as documentaries about chicken farming) can transform markets. The opportunity is to make fully known what happens at the other end of the supply chain. And for consumers to encourage improvement through 'joy-cotting'. You could read this section and get ideas about new kinds of eco-label, social change campaigns or consumer co-operatives to create change through what they buy.

Economic resilience. The bottleneck is the current free market model whereby speculative investment benefiting narrow interests, rather than common wellbeing, drives the economy. This demands GDP growth at all costs; climate change, poverty and other effects could be seen as 'manufactured' by this arrangement. It is also narrow in who it benefits, who has access. The alternative is co-operative economic systems – like microcredit, co-operative societies, community choice aggregation and local economic trading schemes. These work for the common good although viable in economic terms too. You could read this section and come up with ideas for anything from restoring trust in banking, to a community scheme to support renewable energy.

Abundance rather than 'lean and mean'. The bottleneck is a narrow definition of productivity as a mechanical return on investment or ROI. By shifting to WROR (wellbeing return on resources) different systems designs emerge, which are abundant (for the common good). WROR sounds like business school jargon gone mad, but it is also the fundamental principle of healthy living ecosystems. Not only are abundant systems more productive of wellbeing, they also restore human participation. We'll see the same pattern applying to regenerative agriculture and also Web 2.0 and social production. You could read this section and come up with new ways of organising for service or supply systems – or equally use it to think differently about the design of the organisations themselves.

Each section of the book divides into three: (1) exploring the issue; (2) looking in detail at a couple of major case examples that have achieved critical mass; (3) taking in a wider variety of tactics – intended as a pick and mix of examples readers could re-apply to their own projects.

There is one further implication of regarding the solution to climate change (and other 'running out of world' issues) as mass co-operation. It means we can't wait for government, big business, or any top-down solution. Large organisations may still play a key role, not least in opening up to participative forms of organisation. But it is up to all of us to build solutions. As Bill Drayton puts it: 'Everyone a change-maker'.

Opportunities to be a change-maker – and to recruit others to follow suit – have never been as accessible. For instance, it takes minutes to add a new idea at http://www.pledgebank. com. Whatever the external result (how many people join you, what you achieve together) it's about being a citizen who can and does come up with solutions. And the question of what one person can do to make a difference has become an open one. Consider the case of Dave Carroll's broken guitar. Dave had no luck in his complaints to United Airlines about this, so he made a humorous song and YouTube video of his complaint. Four million views and some extensive media coverage later, United's share price fell by $180 m.[4] And Dave got his guitar fixed. It's not about sustainability, but it's encouraging as a 'Dave and Goliath' example!

I think of the challenge as partly about redefining 'work'. Many social production phenomena (open source software, Wikipedia) are put together in a serious, methodical, skilled way by unpaid amateurs. Within paid work we have seen a progression from 'job for life' to people who tend to have a range of roles and projects. Charles Handy called this portfolio working, and like an investment portfolio it is partly to do with speculating about what will take off. That frees you up to try bolder or more off-beam stuff – pet ideas, collaborations. At a sustainability innovators dinner I went to recently, most people had three to seven projects on the go, in some cases including a 'fulltime' job. It's about seeing beyond a current job to 'your life's work'. Tamara Giltsoff, one of the founders of Abundancy Partners (our new consultancy), calls this the 'slash-slash' trend. Slash-slash as in 'I'm a designer/blogger/social venture founder/...' Tamara wrote to me, in response to an early draft, about her experiences with the green ventures scene in New York: 'They don't wait around for policy or the market to enforce decision-making, instead they are a community of their own, shunning the traditional route to riches – MBAs and consulting/city jobs – and instead funneling their energy into creating a new socially led economy. Together.' There does seem to be a new generation emerging. The Ecologist magazine called this the most politically and socially aware generation of students since the 1960s.

The idea of being a world builder is a commitment to getting on with it. Not protesting (although that has its place). Nor sitting in committees trying to persuade people that aren't interested in change. But simply making stuff happen. Trying things. Starting small if necessary and working around existing systems. Creating real change that could cascade or otherwise catch on.

Andy Gibson, an award winning social entrepreneur as one of the founders of School of Everything, has in his spare time developed an idea called Mind Apples. 'What would be your 5 a day for mental health?' was Andy's core initial question. He started by asking around (I first heard about it in the kitchen at Social Innovation Camp). Then Andy started getting people including me to use a little quiz widget and stuck their replies on his blog http://mindapples.org. Now the idea is sprouting. It's no longer just Andy, it's a team of collaborators. One of their ideas is Mindapple Zones – 'by tagging places in cities and offices places that make you feel more mentally healthy, like a park, a great view, or a really relaxing cupboard'. They also got some famous '5 a day' respondents to take part; including Alistair Campbell, Tony Blair's spin-doctor, who had written a book about his own struggles with mental illness called *All in the Mind*. The Mind Apple team spread their idea through a blog meme – inviting five bloggers to share their five a day, and then invite five other blog friends to do the same. It's a really simple idea. I think what's really impressive is that they just went out and did it. One reason that's possible is that we have public tools to share ideas through; you no longer need £5 m in funding. Even if you want to build your own unique website it's much more affordable – costing thousands, not millions.

There's also been quite a shift in tactics from protesting to co-operative change from within. A generation had bought the wristband, waved the placard, signed the petition ... and what lasting change did it bring? Greenpeace faced with trying to get Apple to improve its environmental record could have led a boycott. Instead the 'Green My Apple' campaign worked with the community and creativity of Apple fans. And it was effective. Apple adopted significant changes in manufacturing and are now far from the bottom of Greenpeace's survey of the electronics industry, where they once sat.

Those creative campaigns are catchy and involving. They seem a far cry from what people imagine when they hear the word 'Sustainability'. It hardly sounds inviting, playful or exciting. You could argue that it's more of an issue than the name though. 'Sustainability' is policy committee jargon (like the word 'Subsidiarity'). And you could argue that committees, think tanks and corporate departments are precisely where it has got stuck. That it has failed to cross over into mainstream consciousness.

Sustainability ought to be the most popular idea around. I've argued we should perhaps rename it 'Ustainability' – as it requires all of us co-operating for the common good. The original definition of sustainability that most refer to is from the UN's Brundtland Report Commission report *Our Common Future* (1983):

> Sustainable development ... meets the needs of the present without compromising the ability of future generations to meet their own needs. It contains within it two key concepts: the concept of 'needs', in particular the essential needs of the world's poor, to which overriding priority should be given; and the idea of limitations imposed by the state of technology and social organization on the environment's ability to meet present and future needs.[5]

This goes back to the idea that our societies are supposed to be based upon; the government of society for common wellbeing (The Common Weal). You'll find that idea in the American Constitution, in the classic historical texts behind both the English Restoration (Hobbes) and the French Revolution (Thomas Paine). According to all modern accounts of liberal democracy, society should be organised to support the common wellbeing. The enthusiasm for modernism was based in the well-intentioned belief that the technologies and machine-like forms of human efficiency would improve wellbeing. But as Prince Charles pointed out in his recent Dimbleby Lecture, at some point we lost sight of this and came to confuse means and ends, seeing GDP growth in particular as an end in its own right. As we explore the effects of climate change, degradation of natural resources, barely functioning communities, brittle financial markets ... we realise that our systems not only fall short on wellbeing, but positively work against it. That means that we can't just deal with the symptoms, we must tackle our systems and the worldview that sustains them. France, following the Stiglitz Report, has recently joined the growing number of countries committed to finding better measures than GDP for national wellbeing and prosperity.

Mohammed Yunus, founder of the Grameen bank (pioneers of microcredit) says that in focusing on self-interest our economics is too one-dimensional. 'It is the failure to capture the essence of a human being in our theory. Everyday human beings are not one dimensional, they are excitingly multi-dimensional and indeed very colourful.'[6] Grameen is featured in a later section on co-operation and economics; we will see that it is both economically viable at a large scale and also abundantly supporting the wellbeing of its customers, who are also its owners. Yunus is an economist, and far from creating a charity, Grameen hasn't needed external funds since the early 1980s. To create a bank which also provides interest-free, zero collateral, no time limit loans to their very poorest customers – and even gives them free life insurance – is to put human wellbeing in charge of banking (and not as is usually the case, the other way around). Grameen is the kind of bank that the people would have invented. And substantially it is the way it is because its customers are also its owners, and played a big role in shaping it.

The global challenges to wellbeing (like climate change) are so extreme that even those who quite liked the current system, because it did suit their interests, are being forced to take notice. As senior corporate executives on the recent Tomorrow's Global

Company enquiry team noted[7] it's no good carrying on with business as usual when there may actually be no markets in 20 years' time. A point spelled out in detail by the Stern Review of the Economics of Climate Change, which offered a stark choice between spending 1–2% of GDP now, or losing up to 20% of global GDP later.[8]

I've framed the sustainability challenges as bottlenecks to be opened. For individual human actors each of these 'openings' also represents an expansion of thinking and action. That's not to say everyone needs to become saintly, or nice. Responsibility carries the sense of an attitude of being answerable for (as in response). It also carries a definite sense of the scope. A responsible parent is someone who takes this position relative to their children. A responsible community member takes this position relative to their neighbourhood. In a Brazilian MST farming settlement, each adult has two jobs – one is their farm and the other is a specific role (a 'tarefa') in the community. It's a reminder of what citizenship means.

Many of the difficulties we face are a result of a narrowing of responsibilities – of demanding results without oversight and involvement. We buy a product without considering its broader effects. That's because our scope is limited to the immediate costs and benefits in a narrow setting. What the crises of sustainability demand is a broader view. One which takes as its boundary the real limits of all communities, not just our town or country. Narrow definitions of interest, such as nation state, or consumerism, or corporation ignore the broader real world context. These structures are inevitable – human beings derive identity and meaning from tribes, enclaves, locales. Yet this narrow focus is counterproductive in a world fast approaching natural limits. To achieve a sustainable, resilient, prosperous society means that we must adopt a broader view of the scope of our responsibility. It's as simple as knowing that you can't succeed at football if you only look at your own feet.

It's this sort of reframing, or expanding of scope, which says why we need a fundamentally different worldview. A common humanity worldview – what sociologists call a cosmopolitan outlook – is essential to the success of a politics of the future. The idea is not to create a single globalised, homogenous culture, but to build agreements based upon tolerance of diverse beliefs and cultures, and also some basic common values and equity in relationships. Philosophers have described what is needed as an attitude born out of feeling for others' vulnerability (Levinas) or a simple hospitality (Derrida). The opposed position to cosmopolitanism, still very much an active force and a danger to the prospects of all, is protectionism. Nation states are a key block to this common humanity view, as are to some extent corporate interests, although it could also be noted that corporations as transnational institutions are also potentially part of a bridge to a global citizen worldview. Hence the importance of the way corporations are accountable to universal standards, whether in law (such as the Alien Tort Act in the USA), or in media monitoring (such as the challenges to Google and others over censorship of search terms such as 'Tiananmen Square Massacre' within China).

In solving the five big sustainability challenges we could also be developing a new phase for human societies. One which in hindsight is qualitatively 'better' in common wellbeing, cultural progress and what Buddhist That Nich Than calls 'interbeing'.

In introducing the book I need to add that it is a work in progress. This is far from the last word on co-opportunity and each type of co-operation described in this book deserves whole books to be written about them, as well of course as action rather than just writing. I see this as more of a field journal from someone who – like many readers – is working on co-opportunity.

To keep up with the debates, to challenge or build on what you have read, or let me know about your own schemes – or indeed simply to say 'hi!' – do come and join the ongoing conversation at my new blog for this book: http://www.coopp.net.

Finally (because I've put the acknowledgements at the back this time, so as not to break the flow) I must point out that this book itself was a collaborative effort. Both because it draws on many of the inspiring conversations and characters I'm in contact with. And because quite a number of people helped with the drafts, including those among the PSFK.com readership who joined an experiment in collaborative online editing. It seemed only natural to do this with a book on co-operation. But – rather proving the point on open source systems being more effective – if the book has any quality, I'd say it's mainly because I've had so much helpful input, for which I am hugely grateful.

John Grant, September 2009

PART 1

A CLIMATE
FOR CHANGE?

WHY DON'T WE HAVE A CLIMATE FOR CHANGE YET?

Barack Obama (has a) fateful choice that he – and we – must make this January to begin an emergency rescue of human civilization from the imminent and rapidly growing threat posed by the climate crisis.

Al Gore, 'The Climate for Change', *New York Times*, September 11, 2008

ONCE UPON A TIME IN AMERICA, a student was taking part in what they believed to be a research project about 'life in the university'. They had been shown through to a waiting room and given a questionnaire to fill in.

A wisp of smoke trailed into the waiting room, through an air vent. Then another. A few minutes later, so much smoke had come into the room that it was becoming difficult to ignore. Yet they remained sitting there, stoically filling in their questionnaire and shooting occasional anxious glances at the other two young men also sitting in the waiting room. The subject did not leave the room to report the smoke – even after six minutes when the smoke was so thick that it was hard to see, or breathe. And according to experts – if this were a real fire – their chances of getting out alive were now very low.

They just sat there. Why? Because the other two people in the waiting room with them were actors. The actors had been instructed to ignore the smoke, sit calmly, pretend that nothing was happening. 90% of the time, given two stooges in the room who do nothing, the experimental subject would follow their lead. Only 10% of the subjects ever left the room to report the smoke.

These experiments were first performed in the 1960s by American social psychologists Latané and Darling, investigating a phenomenon they labelled 'Bystander Apathy' (*American Scientist*, 1969[9]). Latané and Darling repeated the experiments with all three interviewees being genuine experimental subjects, and no actors present. Even now, only in 38% of cases did someone leave and report the smoke. Presumably with three volunteers, each subject was still waiting for another to respond? Whereas when the experiment was conducted with a single interview subject, sitting on their own, 75% left the room and reported the smoke.

It sounds incredible. But the experiment has been repeated numerous times with similar results. You can see for yourself – there is a video of this experiment being repeated on YouTube[10], with one experimental subject and a whole semi-circle of stooges. In this case the subject sits in the room for over 20 minutes, while all the time smoke is pouring into the room.

The experiment shows our reliance on reading others' reactions, when assessing risk and the need to take action. Especially in emergency situations, where drastic action might be required. If nobody else seems to be responding, we assume that everything is okay. You can perhaps remember a situation like this yourself, for instance when a fire alarm went off in an office. Nobody else moved, so you assumed it was some kind of 'test'?

All of which may begin to explain why, despite regular reports in the media about climate change, most people carry on regardless. Record levels of ice melting in the Arctic. Record annual temperatures. One in 10 homes in the UK at flood risk. Hurricane Katrina. Climate change is reaching the point where some scientists say it could soon be too late to halt or reverse. And yet here we are, changing very little, not quite believing it is really happening.

Why? Because we look around and no one else seems to be responding. There are no emergency measures being brought in by the government, like fuel rationing. The only people we see responding are ones we can label as 'fringe extremists'. So we can discount their protest marches and stunts. All the real signals indicate there must be no risk. Despite the news. In fact if it was really happening it wouldn't be in the regular news (which is about things continuing as they are). It would have its own newsflash. Imagine scientists discovered a large comet on collision course with earth. They'd hardly stuff this in the middle of *News at Ten*, just after the human interest story? As one woman said, in research groups I was conducting for the UK government 'If climate change were real, there would be mass hysteria!'

The lack of public engagement and action worries politicians a great deal. It has given rise to many a report about 'behaviour change'. The question is: how can we get the general public, in large numbers, to respond to the danger signs? Attention often focuses on the gap between intention and action. It might better focus on the gap between politicians and people.

In 2006, on the publication of their handbook on climate change, the Rough Guides editor sent a copy of the book to every MP in the UK, along with a letter asking three questions:

1. How important an issue is climate change?
2. What can Britain do to make a difference?
3. What steps do you plan to take (or have you taken), in your constituency, and as an individual?

The results of this survey were published in the *Independent* newspaper, their headline being 'How Green is your MP?'[11] Nearly half of all the MPs replied (318). That's a notable result in itself, given their packed postbags. And the reason for this (at least among those who replied) may be apparent from their (near) unanimous answers to question 1: that it is *the most important issue, bar none.* Here is a representative selection of their replies:

Nick Ainger (South Pembrokeshire & Carmarthen West, Labour)

1: Climate change is the most important challenge the world is facing.

Richard Benyon (Newbury, Conservative)

1: Climate change is the defining issue of our age. Previous generations had to deal with the rise of Nazism or communism. This is the issue on which my generation of politicians will be judged. This is our Dunkirk.

Edward Davey (Kingston & Surbiton, LibDem)

1: Climate change is the most important issue facing us today – and has been for some time. The consequences if we do not tackle this urgently and fully are potentially catastrophic for the whole human race and life on the earth.

The answers to the other two questions showed strong support for public investment (in renewable energy, efficiency) and also that politicians are making substantial changes in their own homes and lives. Many acknowledged that the public are not nearly as fully behind this issue as they are (so that it's hard to argue that this was an exercise in pandering to public opinion?). For instance, Edward Davey went on to say:

The problem to date has been persuading enough people to recognise the threat, and despite Al Gore et al., I remain alarmed at how few people still really understand the scale of the problem and how fast we need to move.

Building a climate for change, one where the general public do recognise the threat and are motivated to act, is the subject of this section of the book. Before we come on to public and business attitudes, it's worth pausing to reflect on just why the MPs do see this as the most important issue, bar none. One reason may be their exposure to the latest science. Another, I suspect, is their position as people who take responsibility for society- and planet-wide issues. Perhaps we need to move to a position where all of us, not just MPs, include such global issues within our scope of responsibility?

We'll come back to responsibility. First let's look at the science. I know that many reading the book will be well informed. Still, there would be something missing from this discussion if I didn't cover it. Because climate change is ultimately not a political, cultural or economic issue; it is an environmental one. And the scientific case for urgent action is overwhelming.

At the heart of the calls for action by scientists is a probabilistic model; if we do X there is a Y% chance that Z will happen. A recent Potsdam Institute report is typical: 'The study concluded that greenhouse gas emissions must be cut by more than 50 percent by 2050 relative to 1990 levels, if the risk of exceeding 2°C is to be limited to 25 percent.' That's not because scientists aren't sure whether there is a risk. It is because risk is probabilistic. If you jump from a third storey window your chances of dying could be limited to 25%. It's something you'd regard as risky though.

Probability-based reports are problematic for media (and politicians) who deal in certainties. Probability however is not the same as uncertainty or debate. In a 2009 survey,[12] among those scientists who specialise in studying climate change and have published peer-reviewed papers on the subject, 96.2% stated that they believe global temperatures have risen, and 97.4% that they believe manmade causes of this are significant. You will find few areas of scientific enquiry where the view is more certain. (This contrasts with the view often repeated by the media that there is scientific 'debate').

On the question of *how much* of a risk climate change poses there is genuinely a spread of scientific opinions. In simplistic terms the risk assessments and implications for action can be summarised by two positions:

• Economic common sense (Serious). Changes of at least 2 degrees seem almost certain across the next century and we know from the IPCC and other sources that higher levels will significantly curb economic growth. The prudent thing is to invest now in minimising carbon emissions and hence these effects.

- The red line (Tipping points). In this view, championed by James Hansen (head of the NASA Goddard Institute for Space Studies) we may face runaway climate change. This means that if we cross a 'red line' the planet would 'whipsaw' to a new hot planet state rapidly and with little further help from us. It would be like triggering an explosive chain reaction.

Both positions argue for action; with the second it is a case of – as Al Gore put it – an emergency rescue of civilisation (Gore also supports this second view). Let's go a bit deeper into what the human risks associated with the statistical models are. I'll do this by looking at just one (of many) factors – the impact of melting ice. Getting into the detail may help bring the two different positions on risk and response levels to life:

Serious risk. Sea levels are a global temperature gauge – for the same reason we use liquid in thermometers. The IPCC had predicted a sea level rise of 28 cm if we keep temperature to +1.8 degrees, or as high as 59 cm if temperatures increase 4 degrees. Studies show that a 50 cm average rise would mean that coastal flooding events that today happen every hundred years would happen several times a year by 2100. The frequency of these events increases dramatically with small average rises because of storm surges and similar. A 2007 study in *Environment and Urbanisation*[13] found that at the IPCC predicted rises in sea levels, 600 million people were at risk of coastal flooding. The IPCC Report had similarly concluded that '[m]any millions more people are projected to be flooded every year due to sea-level rise by the 2080s.'

What would be the economic impact? Consider that Hurricane Katrina – just one such event – is estimated to have cost $150 billion. That's more than the annual GDP of New Zealand. The cities now at risk include London, New York, Shanghai,

Tokyo and Mumbai. The impact of one tenth of the world's population – and many of its economic hub cities – facing frequent natural disasters would be catastrophic. This economic common sense view is where the new US administration is putting down their marker. I went to a speech (at Tomorrow's Company in March 2009) by Bill Becker, Executive Director of the Presidential Climate Action Project. Becker summarised the Obama administration's key messages to the public on the issue as follows:

Climate change is real, it is manmade and is doing irrevocable damage.

But what mankind makes, we can still unmake.

Forget 2050 it is impacting our lives and economies today; in super storms, forest fires, pine forests decimated by bugs, sea levels.

Not to invest now would lead to a much bigger debt and cost to future generations; there is no possible excuse for doing too little or too late.

It's time for a transition, a tipping point, and not incremental action.

There is a need to lead, in order to mobilise the public will. And the US administration is gearing up for this.

Becker stated (a phrase from Martin Luther King) that their key message was:

THE FIERCE URGENCY OF NOW.

That's the essential credo of this first (serious) risk position; act now or we will (quite literally) have hell to pay later. It is a corrective to previous public presentations of 'things we need to do by 2050' which gave the false impression this was not a present day priority. Mixed with the threat of inaction are messages about the promise of economic prosperity for the nations that lead new industries of the low carbon economy.

Scientists (at the 2009 Copenhagen Climate Science summit) have revised their predictions; converging on 1 m of sea level rises across this century as the consensus. Why so much higher? The IPCC figures were mainly based upon thermal expansion of the oceans. The new figures are based on taking ice melting more into account too; and using the current rates of ice melting which are already higher than predicted by the IPCC.

1 metre rises are five times more than has been seen over the last 130 years. At this level you would see much more flooding and sooner. As well as the cities and their economic and population displacement impacts ... consider that large areas of agricultural land and fresh water supplies could become salinated and hence unusable, creating instant food and water crises.

The red line. A typical sample of runaway climate change thinking comes from *The Last Generation* by Fred Pearce (former editor of *New Scientist*):

> Climate change from now on will not be gradual – nature doesn't do gradual change. In the past, Europe's climate has switched from Arctic to tropical in three to five years. It can happen again. So forget what environmentalists have told you about nature being a helpless victim of human excess. The truth is the opposite. She is a wild and resourceful beast given to fits of rage. And now that we are provoking her beyond endurance, she is starting to seek her revenge.[14]

Let's go back to the ice, this time at the North Pole. The loss of Arctic ice is a well-known climate impact. And people tend to think of it in sentimental terms – pity the poor polar bears. Actually it is a global threat to all of us, not just the poor bears and local peoples, because of its role as a heat shield (the Albedo effect) and a heat sink. As a reflective heat shield, the arctic ice sheet reflects the equivalent of 70% of all the heating caused by atmospheric CO_2. As a heat sink – like ice in your drink, as long as it is still present the liquid stays cool, as most energy goes into the melting (Lovelock, 2009[15]). That's why we should worry about the latest studies showing that all the polar ice will probably be gone by 2037 and possibly as early as 2020.[16]

Ice loss represents a 'positive feedback' effect – at higher temperatures with less ice the warming will accelerate. Another melting ice positive feedback effect is the releasing of methane (from the rotting of ancient peats and forests) from melting permafrost. A NASA study, looking at the geological record for past similar events (Kennedy[17]) shows that only small increases in temperature could be needed to release vast amounts of methane, and that the resulting temperature increase could be 'tens of degrees' and would happen very fast. Methane clathrate release is a common suspect in a number of past mass extinction events (an effect known as the 'clathrate gun'). Another example of how slightly higher temperatures could cause dramatic amounts of further warming. 'Tens of degrees' is known to be both a possibility from past events in the geological record, and also off the scale in terms of its potential impact on human life. Human beings can survive in deserts, but 9 billion can't survive in broken flooded cities, without food.

There are at least 10 such known positive feedback 'tipping elements' that could lead to runaway climate change. Nine are listed in a paper by the Tyndall Centre (2008). Commenting on this report its main author, Professor Tim Lenton, said 'Society must not be lulled into a false sense of security by smooth projections of global change. Our findings suggest that a variety of tipping elements could reach their critical point within this century under human-induced climate change.'

I went to a talk on melting Arctic ice and runaway climate change models in early 2008 at Tomorrow's Company. It was a repeat of a presentation that had been given to a cross-party committee of MPs in Westminster. I was quite simply stunned. The gap between what the scientists (one of whom goes on a submarine under the North Pole every year to measure ice thickness) explained has already happened, and could be about to happen ... and the low public recognition of the risks was staggering.

MPs get this information first hand. But it's not like it has been entirely absent from broadsheet newspapers and TV news. I think the key difference is that MPs feel responsible for problems on this scale. I don't mean they feel guilty. Or that it is all the current administration's fault. 'Responsibility' literally means that you are 'answerable for' – and relates to the scope of matters for which this is the case. A parent is answerable for the care of their children, but not the current state of the education system. A police officer on holiday is outside their jurisdiction. Our current political system means that we delegate public responsibilities to elected governments. This works okay for many of the administrative duties of a civil service and legislature. It's a disaster for facing an issue where the general public do need to take responsibility. Climate change is one such issue – and I'll point in this book to other cases of failing common wellbeing associated with too few seeing it as their responsibility. Poverty is one longstanding example of this.

The taking of responsibility isn't just an individual decision. You can see similar issues being played out in two sorts of crowds. One is fragmented, each going about their own business. The other is aligned and charged with emotion. It's the difference between a crowded train station and a crowded football stadium. And the key component with the latter is each individual taking a group view. Where every person feels an emotional stake in the struggle and the outcome. Where they will throw themselves behind the cause. That's the side of the 'climate change should be like a wartime emergency' argument from Al Gore, James Lovelock and others that I buy into (but not so much the machismo, mechanised side – a 'gearing up for').

Citizenship is not just a label, it's a collective process. When you invite a group of people off the street to role-play being in charge, for instance in consultative planning processes, they quickly pick up all the issues, the trade offs and balanced solutions. It's not some God-given superiority that politicians have – it is simply a position (of power/responsibility) to take a broad view. That's not the same as polling people on their views. You find that these views often shift quite dramatically in what social scientists call 'deliberative forums'. For instance 'voter weekend' experiments in the early 1990s found that people shifted from the default 'hanging is too good for them' public attitude to a more nuanced and liberal position on crime and punishment, simply as a result of taking part in forums where they heard testimonies from all sides: ex offenders, police, judiciary, victims of crime. Here we see another key to having responsible feelings towards a subject, which is the role of empathy; 'There but for the grace of God go I.'

Superficially, there are surveys showing that the majority of the population are 'concerned or very concerned' about climate change. (I for one had become very concerned, so was encouraged to hear that most others apparently felt the same). Synnovate conducted massive annual surveys for the BBC, interviewing 22 000 people in 22 countries. They found the proportion 'concerned about climate change' increased from 68% in 2007 to 72% in 2008. The most dramatic shift was in the USA – from 57% to 80%. Big increases were recorded in other previously disengaged countries including Denmark (62% to 79%) and India (59% to 72%). And people across the world who were concerned also claimed to be taking action: saving power (80%), recycling waste (69%) and buying green (61%) or energy efficient (59%) products.

That's the proportion indicating 'concern'. It doesn't show us *the intensity* of this concern. Another better question is this: where do the environment and climate change *rank* in people's overall lists of concerns and priorities? In a 2009 poll of American public opinion by Pew,[18] 1500 adults were asked to prioritise a list of 20 issues the government should be tackling. The results are shown in Table 1.1.

Global warming ranked 20th out of the 20 priorities. Even in early 2007 (2006 being the year of media climate hype) it ranked 17th.

The survey of MPs said climate change was rated the most important issue to be tackled. This survey says it is the least important. There have been similar surveys ranking climate change 13th–17th on the list of public concerns in priority order in the UK too. (I doubt all American senators and congressmen are as serious about it as their Euro counterparts though.)

That's the general public. What about big business? Over the last few years we have seen many grand gestures like going 'carbon neutral'. Wal-Mart stunned environmental activists

Table 1.1 Percentage rating each policy area a 'top priority'

	2007	2009
Economy	68%	85%
Jobs	57%	82%
Terrorism	80%	76%
Social Security	64%	63%
Education	69%	61%
US Energy	57%	60%
Medicare	63%	60%
Healthcare costs	68%	59%
Budget Deficit	53%	53%
Health Insurance	56%	52%
Helping the Poor	55%	50%
Crime	62%	46%
Moral breakdown	47%	45%
Military	46%	44%
Tax cuts	48%	43%
Environment	57%	41%
Immigration	55%	41%
Lobbyists	35%	36%
Trade Policy	34%	31%
Global Warming	38%	30%

(aka its critics) with a sweeping pro-sustainability procurement and store energy revolution. You will barely find a single large public company that does not have policies in place on carbon and ambitious targets for other sustainability priorities (water, pollution, biodiversity, poverty, workers' rights ...).

However, that's a bit like saying they are 'concerned or very concerned'. The 2008 State of Green Business Report by Green-Biz found that across a range of environmental issues; carbon, water, waste, pollution ... corporate America's achievements were only just big enough to neutralise the effect of economic growth that year. And Greenbiz in 2009[19] found that despite a slowdown, absolute carbon emissions by corporates had grown by 1.4%. We can't afford to stand still, let alone grow our national emissions. In a recent speech in China[20] Nicholas Stern summarised it as follows: we need to cut total carbon emissions globally from 50 gigatonnes now, to 35 by 2030 and 20 by 2050. By 2050 (given 9 billion people) the average per capita emissions would have to be less than two tonnes/year. That would represent a 90% cut for the average American today. Clearly there is a real political discussion to be had about who cuts what and how. But cut we must.

If you ask the priority-ranking question of business leaders, as Accenture did (in early 2008), you find climate change is a low-ish priority. Accenture's survey, reported in the *Independent*, canvassed executives in 500 big businesses in the UK, US, China, Germany, Japan and India – and it found:[21]

5% of companies rated climate change as their first priority.

11% of companies rated climate change as a top three priority.

89% of companies did not rate climate change as a top priority.

Asked to rank all of their priorities, Accenture found that climate change on average 'ranked eighth in business leaders' concerns, below increasing sales, reducing costs, developing new products and services, competing for talented staff, securing growth in emerging markets, innovation and technology'. Yes it's on their agenda. But no there isn't a war-effort-style shift to this eclipsing any of their previous priorities. Most businesses want a win: win – which is another way of saying they will do it *if* it also helps achieve any of the higher priorities.

Overall you have to wonder if people and corporations just don't think that climate change is that big a risk. That was certainly my impression doing focus groups for a new phase of the UK government ACT ON CO2 campaign. I found, as the surveys say, that people have superficial 'high awareness and concern about climate change'. Most would say that 'everyone thinks about the environment these days' – that it has moderated their behaviour. Nobody I met however was seriously worried that it could affect daily life in the UK, or would impinge much upon their own lifetimes. As one put it; 'it doesn't weigh on your mind'. And hence the actions are all of the 'I do my recycling and ...' type. It's a social norm – an 'ought' – but hardly a gripping necessity.

In my focus groups I would ask people to tell me about 'the environment'. They would trot out sound bites from the media: ice caps, polar bears, global warming, greenhouse gases, carbon emissions, poor farmers, floods, droughts, storms ... At this level it seems almost like people have really taken it on board. And then I'd ask them to *explain it to me*. Across all my focus groups I don't think a single person managed to piece it together. They had quite a few of the jigsaw pieces. People in my groups told me that it might be something to do with pollution, or ozone holes or ...? A few did know about the greenhouse effect. But no one could explain it. They would try and then falter. 'Isn't it something to do with ...?' Climate change has not impinged one bit on that model we have in our heads (mine looks a bit like the globe from my geography classroom at school) of 'how the world really works'.

Most studies have concentrated on new ways to communicate this information. But there is another possibility – they aren't taking it all in or taking it seriously because it simply isn't a big risk (or so they assume). A sure sign of where people are with the issue is the question: how much do you think this will affect our life in this country in our lifetimes? People have a clear and consistent view on this; the answer is 'not very much' or 'not at all'.

No wonder they haven't gone off to frantically research the issue (as many have done with swine flu). They don't think it's a worry. So why bother?

A recent report from the Mental Health Foundation made a telling point about our assessments of sources of risk compared to the actual risks in the world:

Excessive fear poses an enormous burden on our society directly through anxiety related illness ... and indirectly through inappropriate behaviours such as excessive supervision of children or failure to invest. It also paralyses long-term rational planning to deal with key future threats such as global warming by diverting attention to more immediate but less important fears. (MHF, 2009)[22]

Reports into the way climate change has been communicated have been critical of excessive pessimism: what think tank IPPR referred to in their Warm Words Report (2006[23]) as 'we're all going to die' gloom, or even 'climate porn' – impending disaster is presented as sensationalist entertainment. The advice from IPPR is to avoid 'alarmism' in favour of 'treating climate friendly activity as a brand that can be sold' and to focus on meaningful actions such as buying a hybrid car, or fitting insulation (rather than actions too small to be meaningful like thermostats, light bulbs and devices on standby). The IPPR had studied 600 media articles and concluded in their Warm Words Report that the two main tropes – alarmism, and small actions – were unhelpful, especially in combination: alarmism led to doom and gloom fatalism, while small actions had little credibility as real solutions to this apocalyptic vision.

A 2009 report by EcoAmerica[24] seemed to conclude that the 'best' approach was not even to mention climate change; changing the language to 'atmosphere deterioration' also switching focus to more aspirational issues such as energy security, health, American jobs, freedom, ingenuity.

I have another view.

Firstly it's a group issue – like the social experiment in the waiting room – we need to see our milieu reacting. It's not an information task, in other words. No matter how much smoke pours in, if no one is moving no one will move.

Secondly every citizen should be given the opportunity to think like an MP. Invited into a space where – as part of a citizen panel inputting to the real policies and decisions – they can take in the information and input to what needs to be done. Staging a mass public debate and forum would in itself have the missing newsflash factor – signalling something out of the ordinary.

Some argue – after the disappointing failures of 'green consumerism' to bring substantial change – that we should move to the opposite approach than free choice. That we should move to rationing. That however sounds like a double disaster. Firstly it will fail in its own terms – no regime, even authoritarian, could survive the likely public backlash against mass imposed rationing. And secondly it's a lost opportunity to build a society that is better at co-operating for the common good, because it's based on active citizenship. I'm not the first to figure this out. Leading political figures I have discussed this with, ranging from Conservatives to the Green Party, are cottoning on.

Climate change – along with other global crises in ecosystems, finance, food, poverty and equity – is a test case of our current political system, where a few people (leaders, MPs) have responsibility and the vast majority do not. And if we want to tackle this sort of issue we need to challenge this basic structure of disengagement, which is at the heart of people not 'getting it'.

Hence I've come to the conclusion that all the advice on 'how to communicate climate change' is misplaced. It's like giving advice about how to write an email telling someone they have a fatal illness. You don't deliver this sort of information that way. You sit down and talk it through with them, over a series of sessions. Giving space for them to own the issue and develop their own responses. And hence you don't need to spin the information into alarmism nor cheerful/meaningful actions in that context.

What we need to have around the risks of climate change is a big chat. Probably in groups so each participant can, rather than stewing on their own with worry, treat it as a collective issue requiring co-operative responses. The Mental Health Foundation Report similarly recommended that we need public forums to air and manage our fears, and convert them into rational action:

> Our social bonds need to be strong if we are to tackle fear. The proportion of us living in situations without strong social support is growing – four times as many of us live on our own as 50 years ago. 'Absence of community' may mean we are forced to cope with social problems at an individual level, rather than confronting them collectively, and our power to overcome them alone may be limited. (MHF, 2009)[25]

This is a radical step, I must admit. For the many to have more power, and more say, means setting in train a process that could echo the developments in Soviet Russia in the late 1980s. If people had a say what other issues would they start to force the pace on? Would a nationwide debate on the third runway at Heathrow have come out the same, or on building new coal-fired power stations, or going nuclear again? I am in the camp which thinks that's a good thing. So in fact do quite a few of today's politicians. All we need is someone with the gumption of a Gandhi to actually push this through.

ORGANISING FOR CHANGE: OBAMA AND TRANSITION TOWNS

WHAT EVIDENCE IS THERE that citizens can be enlisted for change – not just as voters, but in a mass public collaborative movement? Some sweeping political changes of the last few decades happened this way, in East Europe and South Africa. A recent example, showing the potential of social media to amplify such processes, was Barack Obama's 'Yes We Can' election campaign.

Obama's key insight was that the campaign should belong to the people. It was never just about using the internet; it was about an inspiring vision of HOPE. In a country mired in bitter, negative political campaigning this stood out as a light in the gathering darkness of global recession. People put their cynicism aside and made countrywide coach rides to canvass other voters. America got so swept up that voter turnout (56.8%) was the highest recorded since 1968, the year of the assassinations of Martin Luther King Jr and presidential hopeful Robert F. Kennedy.

The key to understanding this campaign – and most of Web 2.0 – is that all about the middle. In old media you have the professionals – the newscasters, politicians, celebrities, experts – and you have the public. Broadcasting was a process by which the public received content from this centre. You could vote, buy, read and passively consume, or resist consuming. However you had no active role in the production of culture and society. The social production revolution changed that. It adds a middle layer of ordinary people acting as connectors, syndicators, enthusiasts, interpreters, editors. In the case of phenomena like blogging there are nearly as many writers as readers.

The Obama campaign understood how to mobilise the middle. Not just by bombarding people with TV commercials (they did that too). But by enlisting active participants. There have always been party faithful, tireless door-to-door canvassers, volunteers. But not on this scale. Here are some of the statistics on mass participation in this middle layer:

85% of the campaign funds came from private individuals. $500 million was donated by 6.5 million people; an average of $76 per donor.

13 million individuals signed up for the email list to be kept informed. That is 10% of the total voter turnout in this election. 7000 separate messages were sent to Obama's email list during the campaign.

Campaigning was mostly done by online volunteers, 2 million of whom signed up to MyBarackObama.com (MyBO). This social network, modelled on Facebook, was responsible for 400 000 blog posts, 200 000 real life meetings and events, 35 000 local groups.

Another 5 million supporters signed up through 15 existing social networks like Facebook, MySpace, Twitter and BlackPlanet.

An Obama iPhone application searched the user's own phone contacts and suggested friends to phone and canvass in order of location relative to the key states where swing votes were most needed.

You can get lost in the details. The genius of this campaign was explained simply by a campaign manager interviewed in *Fast Company* magazine: 'Technology has always been used as a net to capture people in a campaign or cause, but not to organize.'[26] The success was not campaigning at people it was creating the platform for people to do the campaigning.

That's an example of top-down government opening up the bottleneck, to allow greater participation. The hope would be that actual political process might start to work that way too – involving people in more than just who gets elected. Meanwhile another route is for people simply to decide that as citizens they are not going to wait for government, big business or anyone else to sort things out; rather that they will come up with their own plan.

The Transition Town movement started four years ago, far from the Washington media spotlight, in Kinsale in the rural West Cork region of Ireland. Rob Hopkins, then a permaculture lecturer at the local college, along with several collaborators, set out to draw up an 'energy descent plan' for the local council. In the next version of this approach, Hopkins (who moved to Totnes, to complete his PhD at Plymouth University) got local citizens organised to do the planning together. Totnes (population 8000) was a pretty receptive community for this idea, being home to the Schumacher College (a leader in sustainability education) and according to its Wikipedia entry, known for its sizeable 'new age and alternative community'.

By now there are 400 Transition Towns in the network, and they number among them the City of Bristol, the London Borough of Brixton and the Isle of Wight. One is starting in my own area of North London and is holding an 'eco week' of awareness-raising events as I write. The process starts with a small band (of at least four people) agreeing to engage their community in a transition initiative. The aim is to increase local resilience (by reducing dependence on oil) and reduce carbon emissions (causing climate change). While the process is open, collaborative, patient and informal, it also relies on a well-formed structure and sequence of activities. Hence new towns joining the scheme benefit from not having to invent their own process.

The first step of the process is to raise awareness of the need to rebuild resilience and reduce carbon. This involves a lot of watching videos, attending talks, discussing it among the community. Quite rightly, as it takes time for people to internalise this information, to grasp the reality of the need to change. Early work in a Transition Town also involves connecting with existing community groups, local government and the transition network as a whole.

When the movement is properly bedded in, working groups then start looking at key areas of local life. Hopkins reckons that food is one of the key ones, not least because with food supplies so oil-dependent it is pretty clear how dramatic the impact of future oil shocks will be if changes aren't made. But also food takes people back to nature and – done local and done right – can be a major climate change lever. In addition to food, Transition Towns look at energy, economics and livelihoods, transport and health. The group also look for projects which can engage the broader community and spark some insight and understanding into the issues; for instance in Totnes they launched their own currency (the Totnes Pound) – with a focus on supporting local independent shops. In a workshop I ran at the Design Council recently as part of Greengage we heard all about the latest currency initiative in Brixton. Josh Ryan Collins from the New Economics Foundation explained that 90% of money spent in a local community usually leaves the community. A local currency only accepted in local businesses can make money less 'flighty'.

The (im)modest aim of every transition town is to launch 'a community defined, community implemented Energy Descent Action Plan over a 15 to 20-year timescale'. That quote is from the Transition Wiki, which stresses two key points:

- That we used immense amounts of creativity, ingenuity and adaptability on the way up the energy upslope, and that there's no reason for us not to do the same on the down slope.
- If we collectively plan and act early enough there's every likelihood that we can create a way of living that's significantly more connected, more vibrant and more in touch with our environment than the oil-addicted treadmill that we find ourselves on today.[27]

One of Hopkin's fellow founders in Kinsale, Louise Rooney, points to the slowness of the process as an absolutely key component. Rooney quotes a Dutch study into Transition Management and its application to public policy:

A characteristic of transition management is that it achieves structural change gradually, without too much destructive friction in the form of social resistance. The rationale behind the gradual approach is that a transition can be brought about by the gradual transformation of an existing system, instead of the planned creation of a new system. (Rotmans, Kemp & van Asselt)[28]

Rob Hopkins has written a detailed instruction manual, first as a download and now published as a book – *The Transition Handbook* – which benefits greatly from real life stories, photographs and ideas from the Totnes programme. The book itself has proved immensely popular (last time I checked it was the best selling ecology book on Amazon UK).

The most difficult challenge within transition is that people have to change themselves, their worldview and the workings of their community. Transition involves giving up a secure identity and story about the world around you. Accepting the ending of the old phase. Stepping into an uncertain 'in-between'. And only much later arriving at what, in retrospect, is a secure new beginning. Imposed change like management restructurings can make people feel powerless; transition is about drawing them into leading the change.

That description makes Transition Towns sound heavy and demanding. Whereas when you meet Transition Towners what strikes you is more their exuberance. The whole movement is spirited, meandering, intense, funny, epochal ... about as chaotic as any process involving a normal town inventing a new version of society. The whole thing reminds me slightly of the old pre-industrial London; a society organised around coffee houses, reformers, back room scientists, religious dissenters and political pamphleteers. There's something of this in the language used by Transition Towns; for instance 'The Great Unleashing' is how they describe their official kick off meeting. Usually you'd expect such movements to have a charismatic cult-type leader. But actually Hopkins is as quiet, down to earth and unassuming as they come. And the Transition Town movement doesn't believe in having big leaders; everything is more consensual. In fact if you are setting up a Transition Town you have to find three other co-leaders from the start, and also plan for your succession. So that it can't become a personality-driven thing. A Transition Town has functionaries (like a treasurer) but is led by the membership.

The early months of a Transition Town are spent pretty much meeting up and hearing talks and watching films called things like *How Cuba Survived Peak Oil* (a great documentary by the way). Why so slow? Because people have to decide, together, for themselves that the game is up with their old way of life. This is not like learning for a school exam. It has to sink in. Once they have reached that point together they start work on an energy descent plan.

The word 'descent' comes to the Transition Towns via the deep thinkers in permaculture, such as co-founder David Holmgren. And in turn Holmgren (as he acknowledges in *Beyond Sustainability*) got it from a biological mathematical genius called Howard Odum. Odum saw a pattern in peak oil. One he recognised from a lifetime of modelling the dynamics of ecosystems (see Figure 2.1). Odum's analogy was that (with our recent use of fossil fuels) we were like a shoal of fish happening upon an algal bloom. When this happens the fish population soon overshoots and runs short of food. And then the population collapses roughly back to its original level. So basically human history for the next 200 years could look like a reversal of the last 200 years; a descent in energy use, complexity and population.

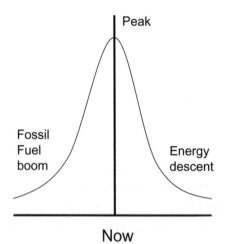

Figure 2.1

Nobody likes to be told that what went up might come down. People usually in my experience try to wriggle out of this descent view in three ways.

1. Close your eyes, cover your ears and shout 'La-la-la I'm not listening'. Or use the adult version, which is to ignore the evidence and label the messengers as green ideological extremists.
2. Assert that there must be a new energy source, perhaps a version of what we already have but with a techno-babble new spin. 'Nanotech solar' is one that futurist Ray Kurzweil has been touting around.
3. Explain that while oil supplies may be peaking, we have 200 years of coal left – we will figure this out by then.

Odum admitted that of course option 2 was possible. But we had better discover it quick. Wouldn't it be brilliant if under the Christmas tree Mother Nature had left us another stored

Now

Figure 2.2

energy glut which we just haven't unwrapped yet? Not an argument for not looking for new energy sources. But Odum modelled the complete energy inputs and outputs of known sources – including wind, hydro, geo, tidal, solar, nuclear and others – and on his calculations the only two which delivered an abundant surplus of energy compared to their total energy costs were fossil fuels and photosynthesis. Odum hence concluded we needed to reforest the earth, which doesn't sound a bad idea. This is a simplified summary of his work. Odum won the Crafoord Prize (equivalent of the Nobel Prize for life sciences). If you want to argue with his conclusions it is well worth reading some of his books, to find out how he arrived at them.

The answer to 3 is simple – I got this from a talk by Michael Pawlyn, a brilliant biomimicry architect. Pawlyn says; 'Okay, we might or might not be at the peak yet. We do have another 200 years of coal maybe. So let's just look at the graph on a different scale ...' (see Figure 2.2):

If you accept that fossil fuel reserves are finite, we do need to make provision for a post-oil world. Ideally investing some of the current surplus of cheap energy in building towards that. Without getting too far into energy politics, another point Pawlyn made is that – for all the highly politicised pros and cons of going nuclear – we do know for sure that the global reserves of fuel grade uranium have already peaked.

What people see perhaps when they notice the outer signs of the Transition Towns movement is a lovely, local, slightly eccentric 'citizen engagement'. Which fits comfortably with current political perspectives – and the movement is seen as something good to be associated with. Ed Milliband, a UK government minister, came down to their last annual conference. He told them he didn't share their optimism that the general public would ever willingly accept anything but GDP growth (although he conflated this with local quality of life, something challenged by many, including Nobel Prize winning economists Joseph Stiglitz and Amartya Sen in a recent report).

I look at Transition Towns and see something much more radical – it feels like a glimpse of the future. This is what it could look like if we really did create a climate for change. I know many others feel the same way. For the last couple of years we have tended to fall back on Transition Towns as an example of how at least some progress is being made. Hence the particularly enthusiastic ovation when Rob Hopkin's name was announced as a winner at the 2009 Observer Ethical Awards. And – as Hopkins more than anyone would be keen to stress – they have barely got started yet.

3

PUTTING ORGANISING FOR CHANGE INTO ACTION

IN THIS SECTION I WILL OUTLINE a range of typical project starting points, large and small, for engaging citizens in self-education and change-making. This is a menu of ideas to dip into rather than the traditional book prose. One thing I'd say though is that even if an idea or case study doesn't appear relevant to what you are working on or passionate about getting into, sometimes ideas can leap. For that reason it's good to have a scrapbook of diverse possible ideas that might be useful one day in a completely new context.

FORUMS FOR CHANGE

I got a chance to explore what creating a climate for change could look like in the course of focus group research, which I conducted to help in the development of the next phase of the ACT ON CO2 personal transport campaign. In these focus groups I observed that there was something about the actual group discussions themselves – as small public forums – which seemed to be quite compelling. A deliberately chosen mainstream and in some cases cynical group would often leave actually quite engaged and inclined to explore climate change further and make some adjustments. Another government department (DEFRA) had come to a similar conclusion from research in 2006. Ed Gillespie from Futerra, involved in this project, explains it thus: 'that going to focus groups and talking about the issues seems to be the most effective way to get people to change their behaviour'.

One marketing model I've been interested in for some time – see for instance a write-up in my book *After Image* (2002) – is evangelism. I know it is difficult to separate out the content (religion) and where you sit with this. But when you want to change deeper values, many historical and current examples do point in this direction. For instance for a client project (Napster – back in its 'Supreme Court' days) I did a study of the marketing tactics of cult religions. We had needed to learn from examples where it wasn't possible to broadcast your message. What struck me – putting value judgements about what was being marketed to one side – was how attuned to human social processes these movements were. One simple example. If you ever invite those two nice visitors who come to your house from the Jehovah's Witnesses in for a chat – and agree to meet with them again – you'll notice next time that one of the people you met last time would arrive with a new companion. The same the next time. And so on. After seven visits you'd be invited along to Kingdom Hall. On arrival you would see both the person who has become your constant mentor, but also quite a number (seven) of familiar faces who would catch your eye and smile with recognition. Given which you'd feel instantly at home.

Another example that caught my attention around the same time (through a former BBC client of mine who went to work with the Church of England) was the Alpha Course. The Alpha Course takes people through nine evening events at their local Anglican church, followed by a weekend away. It was started by Nicky Gumball, an evangelist minister based at the Holy Trinity Brompton Church in London. Each of the evenings focuses on a key issue, question or feature of being (or becoming) a Christian. The course, generally run by the local vicar, takes about 70–100 people at a time. The main action is in smaller breakout discussion groups who stay together across the whole course, each group being hosted by two Christian volunteers. The course is advertised as being about the 'meaning of life'; Gumball says it is for people who have reached the point when they say 'is this all it's about?' (for instance; is life only about achieving material ambitions?). The course has a high success rate of converting people to Christianity (about one in eight attendees) and most of those involved seem to find it enriching or satisfying, whether or not they 'convert' to involvement in organised religion. The key success factor seems to be a well-developed format, supported by videos, scripts, speeches so that any local church can adopt and apply the scheme with a high degree of consistency. It taps into how people can use social groupings to incubate a deep change in personal orientation.

I am currently exploring whether something similar could be developed with *Resurgence Magazine* and other collaborators. Resurgence is one of the most thoughtful publications on sustainability, with a 'spiritual' strand: exploring tribal wisdoms, sacred sites and so on. Running an Alpha Course-style programme would be a chance for people to hear what their expert contributors are saying and explore what it means for them, in practical terms but also morally, as part of a community.

Drawing upon local organisation volunteers, including Resurgence reading groups. And also Freecycle, Friends of the Earth and other organisations with a strong interest in sustainability and community – like the Women's Institute. Going through partners to administer the course could get good coverage of the population quite quickly. Two million have attended the Alpha Course in the UK.

WORKING IT THROUGH

Why not just give people information packs, or make some nice BBC documentaries? The answer may be that for psychological reasons climate change (like other issues of that scale – peak oil, global poverty ...) is difficult to face up to alone. Films like *Age of Stupid* or *The Inconvenient Truth* have had most impact, one suspects, among those already socialised into an environmental point of view.

Some describe this as (psychological) denial. It carries with it the acceptance of limiting human impacts on the environment. That's different from accepting a new horizon of possibility (such as the internet offered). The loss of meaning, social dislocation and reported unhappiness of former communist states in the mid 1990s might be a better reference point. Although I'm arguing across this book that society could get better as a result.

Last year I attended a session about the psychology of the climate crisis. Invitees were a mixture of WWF staff, psychoanalysts and people (like me) from the creative industries. A key realisation that emerged in the discussions was that if you figured climate change as a kind of 'crime', then the psychological difficulty is that 'we done it'. Guilt, the emotion of self-accusation, is difficult to bear. It isn't necessarily conscious either, rather it may be something we cannot be fully conscious of – the founding myth of psychoanalysis (The Oedipus Complex) being the story of a 'detective' who discovers he murdered his father and slept with his mother! Nonetheless some have managed to take this on board, and we weren't all 'born green' either. I would say from my own experience that having an outlet for action and a community to share this with is key. It allows you to accept quite a heavy dose of reality (and guilt) but not be left to stew with it. The main thing is to accept that very big changes are looming and to decide to be part of them.

TRAINING EVANGELISTS

The other way to approach change is to change what people do – and let what they think catch up with their new habits and customs. This means getting out there and teaching people to live better, for the good of their health, pocket and the environment. To make it part of their common sense daily routines. There's been a lot of work done on this kind of social marketing, particularly in the area of health campaigns. They have generally found that you do still need to teach people why a new behaviour is better.

The Environment Ambassadors scheme in Copenhagen founded by Bettina Fellov trains unemployed people (usually Somali women) to go into their communities and teach residents how to save water, energy and waste. Not only does the scheme have great behaviour change results, it has also won awards for employment creation with nearly all recruits going on to fulltime work or study. I ran a workshop with the founder and what's really special is her style of teaching and the down to earth examples she uses. Fellov will open a tin of food in the middle of talking about something else and without saying why start spooning it into the bin. 'What are you doing?!' the audience asks, outraged, 'The same as what you are doing when you leave the tap on.' Fellov replies. 'You are paying for the water, and it's really precious, but you are just throwing it away.' This kind of teaching story really brings things home to people. It's like good science teaching. They are not just changing because they 'ought to', they are learning why – about how the world works – and to have more consciousness and control over their lives.

NARRATIVES AND MENTAL MODELS

From my focus groups on sustainable (transport) behaviour I found that what people most seemed to lack with climate change was a satisfying narrative account or mental model. They could parrot phrases and fragments from news reports: climate change or global warming, greenhouse gas, CO_2 emissions, polar bears and poor farmers ... but few could piece this together into a coherent explanation ('something to do with the ozone layer?' was a common suggestion).

Cognitive psychologist George Lackoff has pioneered understanding how culture is 'framed' by metaphors. He makes a telling point in a 2009 post on Alternet, entitled 'How We Talk About the Environment Has Everything to Do with Whether We'll Save It':

> Climate and weather are usually understood as beyond immediate causation, something you are subject to, but can't just go out and change right away. Climate is not directly and causally connected to the values that underlie our concerns about our planet's future: empathy, responsibility, freedom, and our ability to thrive.[29]

One helpful alternative frame I found in my group discussions was to put things in economic terms. Here is how I explained the Stern Report to the focus groups:

Climate Change will impact this country economically – in higher food and fuel prices, the costs of flood damage, in economic disruption, lost jobs, that sort of thing. And if climate change gets worse these impacts would grow. It is a bit like when you notice you have a leaking pipe in your house. It may only look like a small drip. And could be a hassle and expense to get looked at. But if you leave it 10 years it could bring the whole ceiling down. A government economist (Nicholas Stern) looked at the cost of acting now compared to leaving it. He said it would cost 1–2% of GDP now, but if we left it we could permanently lose 5–20% of GDP.

This straightforward way of piecing it together in a story, with a memorable visual metaphor, seemed to really bring it home. Here are some quotes taken from their responses to this:

'I'd go along with that, it's common sense.'

'The dripping tap argument works – 'we need to fix it now' means more to people.'

'The economic angle makes it more real.'

'This 'brings it home' – the impact of flooding, crops failing, prices, insurance ...'

'You don't begrudge paying for these benefits.'

'You want the economy to all run smoothly.'

'Better to do it now than wait for the price to get hiked right up.'

'I want a decent future for my daughter.'

This explanation made the issue seem real to people. They already understand the human world at an economic level. They understood why floods, failed harvests, economic crises (financial losses caused by natural disasters and insurance claims) *would* impact life here. And they could piece together existing evidence; two million homes flooded in the UK, the food prices in 2008 and so on. They could readily see how all of this could affect work prospects, prices and taxes. All they needed was a story, a metaphor to hold it all together. Also notice that the story is not 'catastrophism'. A leaky pipe is not the end of the world. It connotes a rational process of responding to something that needs fixing. It is talking about something that human agency can actually affect. Even the physical metaphor of pipes, ceilings, water and so on seems to work somehow (ceiling as sky ...).

There is still something of a dilemma in the success of this story. We have come to accept money as what anthropologist Margaret Mead called the 'tree trunk concept' of modern culture. Everything radiates out from and ultimately refers back to money. What people are saying is that if you translate sustainability into monetary terms (better £1 spent today than £20 lost tomorrow) they 'get it'. The larger task though is to attempt to move beyond a 'money makes the world go around' view. Not least because it doesn't! (You could live on an island without money, but try doing so without water.) Really the living earth should be our tree trunk concept.

IMAGINATIVE FRAMING – THE ROLE OF FICTION

To shift the culture is to shift the stories that we tell ourselves. How we talk about the science and frame it – for instance in economic terms – is important. But we should also bear in mind the role of fiction: novels, movies and so on. Think back to the Kennedy era, when the Space Race (arguably quite a good parallel for the amount of public enthusiasm needed – perhaps we could call this The Earth Race?) was seeded in the public imagination as much by Star Trek and Kennedy speeches as the news stories from NASA.

Stories are how we connect the life world with our own life story. As author Terry Pratchett put it (in his novel *Witches Abroad*): 'Stories are important. People think that stories are shaped by people. In fact, it's the other way around.' The Dark Mountain Project is one response; created by writers and aiming through their manifesto and journal to help other writers to help the rest of us re-imagine. Here's an excerpt from their opening statement:

The Dark Mountain project began with our feeling that, if you go deep enough, you'll find the roots of this situation in the stories we have been telling ourselves: stories that go back beyond the latest episode of irrational exuberance, down through the history of industrial society and even further. Stories like the myth of human centrality, which tells of our destiny to separate ourselves from and subdue this thing called nature; which makes history a machine for the production of human progress, as measured in the production of ever more and better goods. What makes these stories more dangerous is that we have mistaken them for reality, insisting that we have put away such childish things as myth. As a society, we no longer acknowledge the role of stories in shaping what is real to us – and so our storytellers become entertainers, our poets harmless eccentrics, our artists cynical manipulators of the market, all taboos busted and everything for sale. This won't do. The times we are living in demand something more.[30]

One popular author with a profound interest in climate change, society and appropriate technology is Philip Pullman. His best-selling *Northern Lights* novels revolve around the mission of a plucky girl (Lyra) to save a polar bear. Pullman talks about stories being inspired by science rather than trying to explain it. It's more about giving people inklings and ways of looking at things. The allusions in *His Dark Materials* to climate change include the sky being torn open by an explosion. He also has a keen sense for the machinations of power and greed in alienating ourselves from our true selves; the idea of a machine that cuts children from their soul (or daemon). In interviews Pullman talks about modern technology cutting families off from each other and also the 'universal acid of the market system'[31] that dissolved social bonds and wiped away so many structures that should have been more permanent. His passion for steam punk (steam rather than electrical technologies) is contemporary green too; we quite possibly will be revisiting steam engines, linked to solar thermal. So there are plenty of allegories and ideas in there when you look for them. But it is first and foremost great storytelling rather than a lecture: giving a richer set of ideas to think with.

THE SLOW MOVEMENT

The slow movement started as a dining club. But by now it has become a whole lifestyle philosophy. It was triggered in the late 1990s by the arrival of a fast food outlet in a famous piazza in Rome. The original slow food movement encouraged people to sample local regional cuisines. The local organising groups gathered people to enjoy the diversity of these traditional foods together in a relaxed way. But the broader philosophy is of finding the right (slower) pace to form deeper human relationships and to experience life, reflect and belong. It has spawned splinter movements such as Slow Travel and Slow Cities. A related idea is that of, for example, the Long Now Foundation – taking a different view of time than 'frantic', 'last minute' and 'short-termist'. One of their early ideas was changing the way dates are written (from 2009) to 02009.

NEW FUTURAMA

Another imaginative approach to helping people envision sustainability is the proposed New Futurama exhibition, something Bill Becker (Obama environmental policy adviser) has been championing. The original Futurama was an exhibit at the 1939 World Fair, sponsored by General Motors, that Becker says has 'dominated the American imagination of what a city should be like ever since'. At the original exhibit 23 000 visitors a day were taken on an amusement park-style ride through a model of the city of the future complete with multi-lane highways. Becker called a 2009 gathering of 'some of the most creative people in America' – engineers, architects, planners, museum directors, writers and others. They met to discuss staging a new Futurama – a city in 2050 with sustainable transport options, energy-efficient buildings and renewable power.

On a low tech level a group of us (called London United) staged some public workshops in 2008 where attendees were taken through a creative visualisation exercise, to imagine

London in 2050. We then all drew on a huge shared sheet of paper an annotated and illustrated map of what we envisioned. People imagined all sorts of things; genetically reconstituted woolly mammoths trudging up the Euston Road, houses powered by wind turbines and a series of pulleys, open air schools, market garden-based housing communes ... A wilder version of Futurama perhaps, but a space to explore the inklings we all carry that guide our rational thoughts.

ADVENTURE ECOLOGY

Why can't sustainability be a romantic/heroic adventure? Wouldn't that be a more engaging public frame to spread ideas and raise awareness of issues?

Adventure Ecology founder David de Rothschild's latest adventure is Plastiki. Modelled on the Kontiki expedition (itself a remake of a pre-Columbian expedition from South America to the Polynesian islands), Plastiki is a 60-foot catamaran made entirely of plastic waste. Plastiki is being sailed by de Rothschild and a small crew to the Medway region of the Pacific where a large floating raft of plastic waste – known as the Great Pacific Garbage Patch – has been gathered by ocean currents. The overt aim is partly to draw world attention to the problem of our garbage in the sea. But also through the symbol of the boat made of waste products such as old plastic bottles, to draw attention to a solution, using our waste as a material rather than throwing it away (as the floating garbage patch shows there is no 'away').

In a similar spirit (opening out horizons) is Cape Farewell, who lead expeditions of artists into some of the frontlines of climate change to witness it for themselves. Boat trips to the

Arctic are now being followed by a mountaineering expedition through the forests and up the Andes. They visit science stations and get to understand the processes and witness them. The artists include musicians, theatre writers, film-makers as well as visual artists. The artists broadcast and blog from the expeditions as well as creating artworks on their return for an exhibition.

In one of these artworks Sunand Prasard used balloons to mark out a space between their tether lines that shows the size of one tonne of atmospheric CO_2. Prasard originally tethered these balloons on an Arctic trip to a place called Diskobay – the photos are online.[32] A replica was created in London by arts students in a parade ground as part of a Cape Farewell season at the Tate Gallery.

INTRINSIC GOALS AND CHANGING VALUES

The WWF paper *Weathercock and Signposts* (2008)[33] by Tom Crompton pointed to problems with what had become a standard NGO and government marketing model – persuading people to make small behaviour changes out of enlightened self-interest. One sticking point is the rebound effect. If every £1 spent ends up (roughly) as 1 kg of CO_2 emitted then 'save money save energy' campaigns only free up disposable income for other equally harmful purchases. Shifting behaviour in a meaningful way, Crompton concluded, requires engaging people at the level of values. What this means in practice he added would be addressing intrinsic rather than extrinsic motivations. This distinction comes from a (1970s) model from cognitive education, and I agree it fits with my experiences of working with this issue.

If motivation comes from other people then it is *extrinsic*. The external rewards might be social qualities like prestige, glamour, charisma and so on. What's interesting is that extrinsic rewards in studies of education have proved less lasting or effective. In one study, lavishly praising children (for their art) was actually shown to actively put them off the activity.

Intrinsic goal setting is self-initiated and self-directed. It is following your own interests and being your own motivator; mastering a subject rather than rote learning. This, studies of cognitive education have shown, leads to better and more sustained outcomes. In a classroom setting it means a teacher helping students initiate the enquiry. After reading a story, the teacher would ask 'what questions does this raise?' – if a pupil said 'why do stories have happy endings?' this could be a discussion thread followed for a while, before it would lead onto other questions. It's rather like the way that we find out about things online, where one answer often leads to another question.

SUPPORT GROUPS AND SUPPORT NETWORKS

The difference in working co-operatively is that it engenders solidarity. It's a different matter than being in a passive community based on self-interest (even if aligned). This accounts perhaps for all the support networks springing up. Literal support groups include a 'weight-watchers of carbon' being trialled by Timebank (working with a Cambridge academic), to see if groups attempting to reduce their footprint to two tonnes could provide the same mutual support and encouragement as with WeightWatchers clubs.

Mentoring is another way of learning within a community. One variant of this is co-mentoring schemes, such as the one being developed by The Hub (a managed office space and social network for world changing people and businesses). In co-mentoring I can teach another group about marketing, while another group gives me helpful info on freelance coder contracts ... and so on. I'd suggested to The Hub that they develop this into an ideas bank, with its own Timebank-style currency, to enable a more convenient approach to this (than the current co-mentoring events which are not always easy to get to). I've since discovered that Hub Culture, another network with a similar name, already does this and much more, using its own currency, the Ven.

Social networks can enable people with similar projects in different regions to compare notes. i-Genius is one example; a world community of social entrepreneurs. Using quite standard (Facebook-style) facilities they can check each other out and make new connections. i-Genius organise events (including a 2008 world summit with the UN) and have attracted members from over 90 countries across the world. As their slogan says it's a good place to 'Meet Amazing People'.

Emotional solidarity and informed advice is all very well, but sometimes what's needed is more practical tools and support. Project Dirt is a community linking projects on the ground, initially in South London. The organisation itself is positioned as a catalyst and a community, but neighbouring projects are in a much better position to muck in.

Big tribal get-togethers and training camps also abound. Ranging from Social Innovation Camp where the aim is to build websites or similar for six social venture ideas in a weekend (and they are looking at extending this to a six-month incubator-style 'project' with its own building), to the Do Lectures which are all about inspiring content that gets people 'doing' stuff (their camp is quite small, but they also broadcast the videos) and Climate Camp which interestingly combines activism (at Heathrow, Kingsnorth, the City) with educational workshops. Bigger events include Reboot Britain and the Skoll World Forum in Oxford. Suffice to say we are not short of summits!

What we are also seeing is the development in these spaces of new ways of meeting, organising conferences to be more about learning from each other. One example is the BarCamp format, originating in 2005, that has spread to over 350 cities worldwide. BarCamp is based on 'user generated content'. It asks everyone to meet as equal participants. If you want to make a presentation then fine. The idea is to make summits more open, participative – unsurprisingly as they started in the Open Source Community. They are organised by using wikis and attendees are all encouraged to contribute content after the event; it's becoming common to all twitter using a shared #hashtag, but wikis, IRC, blogging, photo sharing, social bookmarking and other social technologies to create a 'shared text' are also used.

Transition Town uses a similar Open Space[34] format. One amusing twist within which is to invite 'Keynote Listeners'. There is one law of Open Space – the Law of Two Feet which encourages people who find they are neither learning nor contributing to move to another place in the event. There are four rules:

Whoever comes are the right people.

Whatever happens is the only thing that could have.

Whenever it starts is the right time.

When it's over, it's over.

The key for any such open session is to have a great question as the heading for the event. For instance one Open Space meeting had the question 'How will Totnes feed itself after the age of cheap oil?' I ran a session at the Design Council recently where the question was 'How can we reinvent banking for the common good?'

Climate Camp have an etiquette within their meetings aiming to ensure good consensual decision making. This includes the hand signals (silent clapping, 'T' signal for technical contribution and hand up for 'I want to contribute'). For large meetings the camp uses a Spokescouncil system where a large meeting breaks into smaller groups – the 'spoke' refers to spokes of a wheel radiating out; and also people at the front of each 'spoke' of discussion contribute into a central circle and compare their ideas with the other spokes. The system is designed to support both creativity and consensus (in more traditional meeting structures you tend to get one or the other). And it is a living embodiment of their broader philosophy:

> Climate change is actually the symptom of a systemic problem and we want to change that system. In the end there is trust in people's capacity to self-manage and that will be the path to addressing climate change.[35]

UTILITIES

On a practical level, co-operation can be a bit of a faff. Fortunately there are lots of handy tools that make it a snap to coordinate things like meetings, activities, group or communities actions. In my discussions over the last five years with people working on internet social networks two key themes keep emerging about what 'Web 3.0' might mean:

- prosocial networks; communities of people achieving something worthwhile as opposed to collecting lists of friends they 'poke' or '@'
- networks that support and extend real world community, social lives and interactions as opposed to online interactions only.

PledgeBank is an example of what you could call a new ritual. The principle is that one citizen writes: 'I pledge to do the following if X other people will join me.' It could be an action such as 1000 of us switching to renewable energy. It could be a fun thing, like a dare. But the majority seem to be local initiatives like (an example picked at random):

I, Natalie Adcock, will always dispose of waste correctly and help clear up Bromsgrove but only if 15 other local people will do the same.

The group behind PledgeBank are called mysociety.org and they have been behind a string of really excellent websites, all of them about promoting democratic involvement. Through mysociety.org sites, 200 000 people have written to their MP (They Work for You), 25 000 people have got something in their neighbourhood fixed by the council (FixMyStreet) and a new service (GroupsNearYou) helps you find what community groups exist in your area and also help these to share resources like email lists. The potential to start to link up local groups across numerous online platforms and private websites is extraordinary; if it succeeds it could do for getting involved in your local community what eBay did for clearing out the attic.

Another way the Web has been helping to get people together is Meetup.com. The idea was born out of a desire to help people reconnect, not in internet chatrooms but in real life. Five million people (90% of them in the US so far but it is growing in popularity internationally) arrange to meet people with shared interests locally. Meetup arranges over 100 000 meetings a month. I went to a Meetup with a group of people interested in the future of money, and heard a talk from Dave Birch, one of the developers who worked on MPesa, the Kenyan mobile currency. It's not just the invites, reminders emails and so on. It is the formatting of a soon familiar ritual, which makes Meetups with strangers out of a shared interest or purpose feel safe and routine.

Because of the importance of rituals, existing tribal communities can make a great platform for behaviour change. Ipswich Football Club turned out to be a surprising pioneer in reducing carbon emissions. Ipswich Town started by cutting their own carbon emissions by about 20% through sensible efficiencies. Then they launched a campaign to the fans called www.saveyourenergyfortheblues.com which resulted in 14 000 pledges of sufficient magnitude to offset the rest of the club's emissions. The scheme was mostly about pride and achieving a first together. It was later replicated by the Football Association under a UK wide scheme called CarbonFootieprint.

MEMES

Word of mouth is a slight misnomer because things more often spread by imitation rather than a process of verbal messages being passed on. In the original description of memes (a unit of cultural imitation, analogous to a gene) Richard Dawkins pointed to the ways that dance steps and styles of pottery catch on. These days we could point to iPods, wristbands and recycling, perhaps? In the modern, interconnected world ideas spread far and fast. Academic studies into why such memes spread point to urgency (a countdown or similar), an imbalance of risks (low cost of conforming, high downside risk), snappiness or memorability, a mythic pattern following archetypal stories ... All of which for instance explain why the Y2K or Millennium Bug (the idea that when computer clocks reset to 00:00:00 it might trigger catastrophes in nuclear plants, hospitals, banking and so on) gripped our imaginations back in 1999. I do wonder whether those who have been briefing against alarmism have looked at this example; it did rather mobilise whole economies on the sort of scale we could hope for with climate change. Maybe we actually really need to set off alarm bells?

There are some key varieties of memes that come up regularly as being important to climate for change-type projects:

- Identification. The aligning of your identity with a broader trend, position or movement. The wristband or badge factor. Visual icons, slogans, lingo or catchphrases and other signals often come into this, cementing and signalling belonging. Visual memes work because you see someone you'd want to imitate carrying them. Role models, strong leaders, martyrs and other human figures can take the same role.
- The Concept. Ideas like climate change, the long tail or open source gather a following, adopting a new style of thinking. Well described by Kuhn's classic work on paradigm shifts; it's not just the answers that change it's the questions – and hence it's a leap of faith. Management fads (substantial or otherwise) are usually this sort of thing.
- The Happening. Group actions from flash mobs to superpower summits are registered as significant group

events. The staging and experiential factors tend to dominate. But so does the marking of shared time, whether a significant traditional date (for instance winter solstice) or a new historical one (9.11).

Revitalisation movements (as discussed in my last book *The Green Marketing Manifesto*) draw upon all of these. A revitalisation movement (the term originated with anthropologist A. F. C. Wallace) seems to be the characteristic overall way that a society adapts to new circumstances at a deep cultural level. A particular learning from these past exercises in world building is the integral, ritual, often quasi-religious character – they would be regarded in modern settings as cultish, although I would add generally in a good way. Bear in mind that these movements often originated in cultural low points, such as the social dislocation that followed colonisation of indigenous societies. A modern example is The Art of Living, a 20 million person revitalisation movement in India combining yoga principles with social work.

A final thought to counterbalance any impression I might have given that it's all about functionally designing the right group processes. The revitalisation, transition, land rights and other such movements require members to go on a personal journey of transformation. Arguably that's actually their real value. They are social processes that make it possible to re-imagine what it means to be a human being. It comes back to something I often say when exasperated by overly technocratic discussions of policy, sustainability and so forth; all we really need to change is the world in our worldview!

PART 2

RELOCATING THE DREAMS

IF NOT CONSUMERISM, THEN WHAT ...?

ON 2 FEBRUARY 2009, England experienced its heaviest snowfall in 18 years. The country ground to a halt, as many roads became impassable. Over one thousand schools were closed. So that the parents who could have walked to work, or worked from home, were also forced to take the day off.

The result? One of the most fun days of the year. The streets were full of people, looking around or building snowmen (a snow bear in our case). Neighbours who hardly acknowledged each other on a 'normal day' stopped for a chat. People checked in on those who might struggle, to see if they needed a hand. Public parks with hills were full of people using bin lids and similar as makeshift toboggans. Snow fights were staged across the country – one particularly epic one that was organised using social networks and dubbed the 'Battle of Trafalgar' took place in Trafalgar Square.

This 'Snow Day' was reported in the media as a setback. Apparently we lost £3 billion that day from GDP. But the people didn't seem to mind. 'What's another three billion?' was a common view (after the bank bailout). The day seemed to offer something we had all been missing – a day when it was possible to have some old fashioned family fun, and to interact with other members of the community. There's nothing like all being in the same boat.

This incident came up in my research groups on climate change and transport. People talked about it as a return to simpler times. A return to the days when cars were rare. So rare that it used to be safe for children to play in the street. The days when a neighbour used to knock and say 'I'm going up to town, do you want me to get anything for you?' And, for all the benefits of the convenience of having your own car, and the 24-hour supermarkets, the microwave and the giant flat screen TV … you have to admit we've also lost something. And maybe it is quality of life experiences that we miss – the snow day factor – that could pull us to change. Not to sacrifice modern conveniences, but to embrace some of the enjoyments we have been missing: community, nature, taking it easy, play-fulness …

> Marketers will have a role to play in helping society to relocate dreams.
>
> *David Puttnam*

When companies think about sustainability, in my experi-ence, they nearly always think about the supply side – changing energy, reducing carbon, waste, pollution; sustainable and ethical sourcing. If your product is made of bamboo, is sourced locally, or is recycled – then that's seen as being 'green'. But most companies could have a far bigger impact if they helped people live greener, less wasteful and in many cases more enjoy-able lives.

75% of the impact of a car is the driving, not its materials, manufacture or disposal. How it is driven, when it is driven (or not), who it is shared with, alternatives like using city car clubs. Car use alone accounts for 20% of the total national carbon emissions within the USA from all sources, industrial as well as consumer. Yet nearly all discussions are still about the vehicles – hybrids v 4x4s. Rather than being about driving. Alternatives to driving a car on your own also offer the biggest gains for the driver. Studies have shown that commuting in a car on your own is the most stressful mode of transport. Sharing a lift leaves the driver less stressed. Walking or cycling can be positively relaxing.[36]

You could say companies are focusing on what they can manage and control. And of course they should reduce all these damaging impacts. But they also have huge budgets for marketing. And these can be put to good use. Mercedes 10 years ago made a TV ad in Germany asking their drivers to leave the car at home for short journeys. It didn't cost them anything to say this – they were going to do 'some ads' anyway – and it reflected well on the brand.

Marketers think of their job primarily as 'selling more stuff'. But what if consumerism – people 'buying more stuff' – were the key problem? I sat on a panel once at the Copenhagen 'Climate Solutions' conference, with the global heads of sustainability at several corporations known to be among the most progressive. Someone in the audience asked this question. And no one from the corporate side answered it. I think it was perhaps received as naïve or 'green' in the old anti-business sense. Selling more stuff is simply not often questioned as an assumption in a real business context.

Going back to the snow day point. Isn't it possible that people are also a little sick and tired of all this 'stuff'? To the extent that it gets in the way of other things we are missing out on, at least? Psychologist Oliver James thinks so. He says, in his bestselling book by the same name, that we suffer from Affluenza (James gave a new depth to our understanding of the underlying syndrome, but the term itself originated in a PBS documentary from 1996).

The fashion industry is another good example of focusing on supply, when maybe demand is more of an issue. There are lots of initiatives around sustainable sourcing – both looking at materials like organic cotton and also tackling the ethics of sweatshop employment. Less attention has been paid to the business of modern fashion itself – a business model reliant on rapid cycles of obsolescence.

There have been some moves in the fashion industry to challenge the demand side. Howies produced a HandMeDown range of 20-year products, complete with contracts for buyers also detailing their commitment to stock replacement zips and buttons for that time. Marks & Spencer helped their garments find second wearers by incentivising people to give them to Oxfam shops. Philippe Starck went further with what he claims are sustainable nonfashion garments:

> Today perhaps the most avant garde word is longevity. Today when you buy a dress you buy it for you for six months. When you come in our company you buy a dress for you, for your life, for your daughter and your daughter's daughter. It's a different way of thinking. It's the beauty of the timeless.[37]

But the reason these moves are so avant garde or attention grabbing is the mainstream of the fashion industry has been hurtling in the other direction: Fast Fashion accelerates the cycles and promotes disposability through 'cheap' (in every sense except their impact) clothes like the £1 T-shirt. 2.35 million tonnes of clothing and fabrics go to landfill in the UK every year; that's 40 kg per person.[38]

There are few in mainstream marketing who've had the vision (or the nerve) to speak up on the issue of whether selling more stuff is sustainable. Martin Sorrell, head of WPP the biggest agency group in the world, is one, and his admission that we might have a problem with consumerism itself attracted extensive media coverage. Here's what Sorrell originally said on the subject in a speech – as quoted by Ruth Mortimer, editor of *Marketing Week*:

> Consumers are used to the aspiration that you should consume more, the aspiration that you should have a bigger car, the aspiration that you should have a number of holidays, bigger houses, multiple houses ... in other words, it's a lifestyle we're encouraging them to make ... if you think about one of the things Apple is doing, it's encouraging consumers to buy a music player, an iPod, for about $200 and that is an instrument that the consumer will jettison after a year. It's encouraging people to buy these things, then trade up and consume more. The environmental issues of getting rid of that stuff are very considerable. All our habits of clients, agencies, media owners are to encourage people to consume more – super consumption. That is still embedded in the consumer's psyche, so we're going to have to respond by doing things differently and making sacrifices if we're going to deal with issues such as climate change.[39]

Sorrell wasn't arguing that business or indeed marketing must simply wither and die. In fact what he is describing is again fashion, not marketing per se. In the Renaissance the modern fashion industry emerged at a time when the two booming industries were banking and (imported, luxury) textiles. It was also a time of social, financial and geographic mobility – where suitors for your daughter's hand or prospective business partners could no longer be judged by ancestry or solid assets like land. Fashion provided a way of signifying wealth, moving in the right circles (being 'in the know') and status. Anyone could afford (or borrow for) one lavish costume. But to continually have 'the latest fashion' signified deep pockets.

Today new indicator industries like cars have taken on this role. The unintended side effect is the disposability of objects whose key value is signifying that you are up to the minute. There's nothing wrong with 'peacock-esque' display, perhaps? The question is whether we need to fashion $100 000 cars to fan out our feathers. Hybrid or otherwise.

The fashion industry has been in freefall over the last year. The *New York Times* in September 2009 reported that department stores were cutting their orders for the new season by an average of 30%. Everyone blames the recession. When we see the collapse of something in an ecosystem it's usual to suspect that on top of a triggering event (such as a disease) there is a more permanent stress or pressure. People had a choice about what they can cut back on and it's interesting fashion proved such a ready target. I have a theory that what is really killing fashion long term is Facebook. It tells you how connected, how popular, how in the know someone is. I don't mean to say people won't dress up any more. But it's an intriguing example of how something looking nothing like 'sustainability' or 'sacrifice' could possibly have the potential to convert consumerism – meeting the same needs in less resource intensive ways. A longstanding example of this is eBay. Creating desire and bargain hunting enthusiasm around the sorts of objects formerly sold in classified ads and rummage sales, or indeed thrown out in the trash.

The green movement has attacked consumerism as the forefront of creating ugly, unnatural lifestyles. Yet even consumerism's critics often seem to assume that consumerism is a symbolic, cultural issue – the icing on the cake. That we need to address bigger questions about industry, energy and so on.

70% of United States GDP is consumer spending. Consumerism is the cake. Industry, power stations, lorries, mining and so on are involved in making this cake. But the end product of all this industry – including business-to-business sales of IT equipment and consultancy – is mainly the stuff that people buy. The demand side is the ultimate source of nearly all the other demands for energy, resources, cheap labour and so on. Okay, a chunk of consumer spending is on things like housing and driving. But consumerism – our dreams of a better life – influence these too (hence the housing bubble and 'mass luxury' cars capable of double the speed limit).

Strange then that, until recently, buying stuff wasn't even counted by personal carbon calculators, nor audits of national emissions. This seems to me a bit like measuring someone's height, but ignoring the legs.

This situation was challenged by Oxford Economist Dieter Helm in a paper about UK emissions entitled 'Too good to be true?' Helm's paper was based upon back of envelope estimates, but the conclusions have since been confirmed by the Stockholm Environment Institute. As reported in the *Guardian*:

> The SEI has determined that Britain's calculated emissions would have risen by 20 per cent relative to 1990 if imports and international transport were factored in to

the total. In contrast, under Kyoto protocol accounting methods, the UK government says emissions have fallen by 18 per cent over the same period. (17 March 2009)[40]

A lot of the 'net imports of carbon' today are largely imported cars, foodstuffs, clothes, electronics, plastic toys for McDonalds Happy Meals. The reason emissions had seemed to fall was off-shoring manufacturing and farming to places so cheap it more than compensated for the extra transport costs. But the transport does have environmental costs. According to a report by Sustain, a single basket of 26 imported organic vegetables could have travelled 150000 miles, and caused more carbon emissions than all the cooking in a household for 8 months.[41]

I'm not saying all of this from the position of an activist who just wants the Tescos of this world to fail. I'd like them to succeed in new ways – or for new success stories and new corporations to take over. Given the amount of chaos and change in the pipeline, the conditions are ripe for a 'Google of Green' to emerge. But as with the internet, not only will there be pure plays (like Amazon) but also huge shifts by the existing players (like Borders.com). I see myself as part of the third generation of environmentalists (as described by http://e3g.org) working within the systems of this world on solutions to bring change. As Jonathan Porritt has argued, while capitalism is far from perfect, for the foreseeable future it's probably 'the only game in town'. Capitalism has proved so tenacious partly because it is so flexible.

I'm not a big fan of 'eco chic' green consumerism though. It's too much for show. And too close to the old fashion business models that are what really need changing. If we can redefine consumerism, redirect it, then we can go much further forward. The key is recognising what kinds of needs consumerism is meeting now – and recognising a broader set of largely unmet needs that could replace or displace these. On the insight that history doesn't retreat, it surges forward on fresh enthusiasms – or 'relocated dreams' as described in this full version of the quote from British filmmaker Lord David Puttnam (from his speech at a 2008 Royal Mail event, called 'The View From Here'):

> Our ability to address climate change will rely enormously on you; your ability to adapt your lives and change your behaviour to come to terms with a very different world than that of your grandparents. That is what is going to be interesting. My grandchildren will, in a sense, live slightly more cramped lives than I have. And that probably hasn't happened in human history before. Marketers will have a role to play in helping society to relocate dreams – helping people to understand that where their dreams were located was actually not just negative, but actually positively damaging.

I agree with Puttnam – except perhaps about there having been no setbacks in human history before. 'Relocating dreams' is a great way to capture how we can move forward with enthusiasm, rather than retreat with regret. We can relocate the dreams to unmet and unfulfilled human longings. Not superficial whims, but alternatives that support quality of life and wellbeing. Here's how Jules Peck described the contrast in a recent article on consumerism in *The Ecologist*:

> ... wellbeing studies show that people who live their lives framed around extrinsic values of self-focus, image, greed and acquisition, and are suffering from 'affluenza', are

diminishing their own wellbeing as well as those around them. They also tend to have far higher environmental footprints than others. Conversely, those whose lives are focused on intrinsic values such as personal (not economic) growth, emotional intimacy and community involvement, have far higher levels of wellbeing and lower footprints. It's more complex than saying they are 'happier', but they certainly experience far more 'flow' in work and play, better relationships and balance – things to which we could all aspire. The philosopher Aristotle had lots to say about wellbeing. In his view, to be a flourishing individual – one who experiences high levels of 'meaning' and wellbeing – you should aspire to be an active participant in the flourishing of community.[42]

To create a space in our minds for the alternatives, let's regard consumerism through a negative lens, as a kind of infantilising of society. Nothing wrong with us having or indulging our inner babies, per se. I'm not arguing we should all become repressed puritans with global bans on tickling, giggling, chocolate ice-cream and so on. But consumerism, you could argue, taps into inner baby thoughts, states and moods in the way an addiction can. Making us dependent on regular fixes or feeds just to feel whole, secure and human.

What I mean by consumerism being a babyish phenomenon is that it is about feeding omnipotent fantasies. Human babies are psychologically and physically dependent. So much so that, in the early stages, infant observation studies point to a kind of merged existence with their mother. 'Omnipotent' was one of British psychologist Donald Winnicott's words for the experience of this stage (the full phrase is 'subjective omnipotence'; the baby isn't actually a god, she just thinks she is!). Winnicott used this term to describe the state of being prior to weaning – a stage when fantasies are the reality, in that your experience is of a world (principally your mother) that seems to exist for meeting your needs. Hence it's also a stage of magical thinking. When the baby cries a breast appears. Which Winnicott argued would be experienced by the baby as if it had made the breast appear by magic.

The underlying promise of consumerism is similarly that you will never go without, that your dreams will come true; it's the fantasy of cornucopia. Incidentally I'm not really talking about the content of marketing – some ads and brands play on these themes, many don't. What I mean is that it is the relationship between brands and people that can tend to be infantilising. I'd argue most brands – from chocolate to mobile phones to the National Lottery – are offering to make your dreams come true.

Another term closely associated with omnipotence in Winnicott's theories is 'rage'. To be let down in this infantile state is more than distressing – it is somewhere near 'maddening' on the anger spectrum. The same goes for consumer society. Road rage is surely related to the (marketing) promise that as the driver of a car we are in a position of mastery; the king of the road. And we've all been witness to distressing scenes of consumer rage. It can be maddening for a customer to be let down. To be told your credit card isn't accepted (a consumer version of impotence?), that the item isn't in stock, the flight was overbooked and you don't have a seat ... It runs against not just the fact that you paid for something which isn't right, but the implicit contract establishing your omnipotence in this relationship.

The prospect of disturbing the infantilised consumer; enraging them by telling them 'no' – or daring to wean them off addictions such as oil and driving – terrifies politicians. George

Bush Senior's response to the uprush of concern about the environment at the 1992 Rio Summit was that 'the American way of life is non-negotiable.' A view taken forward by his son's administration as: 'the American way of life is a blessed one.' These statements were received in some quarters as 'grotesque'.[43] But they could (also) be true to the political realities. People do protest against fuel price rises. They vote against parties and policies that raise taxes. That's the deal. We elect others into power – enjoyment, entertainment and ease are what we expect in return.

If we are going to create a climate for change we need to take a long hard look at how we got into the position of infantilised 'subjectively omnipotent' consumers, when we should be stepping forward as citizens?

People I'm often told are 'not willing to sacrifice'. Which is total rubbish. Parents do this every day to provide a better life for their children. People have also flocked in droves to charity shops, to camping, to home grown food in the last year. Not in the main because they had lost their employment and incomes, but out of a wave of positive enthusiasm for 'thrift'. Culture is not simple. It's not primarily about behaviour, but about the meanings of behaviour. What looks like thrift has been embraced as a kind of liberation; tapping into nostalgia, simpler and slower times, health, freedom from anxiety. Bush's metaphor of negotiation assumes a fixed counterparty that wants to stick with what it has. It lacks any sense of human playfulness or fickleness, any hope for society improving and individual growth.

Calling consumerism infantile is not intended as a slur – rather as a model. One that suggests that consumerism is just an early stage. We've only had a hundred years of mass media. Babies do not stay as babies. They grow up. So can we. Yes this may mean weaning ourselves off a babyish omnipotence. But it can also mean being pulled forward (like real babies) by more fulfilling drives such as curiosity, exploration, the delight in achievement and agency, having real relationships. What pulls a baby past the mother-as-world phase is the whole world beyond her, beckoning. A world of such fascination, that it overcomes the 'oceanic' bliss of staying put.

Consumerism (like infanthood) is seriously confined. Its individualism so easily lapses into isolation. One need that can pull us forward is community:

> There is no such thing as society, only families and individuals
>
> *Margaret Thatcher*

In the Thatcher era, a new generation in the UK bought their former council house, fitted a nice new front door with added security bolts and got themselves a Sky television dish. They also took out a string of credit cards. And experienced a change in standard of living too, there's no denying it – a nice car, foreign holidays and so on. But they also paid a price, and that price was the shadow of individual materialism; a loss of meaning, community, embeddedness. According to BBC research nearly 60% of people in Britain don't know the names of their neighbours.[44] This is perhaps why neighbour noise is so intolerable – it shatters another consumerist illusion of omnipotence, of having your own space? I've heard similar laments from a client who grew up in East Germany. More than pursuing freedom, they had been pulled forward by the Western consumerist dreams; of jeans, Coca-Cola, satellite TV. But what they lost was the community enjoyment, the summers that seemed to be one long picnic with family and friends. Many of his peers by the late 1990s were nostalgic for this gentler quality of life they had lost.

We have different individual circumstances and countries are far from all the same. But averages can be revealing. The American Time Use Survey (from the Bureau of Labor Statistics – see Table 4.1) shows that what people lack is social time.

We are so used to lack of social integration it probably doesn't come as a surprise that Americans spend 12 minutes a day on civic activities compared to 157 minutes per day watching TV. According to the same study, four of the top five adult leisure activities were things typically done alone.

Table 4.1 Total time spent on leisure activities per day (average, adults) i.e. excludes sleeping, eating, working, commuting and education

PRIVATE TIME	Minutes
Household Chores	110
Shopping	47
Childcare	30
Watching TV	157
Other private leisure	<u>65</u>
	409 minutes

COMMUNITY TIME	
Civic & volunteering	12
Religious	9
Care non household member	12
Socialising/communicating	44
Sports	<u>21</u>
	98 minutes

Ten years ago Robert Putnam's book *Bowling Alone*[45] appeared, a shocking portrayal of just how atomised American society had become. The famous soundbite was that 'more people watch Friends (on TV) than have them'. Putnam pointed to the decline of socialisation, involvement in groups and social interaction: falling voter turnout, church attendance, parent teacher association attendance, even participation in activities like card games. Here are some of the book's arresting statistics, comparing the 1990s and 1970s:

- a 25% decline in voter turnout and a 50% decline in participation in petitions, speech making, writing to public officials or a newspaper;
- a 16% fall in membership of social and civic organisations, and a 50% fall in participation rates;
- 2/3 of adults attended not one single organisation or club by the late 1990s (whereas in the 1970s, 2/3 did attend).

Anthony Giddens' *Sociology* (2006[46]), puts this in historical context. Five hundred years ago people in England spent their lives mainly engaged in social and community activities. That's not to say they had no leisure time; a study quoted later in this book shows that working hours were similar to today. It was only in the industrial nineteenth century that working hours nearly doubled. The shift from socially embedded to isolated households stretches back to the 1500s. At the start of this period, Giddens writes, households 'maintained deeply embedded relationships in the community'. Family ties themselves were more perfunctory, unemotional, low key. Children usually left home by around 12 years, heading for service (i.e. becoming a servant) or if they were lucky apprenticeship. Twelve years was also the time span of the average marriage (before death did them part). Only around 1800 was the idea of marrying for love and family as an enclosed circuit emerging, a situation Giddens describes as affective individualism.

What seems to have happened in the last 50 years is that affective individualism has gone further and isolated members of households from each other, with less shared mealtimes and home or leisure activities. People don't need to compromise (to all watch the same TV programmes, eat the same food, or use the same shampoo). But they barely need see each other then either. The head of a large UK retail chain once told me that when visiting her teenager's bedroom she would knock on the door and shout 'room service'!

The numbers living alone have increased, through divorce and ageing populations. There is a lot to be said for solitude, as a positive choice. I'm not saying everyone should live in some sort of 'nuclear family'. But I do know that along with neighbour noise, one of the most frequent problems I used to hear as a Samaritans volunteer was straightforward loneliness. There are too many who do not speak to another human being from one day to the next. In primitive societies such a state would mark extremes of grief or punishment by exile. And that's pretty much how it can be experienced today, with your nose pressed to a window (like TV) into a world many of whose consumerist media fantasies are based upon social popularity (also known as celebrity).

Over the last decade things have seemed to improve on this front. There was a rush of communitarian feeling in the USA following the shock of 9/11. The founders of Meetup.com cited a desire they felt as a result of this experience to gather with people in real life, not just online.

The current recession seems to have had some of the same effect. It was certainly a great year for Tim Smit to have launched

The Big Lunch, a national day on 19 July when neighbourhoods were encouraged to sit for a shared meal.

Community is just one example of an unmet need that creates the basis for exciting ways to relocate dreams. I've grouped seven such needs with examples under headings. We will explore each need in turn in later chapters. Here I just want to introduce each one and say why it perhaps has the potential to pull us forward from our infantile (passive consumer) state.

Reconnecting with nature
I'm convinced that every four-year-old is a potential avid naturalist. Young children can spend hours enrapt watching bugs, birds, a rock pool, even just lying and looking up at trees. Even better is exploring; climbing, biting, prodding, sniffing, stroking ... One of the drives that pulls infants forward into separating from mother is an urge to explore the living world. E. O. Wilson sees this as much more than a stage. He calls it biophilia – a human instinct to be passionately fascinated with other living creatures and systems.

Community
Children emerge from early merging with the main care-giver, to develop a broader network of relationships. First with immediate family members. Then familiar figures in a nursery, or among parents' friends and extended family. Later with the society of peers at school – there being enough social dynamics in most playgrounds to rewrite the complete works of Shakespeare.

Lifelong learning
What pulls babies forward from a state of contentment? Curiosity is a key component. Curiosity is the feeling that goes with

the experience of incomplete information or understanding. You half glimpse something through an open door. Who can resist staring? You find footprints on a deserted beach – who doesn't want to know where they lead? Many behaviours we recognise as childish – like wandering off after something they have glimpsed, or asking 'Why?' repeatedly – are born out of curiosity.

Play

Play is situated by psychologists right at the split from the early symbiotic relationship with mother. Winnicott pointed to a transitional object – a teddy, blanket or other comforter – which the baby would start to use as if it were the mother meeting its need, to self-soothe. Play starts with such 'objects' but elaborates into an internal theatre of Peter Pan proportions. If you watch young children playing make-believe games where they take on characters they often spend 80% of the time sketching a scenario and 20% actually enacting it. Play soon also incorporates the sheer delight of attaining physical skills and a sense of agency and self-mastery. Play is like work, except in its lack of an external purpose. So many consumer markets promise intense enjoyment or pleasure, yet seldom live up to the sheer fun of climbing a tree.

Social production, crafts

A key developmental emotion is pride. The glow that we feel when we make it to a milestone, be it an early childhood one like standing up on our own, or a later pride in something we have made, painted, sung or figured out. Carl Jung having rummaged his way around the human psyche for most of his life, spent some of his last years making stone carvings for the garden. It's something I am growing to understand – for instance that we evolved as a species adept at such crafts as working with stone and we feel incomplete in a 'convenient' world where the making is done for us. Craft is another subject that goes to the heart of what's missing from modern life, compared to human nature (the world we evolved to expect). I don't mean buying or appreciating handmade crafts, but rather the performance of craft skills – as evidenced by many hobbies from angling to music-making – as well as new crafts like software coding and multimedia.

Citizenship

This one is slightly harder to argue as a development on from infantile dependency. Toddlers don't vote. But the transition from baby to toddler is all about empowerment and agency. And that's the core of citizenship, taking an active responsibility for things, starting with yourself but extending slowly from there. It's no coincidence that lifelong learning and democracy go together – they are both about empowerment. What we are seeing through new media structures is the emergence of ways for people to get involved in issues which it was formerly more convenient to leave to elected representatives. There is an emotional payoff that goes with having agency; and it outweighs many of the consumerised versions offering 'control'.

Generativity

From an early age we teach children to share; to consider others' needs than their own. It's not just that we think all children should be nice. But actually it is for them too, to help them avoid the (infantile) trap of being 'spoilt'. Too much selfishness, we realise, will impede their social dealings later on. Relationships are all about give and take. Co-operation and altruism are important life skills. Later in life we reach a stage

(Eriksson who named this life stage said it could happen any time from 35) where we start to weigh our actions differently. If previous stages have gone well we have established an identity, relationship, role in life. Now it begins to dawn on you that you aren't going to live forever. You then have a choice. You can stagnate and try desperately to cling to your youth. Or you can deal with the fact that you will die someday by transferring your ambitions to things that could survive you – be it a business, your grandchildren, writing, mentoring … Eriksson said at this stage you start thinking and acting for 'the good of the species'.

There couldn't be a more apt 'relocated dream' than generativity for the times we live in. Movements like Transition Towns act as beacons for people with this mindset – offering a place for pioneers wanting to make a pivotal difference at a key point in history. On a cultural level there is an argument that the transition we need to make could be from an 'eternal youth' culture to a generative one. Certainly there is a case for a wiser, more responsible prevailing attitude, as Robert Bly argued in *The Sibling Society*.

That is a brief survey of seven candidates for new aspirations to link with. These fall between existing defined areas of our modern lifestyles. Many fall into the gap between life and work. And play a role in bringing those ideas together again – under the provisional heading of 'your life's work'. People approach generative projects, community projects, designing their garden or craft-based hobbies as if they were work. As indeed they can be. George Monbiot wrote a great piece in the *Guardian* about taking up sea fishing, not as a 'sport' but for food. Reskilling of this sort is a major cultural trend; driven by some inkling of what may lie ahead; but also by a realisation of what was missing. The days of having everything done for us – babyish convenience consumerism – may be passing. It's crazy for one thing. People scamper through tasks like shopping, housework and cooking in order to hoard some time ... for what? Watching TV? Probably to watch cooking shows! Similarly we skulk home avoiding eye contact on public transport to watch soap operas or check in with our Facebook friends (many of whom are strangers).

The rewiring of our social, biological and emotional needs to fit into patterns of consumption has alienated us, presented a world of simulation that never quite satisfies the itch or drive. So in many cases, it's a step forward to re-engage with what the need is really about. It's the difference between heating food and cookery. It's the difference between watching reality TV shows and meeting people to do stuff. It's the difference between driving an 'offroad' car and going for a long muddy hike.

Underlying all of these unmet needs is a sense of profound restlessness. Anxiety can be the outcome of this. In general if you look at the ordering of society, we do all look a bit battery farmed. It's the way that we have to fit into the industrial systems of work, shopping, housing, schools, media ... coupled with the hurry sickness that goes with trying to fit it all in. Leaving us not enough free space to exhibit our innate behaviours. That list of seven unmet needs is what we would do more of, left to our own devices – our equivalent of nesting and foraging behaviours free range allows for chickens.

The 'free range' view of human nature – that we feel cooped up and are made sick by the constraints of a modern 'battery farmed' lifestyle – was caught evocatively by Bruce Chatwin, who put forward the idea that 'Man's real home is not a house, but the road, and life itself is a journey to be walked on foot' (in *What Am I Doing Here?*). This constitutional restlessness of ours – the urge to migrate, to move with the seasons – can, as Carl Jung put it, be the 'very devil' upsetting our carefully laid plans. It can be the inner force behind midlife crises, affairs, feuds. And perhaps also drives us to distractions like sprawling collections of shoes or guitars, bought on eBay.

In Chatwin's own case when confined later in life by illness he became, instead of a traveller, a fanatical collector (so much so, his wife used to have to go to auction houses to return things he bought which they could not afford). Chatwin's last book *Utz* was the fictional account of an Eastern Bloc collector of fine porcelain. Utz is so obsessed that despite opportunities to defect while visiting the West he feels unable to leave the collection behind. It is a vision of collecting as a kind of prison. And it is a parable of modern consumerism; as a kind of 'comfort eating' – a cycle of dissatisfaction producing the opposite of the desired effect (which is to be free rather than trapped by possessions). In Chatwin's life as much as his fiction we meet the question of whether what consumerism taps into is not so much status, luxury, glamour and so on, but thwarted human restlessness.

There is recent evidence that human restlessness is related to – and in fact adaptive for – nomadic life. A team of evolutionary anthropologists at the University of Wisconsin (reported in *New Scientist*)[47] studied the effects of a gene associated with hyperactivity among a nomadic people in Northern Kenya. They found that among the half of this tribal group who had settled there were no positive effects. It manifested as classic 'hyperactivity'. But among the still nomadic other half of this people, the same gene was associated with weight gain in males, and other positive developmental outcomes. The report speculated that 'a short attention span and penchant for risk taking could benefit nomads who don't know where the next meal will come from'. The restlessness Chatwin described could be more than an urge to roam, it could our evolutionary inheritance, our hunter-gatherer human nature. For 99% of human history – the Paleolithic period – our stone tool-making ancestors mostly lived on the move. That's not to say they were all explorers or drifters. Most moved within a defined territory or route. Some moved with the seasons, or with the herds, or to winter fishing grounds. Some travelled to trade, in flints, hides and other commodities. But few seem to have simply stayed put. That behaviour emerged only 600 generations (roughly 15 000 years) ago with the emergence of the farm, the town and the settler. In evolutionary timescales that is an afterthought. It may account for most of our 'civilisation'. But the universal feelings we have for wide-open landscapes, for the wind in our face ... these may be our primary orientation.

One common factor among many of those new dreams is that we yearn for authentic experiences. An authentic experience is not staged, manipulated, predictable, processed – it doesn't play to subjective omnipotence. We can find this experience in dating, in getting lost and drenched trekking, in encounters with wild animals. We can also find it in a conversation with a child, an artistic production, a humorous slapstick accident. Where we seldom find authenticity is in the world of brands, services, entertainment and other things, devised to please 'people like us'. Umberto Eco wrote of Disneyland that it seemed to have been created to make the rest of America appear 'real'. The engineering of human environments like shopping malls or media channels can be disorientating, but typifies inauthenticity. To live in a manmade world created just for you is to feel radically alone; like Jim Carrey in *The Truman Show*.

And why do we crave authentic experiences? To feel alive. To be in the here and now. But also to live lives which are rich with meaning. For our lives to be meaningful we do need to struggle, sacrifice, find a way of accepting suffering too. The myth of convenience is that we cannot bear frustration or effort. Studies of happiness by psychologist Mihaly Csikszentmihalyi show that we experience it most reliably when we flow – finding an optimal balance between the challenge of a task and our abilities, stretching to achieve something. That's the spirit that animates many of the examples we will see in the following chapters. Where the meaning of life is filled out by a shift from having, back to doing. And channelled through activities where what we produce, perfect, struggle with contributes to our own human growth.

RELOCATING THE DREAMS: GROWING OUR OWN, NOKIA

I WANT TO SHOW THROUGH some substantial case examples what relocating the dreams towards seven other human needs (than passive consumerism) might mean in practice. Firstly I will look at the 'grow your own food' revolution and how all seven of these different needs are being expressed through a range of developments. Then I will look at how Nokia, a global company, engages with sustainability in a different way than consumer marketing as we knew it; following more of a co-opportunity path. Moving past consumerism is not just a turn away from commerce, but also a potential new turn within it.

GROWING OUR OWN:
CONTACT WITH NATURE

According to reports in the media, vegetable seed sales are growing by between 60% and in some outlets 300%. The

UK's *Daily Express* newspaper reported that 'Seed sales figures have seen vegetables outstripping flowers for the first time since 1939, when the nation was encouraged to tend garden plots to assist the war effort.'[48] Keeping chickens is also popular and urban beekeeping is another trend.

The reporting has suggested this is a credit crunch effect, with higher food prices also pushing people to think of this as a way to save money. I'm not sure this is the whole story as food and grocery retail in general has been subject to price slashing for the last year. Whether it is cheaper to bake your own bread would be a close run thing. Certainly it is in line with the cultural mood though; regressing towards the 'good old days' and a fashion for thrift (charity shops in the UK in March 2009 reported running out of stock). CEO of ASDA, Andy Bond, has talked about this being as big a shift as that made by the post-war generation – a 'frugal is cool' mindset that could last 40 or 50 years.[49]

Whatever the triggering causes it also represents an important step towards reconnecting with nature. Your whole attitude to food changes when you grow some of your own. Also the footprint of home-grown food is much lower; there is less transport and energy involved (according to selfsufficientish. com the energy used to bring an apple from New Zealand may be 100 times its calorific value). Also you pick it as you need it and are much more accepting of 'odd shaped vegetables' the retail sector would not sell.

GROWING OUR OWN: COMMUNITY

Rob Hopkins (Transition Towns' founder) reckons food schemes are the 'royal road' to community engagement.

Growing and sharing food certainly seems to draw people together. In my local Transition Town (Belsize) an eco week is being held and many of the events are about food – not only growing, and local sources, but also a walk and talk by a foraging expert through Hampstead Heath.

A well-established community food format is the allotment – a patch of land made available by a local council for local residents to grow food on. If you talk to people in longstanding allotments it is clear these function as much more than places to grow stuff – they are crisscrossed with mentoring, looking out for each other, cosy sheds to have a cup of tea in. They are places where communities act like real communities – a kind of neighbourliness almost unknown in a modern cul-de-sac. The problem with these schemes is that in an era when land is managed not as a common utility but as a profitable asset, land is hard to come by.

There have been interesting moves into this space by landowning organisations, as part of their Corporate Social Responsibility. The BBC now offer a free allotment on corporation land to any employee who wants one. And the National Trust have offered 1000 new public allotments on their properties. The National Trust are offering these allotments through a community scheme called Landshare (www.landshare.channel4.com) founded by celebrity TV chef Hugh Fearnley-Whittingstall. The National Trust plots are estimated to be large enough to grow 2.6 million lettuces. 40 000 people have signed up to the Landshare community, which aims to 'connect growers with landowners'. Many of those offering land in this scheme are organisations. And in fact members are asked to 'report' any apparently unused public property in their area such as that around a community centre, which could be invited into the scheme.

A more grassroots approach is garden-share. A scheme which is part of Transition Town Totnes involved 20 local domestic gardens being shared with others who could grow fruit and vegetables there. Because of legal issues with domestic land they have developed protocols around insurance, fencing and permanent planting. It's a key learning for any community scheme that agreements need to be well formed and spelled out in advance. A larger scale (than one town) but equally grass-roots scheme in the US is Yardshare, run by Liz from Hyperlocavore – a community promoting local eating. Their site uses social network tools (.ning) to develop a simple community notice board, which is also packed with advice, videos and down to earth content like a competition to name Liz's mother's donkey.

Community supported agriculture (CSA) is an established means in the USA for groups of people to co-operate and own 'shares' in local farms. They are usually paid by receiving a box or bag of vegetables every week during the farming season. This allows farmers to sign up customers at a time when they are not so busy. And to get payment early, reducing the need to take out loans. It also allows farmers to get to know their customers. It's common in these schemes for families to visit 'their' farm and to form a relationship with it. In some versions, for instance in Holland, people may actually go to help on the farm. In others people at least go out and pack their own boxes, enabling them to mix and match what they actually need. CSA is now booming. In 2007 there were 2500 farms registered in CSA schemes in the USA, over 500 further farms joined in 2008 and over 300 in the first two months of 2009. A key principle is shared risk (this is much more than a consumerist 'advance order'). In the original versions of the scheme 20 years ago a group of individuals literally pooled enough money to buy the farm. It's still the case that 'you take what you can get'. According to the CSA website, if the pepper harvest were taken out by a hailstorm, you'd just have to make do with left over winter squash and broccoli. Conversely the farmers take their responsibility to members seriously and if the harvests are poor will make sure they get taken care of first. In the few cases where things have gone completely wrong (for instance through death, divorce or natural disaster) the membership has usually rallied behind the farmer and basically said 'never mind, hopefully it will be better next year'. This is the benefit of a community being involved in the story of the farm; it forms the basis for mutual obligation and empathy and being in it together for the long term. It's a story that is common in ethical businesses – for instance early in the history of Whole Foods, customers turned out to help clear up after a store fire. In these cases you can see that the business is a community.

Fordhall Farm in Shropshire is supported by 8100 private investors; most responding to an article in the *Guardian* newspaper. A large proportion of the money was raised through £50 nonprofit shares – effectively no-interest loans from well-wishers. Fordhall raised over £1 million which gave them enough to repair and upgrade the buildings too. The original tenant farmer was Arthur Hollins, one of the pioneers of UK organic agriculture. The farm is now run by his children, Charlotte and Ben, and it still acts as an organic education centre for other farmers. It all came about out of a rush of concern to keep the farm going rather than see the land sold off by the landowner. It seems likely with social media that we will see causes and crowd funding working together in this way quite a bit in future.

GROWING OUR OWN: PLAY

Guerrilla Gardening is like Landshare, only without permission! It is the act of turning urban wasteland back into productive growing land; to improve quality of life. It can involve throwing clay balls packed with seeds and nutrients into derelict lots. Or a spot of nighttime digging, hoeing, planting and tending.

1 May was International Sunflower Guerrilla Gardening Day. 1200 people joined the Facebook event and digs took place across the world; in Austin Texas, Rome, Dublin and especially Brussels where this particular event originated. Apparently planting sunflowers helps take the lead (from car fumes) out of the soil, preparing the ground for edible crops to be grown in surprising public spaces. That's very playful – the sight of a new bank of sunflowers in an unlikely setting can only bring a smile. But it has a serious point to make about land, landowning and reclaiming public space.

Guerrilla gardening dates back to the Diggers, a co-operative living group who took over a piece of land (St George's Hill in Surrey) in 1649 and started to cultivate it. Their idea was that if *all* the poor people in Britain started communal farming the aristocracy would collapse, because there would be no one to grow their food. That makes them sound like economic terrorists, but actually this was more of a utopian, high-minded religious sect. It was quite legal and above board to do all this. But the Diggers were brutally harassed, despite courts of law ruling they hadn't done much wrong.

This conflict is still playing out today, with the massive land rights movement in the developing world; for instance the Movimento dos Trabalhadores Rurais Sem Terra (The Landless Rural Workers Movement) in Brazil, which Noam Chomsky, quoted in Raj Patel's *Stuffed and Starved*, called 'the world's most important social movement'. According to Patel, this group has settled more than one million landless people since the 1970s – despite repression from armed militia and the state. These are not disorganised 'squats' – they represent a highly evolved form of co-operative community. This is evident in the organisation of their encampments and settlements, where each single member has, in addition to their own farming work, a tarefa – a task which benefits the community as a whole. The communities are characterised by direct democracy. Their approach to farming follows mostly organic and diverse crop principles.

In the UK large tracts of land go to waste because they are held as investments by pension funds, or were bought by (now stalled) developers. In a wartime-style food crisis you can well imagine the common land traditions returning – which allows at least free use of productive land. Perhaps we the people (and also the pension holders) can bring this forward a little?

GROWING OUR OWN: CRAFT AND LIFELONG LEARNING

Food gardening as a craft is a deeply satisfying activity. It is packed with skills and implicit knowledge, something well suited to craft guild-like communities. There are numerous guild-like structures organising education for their members, such as the British Bee Keeping Association. These are today using new media such as YouTube to supplement the traditional evening classes and courses in 'the field'. As with many craft-based hobbies there are lots of blogs and other online resources, forums and so on.

If you want to get away from it meanwhile there is always WWOOF – Willing Workers on Organic Farms. The aim here is to provide labour for the farmer, in return for accommodation, three hearty meals a day and firsthand experience of organic farming and the countryside. Also you get to support the organic food movement. WWOOF was established in 1971 in England by Sue Coppard who wanted to give city workers experience of the countryside (it originally meant Working Weekends On Organic Farms). By now WWOOF operates across the world, and has experienced a surge of popularity in recent years. In the USA the number of WWOOF volunteers increased six fold in the last five years. A spokesperson said that the rapid growth was down to 'local, cheap vacation options that include good-feeling work outdoors'. Some join the scheme to train to be farmers, but most want to 'get more involved with the movement toward local and sustainable agriculture'.[50]

GROWING OUR OWN: CITIZENSHIP

One of the first major symbolic acts of the Obama administration was Michelle's Victory Garden. Named after the garden dug on the Whitehouse lawn by Eleanor Roosevelt during WWII, the First Lady, helped by her daughters and local school children, dug up a sizeable plot of 1100 square feet and planted vegetables using organic techniques. However authentic an act by a family wanting its own vegetable plot, this was also a symbolic way to green the Whitehouse; akin to when Jimmy Carter put solar panels on the roof. And it is also legitimising the 'grow your own' revolution already sweeping the developed world. It was a move as in Roosevelt's day to lead by example and engage citizens in grassroots action. There were some subsequent news stories about the levels of lead in their soil (a sustainability sign of the times). Perhaps they should have planted sunflowers first?

In September 2009 Michelle Obama revisited the whole issue at a farmers' market close to the Whitehouse, talking about the health benefits of fresh seasonal foods, and also the benefits of interacting and learning from the people who produce it.

GROWING OUR OWN: GENERATIVITY

Perhaps the most iconic generative action is planting a tree. It is a symbol of investment in the future. Speaking on this subject Nobel Prize winner Wangari Matthai pointed to the broader cultural needs addressed by her Green Belt community tree-planting programme in Kenya:

> People without culture feel insecure and are obsessed with the acquisition of material things, which give them a temporary security that is in itself a delusional bulwark against future insecurity ... Communities without their own culture, who are already disinherited, cannot protect their environment from immediate destruction or preserve it for future generations.[51]

Matthai's programme in Kenya has planted over 40 million trees in communal areas such as school compounds, churches and farms. This helps in building protection from soil erosion. It provides firewood and building materials. And it offers a source of income to support the volunteers' children's education and wellbeing. Thirty years earlier Matthai had started this movement herself poor, recently divorced and with nothing but the conviction that by rebuilding the habitat African women could rebuild their confidence and culture. Wangari Matthai explained in her acceptance speech for the Nobel Prize how the simple act of planting trees was the platform for a broader transformation and education process: only with a healthy environment could a community support its own health and wellbeing.

My focusing on gardening could be saying the only way forward is 'back to nature' exercise. That's why I want to look at what Nokia have been doing. Not to single them out as perfect (they would be the first to admit there are plenty of areas still to be improved). Only because they do seem to 'get' how to engage with sustainability and community.

I came across Nokia's Power of We programme, as a judge at the Green Awards (where Nokia won the overall 2008 Grand Prix). It was clear from this that they are taking sustainability into the heart of their business. On their corporate website CEO Olli-Pekka Kallasvio comments:

> Thousands of Nokia people have made sustainable, environmentally sensitive practices an integral part of our day to day business. With more than a billion people using Nokia phones globally, we feel we have a responsibility to make a difference. Even in these tough economic times, environmental sustainability is not just the right thing to do, it is the only thing to do and makes good business sense.

If you look into what Nokia are doing as a company you find all the usual supply side stuff. The company has set targets for CO_2 emissions since 2006 and reports publicly how they are doing against these. Their phones are certified as free of conflict metals, such as tantalum from the Congo. Nokia has been named the number one electronics brand in Greenpeace's Greener Electronics Guide. And it has won the phone industry (GSMA) first CEO Award for Outstanding Environmental Contribution. Given all of this it's pretty impressive that Nokia have not been shouting about their green credentials in advertising. Rather than claiming green they have been doing green. For instance encouraging people to unplug their charger (in some popular models Nokia fitted a 'finished charging' alert) and putting recycling collection points into retail, including a major new push to establish this in India in 2009.

As far as green phones go, the Nokia Evolve is one of the best around, in energy, materials and so on. I also like their Remade concept (made out of old tin cans and other waste material). And another concept phone whose case is made from reclaimed wood. This brings the appeal of unique handmade crafts into a space which is almost the epitome of mass production. Nokia say they are also working on ways to make chargers use zero power except when the phone needs it. And developing ways for people to upgrade phones digitally, rather than buying new devices. A fascinating development is that their researchers may have found a way to do away with the phone charger altogether. Instead phones can draw waste power from ambient electromagnetic radiation (like Wi-Fi and TV signals); a trickle but enough to keep a phone topped up. It's a green benefit, which is also just a great consumer proposition; you never need to remember to charge a phone again. (Although it also underlines just how much EM radiation we are exposed to.)

It's when you look on the demand side though that I think their efforts are most impressive; imagining how mobile phones can be part of a world working for the common good. For instance mobile phones play a leading role in African development projects. And Nokia have been in there since 2005 working with Grameen, helping to ensure they can build an accessible mobile network in countries like Rwanda.

Mobile applications have been big news in the last few years and Nokia have been behind some nice green apps and sites. Green Explorer gives you green travel tips and helps you locate local green services. Nokia have for some time operated a partnership with the WWF and IUCN in the connect2earth community site, on the Web as well as mobile. Here you can learn about environmental issues, exchange ideas and content like video and ask experts about key themes and actions. Freecycle is a 6.5 million member web phenomenon – if you are about to throw something away, you can give it to someone else instead. Nokia just helped Freecycle port the same service to mobile. They have also introduced a home management system (currently being trialled) using the mobile to monitor and control your home energy along with a host of other smart home functions.

Nokia have also (like Google and others) been embracing open innovation; instead of assuming they have all the answers, they brief 'the world' to come up with solutions too. They offered a $150000 prize for phone apps that could 'improve life on this planet'. One short-listed entry was a Green Phone app which hacked the Nokia operating system to manage settings on a phone to minimise its power use.

Why I like Nokia's efforts is that firstly they have got the basics right. Despite being the biggest they are also one of the greenest. And they got there by helping every employee see this as a central part of their job, not an add-on – building a community of enthusiasm around their 'Power of We' internal change programme. Their focus externally is on innovation, education, community and great green utilities. And they are not too proud to partner, getting many of their best ideas from outside inventors, NGOs and consumers. I think it is partnership that makes them stand out from most corporates. I really like the way they have quietly been helping great green web communities like Freecycle and DoTheGreenThing get onto mobile. Or giving resources to organisations like Surfers Against Sewage to make and distribute little movies (also partnering with Virgin on this). Of course Nokia are not perfect, they are still a big business with a huge impact and still addicted to the business model where we treat phones as throwaway fashion. But supposedly they are working on that too.

PUTTING RELOCATING THE DREAMS INTO ACTION

USING THE SEVEN UNMET human needs as a framework let's look deeper and explore a diverse set of starting points and examples, as a kind of scrapbook readers can draw upon as starting points for their own projects. Some of these examples are small (compared to growing your own trends or a company selling one billion mobile phones). But they are indicative of what is possible.

CONTACT WITH NATURE

According to psychologist, Peter Kahn 'Children need rich interactions with nature for their physical and psychological wellbeing. However, nature is suffering, and so are our children, who are growing up in increasingly bleak environments far from the natural world in which humans evolved.'

People are starting to find their own ways back into nature. Trends in this direction include camping holidays. British families made about five million camping trips in 2007, according to the BBC but in 2008 that figure rose by about 20–30%. Camping equipment sales rose 40% in 2008. Judging by this hike in equipment sales there must have been a lot of newbies. The reported reasons included saving money, the adventure it represented for the children and the easy sociability of campsites. This is a good result for the environmental impact of tourism. And significant in giving a new generation experiences like waking up to birdsong, mist and a distinct chill in the air.

The burgeoning field of *Ecopsychology* has taken forward the idea that a well adjusted life will be richly connected with nature. It's recommended reading for anyone exploring ways to reconnect people with nature. The term – intended as a psychology informed by and connected to ecology – was coined by Theodore Roszak in *The Voice of the Earth* (1992). The key subjects explored in *Ecopsychology* – according to a new (2009) peer-reviewed journal by the same name – are:

the role of connection to nature in healthy development and self-identity;

emotional and psychological factors that drive environmental issues;

ecotherapy and the use of wilderness for health and healing;

coping with anxiety or grief about environmental destruction;

effective ways to motivate sustainable behaviors;

spiritual and cultural practices that support a healthy environment.[52]

When thinking about this as a therapy I'm reminded of the Woody Allen quote 'Only God can make a tree (perhaps because it's so hard to get the bark on?)' It may be possible for conventional therapy and drugs to curb anxiety and other symptoms by mechanistic means. But it's not so easy to help people become fully human – the equivalent of planting a tree in open ground, not in a restricted pot.

One of the methodologies to emerge from ecopsychology has been retreats into nature. North America is blessed with wilderness spaces, and the accounts of people's encounters with eagles, mountain lions and so on make exotic reading. But similar programmes have been applied successfully in the UK. WWF Scotland, together with several psychologists, created a six-month Natural Change programme which seems to be getting positive results, both in readiness to make personal shifts but also in building a powerful sense of community. The activities used in the Natural Change programme include: using pictures from nature to introduce yourself to the group; finding natural objects and making 'mandala' (circular) maps of the area using these; walking deliberately slowly through an area and becoming increasingly aware of all the sights, sounds, smells around you; exploring what all the constituents are that make up your cup of coffee. The report of the project so far and blogs recounting participants' own experiences are at http://www.natural-change.org.uk.

As far as reconnecting with nature goes, my own experience is that it is not about being in nature, it is about being with nature; how you approach it, interact with it, feel for it. When I was working on an internet bee campaign project (Tweehive), my awareness of bees and my interactions with them became a big feature of the summer. I have been drawn to observe and appreciate what they are up to. And I could swear that the bees have become interested in what I am up to too. I'm well aware of the cognitive bias that would lead me to think this. But it's more of an attitude – something from our animist origins? We are hard wired to participate with nature as if it were just as sentient as we are. It's enriching to do so and was a vital way of grounding my instincts for the creative project too.

COMMUNITY SHOPS

You'd think that shops might work against community (and they can). Yet initiatives taking shops towards community again do seem particularly effective. We'll see in a later section that the co-operative movement really took off in the nineteenth century when it reined in its ambitions (from building whole model community colonies) to operating shops.

Rural Community Shops is a foundation for UK villages which want to buy and run their own shop. Over 180 have already joined the scheme (previously known as VIRSA). The advantage of a community-owned business is that it tends to be responsive to the needs of the community. There are stories about community meetings to reinstate a favourite brand of sausages, or where a shop realising an older customer hasn't been in for their newspaper today has gone round to check they are okay. What the Plunkett Foundation (behind the Community Rural Shop project) have done is create a resource so that the 181st shop can learn from the experience of 180 others about the best way to consult the community, structure, finance and run such an undertaking. Rural Community Shops is a good example of one way to scale local grassroots innovations. Which is to format and structure the learning, then broadcast it to other communities. Transition Towns is another example.

Don't live in a village? Why not create a village shop in the city? The UK government offers a £1000 grant to anybody with a good plan for a vacant shop outlet. Temporary lease agreements make it easy for owners to allow this. Having a tenant can keep the property attractive, maintained, free from vandalism and pests. The key though is that the property becomes rates-free if it is occupied for community uses. Whereas if it is empty the owner will still need to pay rates (that can easily be tens of thousands of pounds). 70 000 shops are predicted to close during 2009, so this could become a feature on the high street. And it certainly beats a depressing ghost town row of boarded shop fronts. The *Guardian* newspaper found that, in the UK seaside town of Margate alone, 12 shops had already been given to local artists.

Anyone looking to turn a disused shop into a beautiful social venture would do well to check out 826 Valencia in San Francisco. Founded by Dave Eggers and run by a small staff plus hundreds of volunteers, 826 Valencia appears to be a store offering pirate supplies – glass eyes, cutlasses, skull flags, compasses. Visitors are even occasionally attacked by pirates with wet mops. The store though is actually a front; get through to the back and you find a centre teaching kids (and adults in the evening) creative writing, and writing and English (as a second language) in general. Six other 826 centres have opened across America by now. Other shop themes include space travel supplies, a Bigfoot (yeti) centre and a robot store. The genius idea of the surreal shops/fronts was originally because of change of use laws for retail premises; the only way they could run an education centre without too much legal red tape was if it also had a shop attached!

A UK concept (which the founder Sophie Howarth freely admits was inspired by 826 Valencia) is The School of Life.

Here you arrive with a problem, be it an unresolved argument, a general worry, a career plan crisis – and are pointed by assistants towards cultural resources that may help you reflect on this; perhaps the sort of history or philosophy book that few these days would usually know to delve into. Howarth explained in an interview: 'The history of human ideas is a great big bumfundling mound that belongs to all of us. It is our heritage. Why shouldn't we be able to access it in a way that matters to us, right here, right now?'[53] You can also sign up for courses. On the six-week course 'Love' guest speakers include a priest and a sex therapist. It's a mixture of heady intellectualism and jokey self-deprecating humour. And has been supported by big name intellectuals such as Alain de Botton.

LIFELONG LEARNING

Lifelong learning literally means the continuation of education throughout adult life. But I see its potential as being about a different kind of learning too; community- and experience-based, self-directed; one big 'school of life'.

One of my past attempts at working with brands to relocate the dreams was a putative scheme called Walk to Learn. This was the idea of creating a joint campaign to support family walking. I invited a consortium of relevant potential sponsors to discuss and help develop this idea; the Campaign for Learning, Clarks shoes, John Lewis, *The Ecologist*, the *Guardian*, HSBC, innocent, Islington Council and Puffin Books.

The aim of the project was to produce a campaign of educational and inspiring materials to encourage families to walk more together. Why? All sorts of reasons; like reducing CO_2 emissions from driving; interactions with nature and community; and supporting family learning.

The title was a play on 'learn to walk'. Walking and learning link well. It is a space in which people have freer flowing conversations – stimulated by what is experienced, not least the bodily experience of ambling along – as opposed to 'talking about' within activities like play, feeding and bedtime. Plato's Academy took place in a garden (the word 'academy' means garden), and many of their dialogues took place on walks. I imagine a robed philosopher presenting his paper and saying 'here the argument turns' while leading the group walk in a different direction. When I briefed design college students I actually took them on a rambling walk across London, chatting about what we saw, what the opportunities would be if our 'family' were on this walk.

The role of the campaign materials would be to propose topics of conversation, games, missions. It could be trying to spot the 20 most common birds, using a chart of silhouettes. Or discussing the history of chimney shapes. Most would have something about connecting with community and the nature that is present even in the most urban environment. Walk to Learn never quite came together, for various reasons, but I always felt (as did some of the potential sponsors) that it had a lot of potential. And 'family missions' certainly do work – this weekend Cosmo and I are taking part in a national Spider Hunt (a census for BugLife).

Another promising idea that didn't quite happen (in 2002) was a plan I hatched with Justin Francis from Responsible Travel to encourage people to get more out of their holidays – by really engaging with local nature, community, food and so on. The idea was to use sponsored content to stimulate mass tourists to become more independent travellers – speaking a bit of the local lingo, trying some local dishes, going for a snorkel. In our (perhaps over-complicated) version of the scheme we

were going to produce customised packs at the point of departure so you could print out walking map guides for your destination, snorkeling guides to the undersea flora and fauna of
that area – and also based on your own interests. For instance
if visiting Barcelona why not learn about their football tradition
too? We were hoping to persuade sponsors to give away goodies
such as compasses for exploring, snorkels and masks for swim-
ming, language and guidebooks.

PLAY

We are losing species at a rate which, according to some scientists, already would qualify as a mass extinction event. And it
may take up to 10 million years to rebuild this lost biodiversity
(reforestation by the way is not the reversal of deforestation;
the species lost will not be recovered that way). Many of the
species under threat are insects. Not surprising since insects are
thought to account for 90% of all animal species.

It's pretty easy to get people worked up about the (potential)
loss of pandas and tigers. Easy even to campaign for tree frogs.
But hard when it comes to insects. Relatively few are parasitic,
disease bearing or otherwise bad for us. Many key functions in
ecosystems from pollination to waste disposal are carried out
by insects. But most people seem to have an instinctive aversion
or sense of disgust when it comes to creepy crawlies.

Tackling this aversion – along with learning from insect life,
appreciation of biodiversity and sheer wonderment – was the
subject of Pestival – a playful blend of art, science, culture and
ecology festival in London's South Bank. I was introduced to
the founder Bridget Nicholls by a mutual friend from *The
Ecologist* to help market Pestival. The festival sounded amazing;
exhibits included the Termite Pavilion (a section of a termite

mound scaled up 15 times), lots of opportunities to interact with and observe insects, along with insect themed art, music, comedy, film screenings, lectures and workshops. The one catch being they had no marketing budget. So I figured it would have to be some sort of online social production.

The idea I came up with is called Tweehive; a Twitter mass role-play of a beehive. It started off as a marketing idea. But actually Pestival got masses of media coverage in their own right – and 200 000 people visited the event. But Tweehive took on a life of its own attracting supporters including several best-selling bee authors, alternative comedians and even Gordon Brown's wife, Sarah. The reason being that this was an opportunity to raise awareness of the disappearing honey bee. An issue that the Pestival event highlighted too.

Tweehive was a mass role-play by human beings of a bee colony on Twitter. What this meant was that a large number of us tweeted describing what we would be doing if we were bees. The aims, besides its links to Pestival, were to raise bee awareness, wonderment, interest, actions – plus generate traffic to bee related sites, campaigns and resources. We ran the event on three separate days. The third of these was live at Pestival – with the online stream projected onto big screens, alongside our 22 pen portraits of the different roles bees can perform in a colony; from nurse, to forager, to mortician. The aim being that rather than just saying 'bzzz', people would learn about bee life. Imagine for instance being a fanner bee whose role is to act as a living aircon and keep the colony cool? You would also then need to interact with water carrier bees (who bring water to put on the fanner bees' backs). Plus the other fanner bees to decide when it's getting too warm.

Also during those Tweehive days there was a flower foraging 'treasure hunt'. When a bee found a flower widget that we had hidden on more than 100 partner sites all over the internet, they told all the other bees – by posting a link on Twitter. The more clicks the widget got, the more it 'fed' the colony. This was a means to create some traffic and interest for relevant partner sites involved in bees and sustainability. But it was also a way to model the way bees really do signal finds of pollen and nectar to each other (through the famous waggle dance). And it also ensured more bee to bee interaction, which was vital to pull the role-play beyond 'look at me I'm a bee' individualism to an experience of co-operative self-organisation.

The other thing about Twitter: many of our bees had 500+ followers (perhaps bee and sustainability nuts are more co-operative and sociable?) And on Twitter if you follow someone you get all their tweets, including the ones tagged #tweehive. The size of the audience seeing Tweehive was hence very much larger than the size taking part. Friends and supporters also helped build the awareness by sending out tweets about #tweehive. Deepak Chopra, the physician, writer and philosopher who has over 100 000 followers on Twitter, helped spread the word. Other supporters included Martha Lane Fox (founder of LastMinute.com) and Sarah Brown the wife of the prime minister. We also had links with bee campaigns such as the Co-operative's 'Plan B'.

The campaign was picked by TrendCentral.com as one of the three 'Twitter trends' of the year. And I even got a message saying the Mayor of Portland, Oregon had been talking about it. It's been an amazing experience of co-opportunity; 30 volunteers were involved in the development of the content and technology; organisations such as the British Beekeeping Association advised us too; as well as our own website we had a mobile application for Tweehive live where any of the 200 000 visitors could simply text 'bee' and their message to a number and have their comment posted within Twitter and tagged #tweehive. We had some live performances at the South Bank too (to break up the experience of staring at a screen all day) which Aladin curated – including live visual art, magic, stand up comedy and also a movement artist who performed a dance based upon watching bees in her garden for three weeks. All of this done by people for the love of bees and also in many cases because they thought the idea was really neat too.

For all the thrill of the new media spectacle, I've found watching bees one of the most enriching aspects of the project overall (as well as chance encounters, there is a glass sided bee colony at the Horniman Museum). I've come to appreciate what Rudolf Steiner said of bees; that 'by way of the hive the whole cosmos enters man and makes him strong and able.'

CRAFT

There is a huge upsurge of craft-like hobbies – from bread-making, knitting and gardening – to new media crafts such as keeping a blog or writing open source code. You could also include growing your own food under this. We seem to have swung from an age of convenience to an age of crafts.

By craft I mean a deep skill and practical know-how; often apprenticed but in the higher levels of mastery self-taught. And it's not just about developing a knack; it is also an anvil on which you can hammer out your psyche.

Rediscovering craft is at the heart of the social media revolution. The clearest descendent of something like the Guild of Stockingers (the real name of the rumbustuous group better known today as the Luddites) is Linux. The parallels include the concept of craft – getting it just right – rather than mean and lean profit, owning the means of production, peer assessment of quality (an applicant to be a full guild member had to present a 'masterwork').

By craft I don't necessarily mean economic work. In fact the craft spirit has flourished in amateur settings; perhaps because it is easier to approach these with a pure motive of dedication, as your life's work. It is also the ethic of organisations like the BBC (a passion for creative quality and public service). Craft is central to human nature. We are not a blank slate. And we evolved (in the first two million years of human development) as makers of beautifully worked tools and artifacts. The deskilling and routinisation of industrial work was hence almost bound to be an assault on the human soul.

There has been a burgeoning market for unique modern crafts, which Etsy.com for one has tapped into. You can find some amazing stuff on there. Like some of the Trashion: little toddler shoes made from Reese's Peanut Butter packaging (they are lined by the way). That all sounds niche but Etsy is the world's fastest growing online selling site; in March 2009 it sold $12.5 million compared to $1.6 million in 2008. It's basically eBay for nice stuff made by nice people. And because it was founded as a service to the makers of handmade goods, it has kept the fees low. Launched in 2005 Etsy now has 2.1 million members, 200 000 sellers, 3.4 million items listed.

Etsy have taken in some major VC investment over the years but their founder Rob Kalin seeming aware of the tension between this and potentially supporting the biggest mainstream craft revival since William Morris, references a children's story called 'swimmy' (by Leo Leonni):

So our vision is to be the eye, to be a kind of organizing principle. We do not want Etsy itself to be a big tuna fish.

Those tuna are the big companies that all us small businesses are teaming up against. Those big companies are holdovers from the days before the Web existed. And any company that is being run the same way now as it was before the Web came about is due for some massive restructuring or deflation. Etsy is a company born on the Web, literally. I see the company itself as a handmade project.

One effect of that is that despite having some big investors on their board, they continue to run the actual business co-operatively, i.e. democratically.

CITIZENSHIP

A G20 summit took place in London in April 2009, where leaders of 20 leading economies met to agree measures to tackle the global economic crisis. Two weeks earlier, in Karlskrona, Sweden 18 people had already met to discuss the world crisis too. Citizens from eight countries were represented in the group: Brazil, Canada, France, Korea, Mexico, Sweden, Pakistan and the United States. All of the delegates happen to be students of both sustainability and systems theory. And they were one of the first to respond to a new prosocial network I was involved in setting up – called 'We20' – where the idea is for citizens to hold their own summits and see what plans they come up with.

The We20 idea was the product of a meeting at NESTA in January 2009 hosted by a lawyer named Paul Massey. Present were a diverse bunch from policy, economics, IT development, the arts, change management and social ventures. Paul's initial challenge to the group was – what can we create, using social media around G20, to get people's voices into the event? We got to the We20 plan via lots of other ideas, arguments, debates and diversions. In essence we realised that the most valuable thing might be for other groups of 20 citizens to have such an interesting discussion as we had had, and come up with their own plan, i.e. to hold their own G20 meeting.

Basically We20 is a three-step 'service system':

1. Invite (up to 20) people to your very own G20 meeting.
2. Discuss the world crises and come up with a 'plan'. The plan could be for your street or it could be global, or anything in-between.
3. Upload a written report of your plan to the website for others to comment and vote on. And check out others' plans.

A little bit of guidance on each step is given on the website. But the group deliberately wanted to make it an open-ended thing; let groups find their own way, their own topics; make it emergent, not constrained – just as we had been in our first meeting. Groups of volunteer coders 'hacked' it together. There was a launch event at NESTA where 80 people held a series of prototype We20 meetings. The word was spread to contacts across the world and meetings started happening. Which brings me back to Karlskrona in Sweden. What this We20 group came up with touches upon many of the main themes of this book. Here is an excerpt:

> Our vision of a sustainable future: Economic institutions and governmental institutions that serve human needs, and are not ends unto themselves. In order for them to do this everyone must be empowered to partake in these

systems, self-organize, and decide the vision and outcome of these systems. Interdependence (strong sense of community). Systems that are simplified and understandable, trustworthy & transparent. Did we mention transparent? Education and empowerment. Laws written for people, not for corporate institutions (systems by all of us, for all of us). Stories of meaning that support these values and can be translated to the reality of our global world. More chaordic, self-organizing 'flat' institutional structures.

And here's what this group chose as their concluding remark – a great quote:

Today, many things indicate that we are going thorough a transitional period, when it seems that something is on the way out and something else is painfully being born. It is as if something were crumbling, decaying, and exhausting itself, while something else, still indistinct, were arising from the rubble.

Vaclav Havel

One of the inspirations for the We20 idea was that the BBC did something like this in another time of economic crisis; the 1930s. They broadcast a series of six radio lectures called 'Life in Our Times' given by leading government figures and academics. There was one on the Great Depression, one on whether war with Germany was coming, one on the idea of a leisure society. What made this different from other factual programming was that the BBC also produced 'listener guides' – pamphlets with instructions for holding your own group discussion after each programme. People gathered in homes, church halls and working men's clubs and took part. If I get a chance I might remind the BBC of this – I wonder if it is time for something like that again?

> Our constitution is called a democracy because power is in the hands not of a minority but of the whole people.
>
> *Pericles*

In Athens, which called itself the birthplace of democracy, every citizen could attend every meeting of the Assembly, propose laws and policies, vote. While Athens claimed to have invented democracy, assembly-style politics had a much longer history in the East. But Athens took it to another level. Out of roughly 30 000 citizens, up to about 6000 did regularly attend the meetings of the Assembly. They had some interesting recruitment tactics to keep the numbers up. One involved ropes dripping with red paint being carried through the markets – anyone marked with paint that didn't attend Assembly could be punished. Another policy was paying attendees, which led to a higher representation of the poorer people, much to the reported annoyance of the conservative wealthier Assembly members. But mainly the system operated on natural enthusiasm for this way of doing things. During the 27-year Peloponnesian War against the Spartans the Assembly was unusually packed.

Roll forward 2400 years to The United States of America – in its prominence and power very much the modern Athens. In Athens 40% of citizens were involved regularly in the Athenian Assembly. In modern America the equivalent figure for central government is 0.002%. As we've seen in a time of crisis there is a need for a much broader citizen engagement. But how to get people involved in political discourse again?

One such scheme in 2008 was with a group that Liberal Democrat environment spokesperson Steve Webb dubbed 'Ten

Green Bloggers'. Webb had called us together to chat about how to use social media to help get more MPs behind the Climate Change Bill and specifically the clause (which has now passed) giving the UK the world's first legally binding commitment to make an 80% cut in CO_2 emissions by 2050. We all sat perched on seats, bits of desk and windowsills in his tiny Westminster office chatting about this. Being inquiring, blogger types, we asked Steve questions. One was: what had ever made *him* change his mind on a free vote? Steve said it certainly wasn't sacks of petition postcards from some NGO, signed by 'crowd sourced' members. Times he could remember changing his mind (and vote) had all happened in his local constituency surgery; when a local resident had come in and told him straight: 'I've been voting for you lot for thirty years but I am really worried about ___ (e.g. the Iraq War, identity cards, embryology) and I want to know where you stand on it?' Steve said you only had to see two or three people like that on an issue and 'it takes up your emotional space'. In the era of mass global media, what politics still comes down to is conversations like this.

Okay, we said. Then we just need to get two or three people who are genuinely concerned about climate change to go and see each MP in the next month or so, and tell them how they feel about the Climate Change Bill. So how could they do this? (Most of us hadn't known you even could just go and talk to your MP.) Steve told us that every MP makes public where and when their surgeries take place and these are either open to the public on a drop-in basis, or there is a number to call to make an appointment. The trouble is firstly (we guessed) that 99% of people don't know this. And secondly the information is buried in constituency and party and local websites.

So what we did, as a group of volunteers, is look up the surgery details for each MP. We then put up a website at www.canvassyourmp.com with all of the information listed. On this site you can enter your postcode, find out who your MP is, look up their surgery details and also – if you liked – report back on how you got on. We also publicised it from our blogs; one of which (Treehugger) was among the top 20 blogs in the world. The 80% clause passed and it would be nice to think we played some role. The biggest gain though would be spreading the idea of just going to chat to your MP.

There are lots of new ways to get your views through to your representative. In the USA the award winning http://tweet-congress.org/ has proved a hit:

> We the Tweeple of the United States, in order to form a more perfect government, establish communication and promote transparency do hereby Tweet the Congress of the United States of America.

In these examples social media are not replacing the real world process of politics. Rather they are encouraging people to rejoin the assembly. The old excuse that it is too inconvenient for everyone to be involved no longer applies. In another such initiative, at www.change.org all you had to do was vote on which, of hundreds of options proposed by campaigners, should be 10 'Ideas to Change America' presented to Obama on his first day in office.

GENERATIVITY

Generativity sounds like a grand legacy concern but it's really about how we apply our values to make lasting changes to our communities for the better. Hence a concept for tackling consumerism I pitched (together with *The Ecologist* magazine) to Christian Aid, with a view to working with their church network. The idea was to provide an alternative to the consumerist frenzy of modern Christmas. Rather than cutting back on the fun, why not have *more* fun by celebrating together? Who else could tackle this, we asked, than the church? It was their brand after all, it was about time they took back control!

Our idea was approaching it at a community level (local churches and their connections into clubs and faith schools) in the hope of relieving that terrible peer group pressure to be out splurging on expensive games, flat screen TVs and so forth.

Christmas represents something like a '13th month' for retailers. It's the prime time when consumerism is aligned not with needs, not even with wants, but just buying stuff for Christmas present rapture. It's stuff that often gets put in the cupboard on Boxing Day, never to reappear until the long walk to a charity shop (at best). But the dream of Christmas present is a strong one; up there with the dream of an escapist summer holiday. Christmas is the heartland of consumerism, the time when children's expectations get set, the 'Hajj' of affective individualism; only here the pilgrimage is to the department stores, toy shops and increasingly the online retailers (whose reliance on Christmas deliveries is amusingly resonant with the whole 'will he/won't he' Santa lore!)

Here are a few 2006 statistics from the British Retail Consortium that we used to support our case:

- Many retail outlets make up to 60% of their annual turnover between November and January.
- Spending in the two weeks before Christmas rose by 8% to £15 billion. The amount spent on Christmas purchases rose by 10% to £11 billion.

In 2006, each person spent an average of £390 on Christmas gifts, up 18% on 2005.

- Christmas day costs approximately £975 per household.
- Approximately 7 million Christmas trees were sold that year, worth an estimated £245 million.

£160 million worth of Christmas decorations were imported into the UK during 2006 to meet consumer demand, with each household spending an average of £25 a year on decorations.[54]

Other records set by Christmas include levels of domestic violence – fuelled by sensational cheap booze offers – intensification of the misery of loneliness for those left out, and (by January) small business insolvencies and divorces!

Our view was that Christmas ought – as it had been up until only 200 years ago – to be a community festivity. That by hemming it into Victorian domestic bliss the restlessness had been unloosed on consumerism. The idea we pitched was based on community ideas located around local churches.

- Craft classes nights remaking Christmas cards by cutting out letters from cards and wrapping paper left over from the previous year.
- The cards would all spell out a more appropriate seasonal message: like 'Less is More' our campaign brand name and rallying cry.
- A swapping fair. Like Swishing (clothes swapping parties) but for kids' Christmas presents. For instance if you have a six-year-old child, bring in their old four-year-old toys and swap them for six-year-old ones.
- Community activities to get people out enjoying themselves; from visiting local grannies and carol

singing, to silly fun in the church car park (like a snow castle building competition, weather permitting).

- A pledge to spend £20 a person maximum (when a group sets a norm it is easier for individual members to take the social pressure). With the option to donate the excess to Christian Aid for those more fortunate.
- Education around the waste and environmental impact of Christmas, combined with practical alternatives to halve your 'stocking print'. Lots of this education focused on faith schools.

The Christian Aid team we met and some of the church organisers seemed keen. But the scheme got slightly lost in upper echelons at the charity – it was not felt to be aligned with their existing campaign on climate change. I've been told since I would have been better off taking it straight to the Anglican Church. Richard Chartres, the Bishop of London, is certainly well-known in sustainability circles to be a passionate advocate. Chartres is behind many a scheme, such as energy audits in local church buildings, and has been one of those promoting a 'low carbon Lent' since 2007. I also appreciate his forthrightness on the moral question:

There is now an overriding imperative to walk more lightly upon the earth and we need to make our lifestyle decisions in that light. Making selfish choices such as flying on holiday or buying a large car are a symptom of sin. Sin is not just a restricted list of moral mistakes. It is living a life turned in on itself where people ignore the consequences of their actions.[55]

If we are to speak with people about their values and broader responsibilities, approaching people through communities like the church seems a sensible approach on all sorts of grounds. It is a ready-made community for co-operative solutions and schemes. It has its own media channel. And it's one of the few places people actually don't mind being preached to!

Similar points though would apply to any sustainability minded network. And I don't just mean green causes, I mean organisations like the Women's Institute and CBI, which are proving some of the more progressive voices urging a change in our society and ways of life.

PART 3

CO-OPERATIVE RESPONSIBILITY

THE WALL OF
IRRESPONSIBILITY

Publicity is justly commended as a remedy for social and industrial diseases. Sunlight is said to be the best of disinfectants; electric light the most efficient policeman.[56]

US Supreme Court Judge, Louis D. Brandeis

IN 1986, US CONGRESS passed the Emergency Planning and Community Right-to-Know Act. As a result of this legislation, companies in relevant sectors became required to disclose the quantity and type of toxic chemicals that each of their facilities released into the environment. Furthermore by mid-1988 this 'Toxic Release Inventory' (TRI) data was to be made public, whereas previously (under the Freedom of Information Act) any data on a business held by the government had to be specifically requested, item by item. Congress took this bold step partly in response to the wave of public concerns raised by the Bhophal disaster of 1984, involving a leak at a Union Carbide plant in India that had killed 2000 and injured 100000.

These reported emissions weren't illegal. But having the information out in the open made some of the companies look worse than others. Newspapers wrote articles with headlines like 'The Ten Worst Polluters in this State'. *USA Today* ran a whole special report naming the worst polluters nationwide. Investment banking analysts picked up on it too, and a subsequent business school study showed that 'firms with lower TRI emissions outperformed their industry competitors in the stock market'.[57]

Within two years of the data first being published, the recorded emissions of toxic chemicals by the same companies fell by 40%.[58] Without the need for fines or lawsuits – simply through being accountable through information in the public domain, companies started doing the right thing. Some companies launched policies to reduce their emissions by far more than 40%. The head of Monsanto stated on the eve of first filing their TRI data that he had been 'astounded' by the 0.17 million tonnes of toxins his company was releasing. And he promised to cut these emissions by 90% within four years.

The responses to the Californian Proposition 65 (also in 1986), was if anything more dramatic. The idea behind this legislation was that companies would have to warn consumers in advance if their products contained more than a certain amount of substances like lead, known to have harmful effects on human health. As a result a number of companies scrambled to remove these chemicals from their products altogether, to avoid having to make such a brand-damaging admission; for instance, removing lead from water taps, calcium supplement tablets and the solder used in some food tins.

All of which explains why a number of us looking at sustainability and food got excited when Wal-Mart announced in mid-2009 that all of its suppliers were going to have to disclose full details on the sustainability and sourcing of all their ingredients, to be released into a public, open source database. Of course details of how this is done and what is covered will be important. But as judge Brandeis said such sunlight can often be 'the best of disinfectants'.

A lot of the bad stuff that happens in the world only happens because people are not aware of it. We catch snippets in the news. But we are shielded from knowing how the world really works. Poverty is a case in point. We know it exists, but few appreciate how much of it there is. If you read the entry on poverty in Wikipedia you find a common view that poverty is one world problem which we are actually well on the way to solving:

> We need global economic growth in order to lift the poor nations out of poverty. And this say the proponents of the current system is working. The number who live on $1 per day has halved since 1981. Life expectancy has improved 'greatly'. Child mortality has decreased in every developing region of the world. Similar trends can be observed for literacy, access to clean water and electricity and basic consumer items. (Wikipedia)[59]

Poverty is something we think of as happening at the extremes; refugee camps filled by conflict or natural disaster. It can be exacerbated by conflict, famine and so on. But sadly it is also the majority human experience.

First of all, let's put the record straight on $1 per day.

You might imagine that a US dollar would actually go quite far in Darfur or rural China. As indeed it would. But that's not what the $1 per day figure means. The $1 per day calculation is adjusted for spending power. It is what you could buy in the USA in 2005 for that amount of money.

The researchers use the relative prices of goods and services to translate what an income means in different parts of the world. It's an entirely valid statistical method – otherwise the figures for two countries wouldn't really be comparable. But it is widely misunderstood.

You can check for yourself what proportion live at what income using the World Bank's own database: http://iresearch.worldbank.org/PovcalNet/povDuplic.html.

Here in Figure 7.1 is a chart with some examples of what you will find:

Imagine living on $1.25 per day in the USA (that's the new standard measure of extreme poverty used by the World Bank). It's a level of poverty seldom achieved in the West, even by those sleeping rough. The decrease in the numbers below $1.25 per day is welcome. But you notice that it does not greatly affect the overall pattern, which is one of staggering inequality. The global distribution of income has twin peaks; 'us' (the 7% living at or above the average income in Portugal – the poorest country in Europe); and 'them', the other 93% – with around 80% living below a $5 per day equivalent. And you can see from the

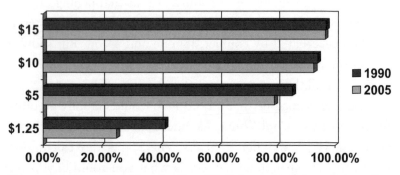

Figure 7.1 Household income/day (% living below these $ spending power levels at US prices)

graph that there has been very little change in the proportion living on the equivalent of what $5 per day would buy you in the USA.

Within the USA the poverty line is defined as the threshold below which families or individuals are considered to be lacking the resources to meet the basic needs for healthy living: having insufficient income to provide the food, shelter and clothing needed to preserve health. That level is currently estimated to be $22 000 for a 4-person household – i.e. $60 per day. A household income 0.14% of the world's population achieve.

One thing I worked out from the database was what percentage of households in the world earns more per day (in USA spending power equivalent) than the cover price of this book? The answer is 3%. If you bought this book without thinking, because it was only $15, then you are in a *tiny* minority.

Hence we are all modern day Marie Antoinettes. As with this famous queen of France, what is shocking is not just us living it up (while so many others suffer deprivation) but also our total ignorance of the true situation. We could hold our hands up and protest that poverty is something that mainly happens in distant countries. Our governments and charities do supply aid. Our GDP growth offers markets for their produce and employment for migrant workers. How much more can we do?

The trouble with that excuse is that our companies, governments, banks, agencies and markets perpetuate global poverty. It's not that we got rich and others haven't caught up. The standard of living for a worker in India, for instance, prior to colonisation was similar to that in the UK. The wealth gap is not just born out of unequal success, it is also the result of a seesaw. Or to give it a more straightforward word, the result of exploitation.

As well as scale and distance, rapid change is something that seems to fox us. Few realise how rapid and recent the 'offshoring' of Western manufacture to developing world countries has been. In the 1960s, 60% of clothes bought in America were produced in America. Now the figure is under 5% and those produced in America would often be produced by migrant workers from Ecuador and similar places, working in true sweatshop conditions within American cities. Why are corporations doing this? Again people do not often realise how big the differences in wages are. The current UK national minimum wage is £5.73 per hour. The rates paid by UK companies Matalan and Mothercare in the developing world, as highlighted by a (2007)[60] report *Let's Clean up Fashion* were as low as 13 p per hour – a level so low even in these developing countries that workers had to rely on government food parcels. If you adjust the figures for spending power you find that fashion workers in Bangladesh earned about 7% of a UK living wage, and the situation in India (9%) and China (11%) isn't much better. What the report points to is a systematic paying below a living wage, as opposed to the image projected by industry of an ethical operation with a few (hard to police) malpractices.

It's the same with child labour. We see this as an abuse limited to specific cases. According to the International Labour Organization there are 250 million child workers worldwide. Over 70% are involved in hazardous work, slavery, sex trafficking, soldiering and so on. Not a pretty picture.

From a company point of view, with competitors 'racing for the bottom' (the lowest wages and costs, the highest margins and profits), it is impossible not to follow suit. I met an executive from a manufacturing company at a marketing conference last year. He told me that one of his competitors was manufacturing a product for around £10 that they sold in the market for over £1000. His local manufacturing costs were much closer to the selling price. And he had reached a point when he couldn't see any alternative to following suit and moving production to China. That or go out of business.

Off-shoring is presented as a positive development. In time its proponents say that China will become Japan. But look again at the wages – 13 p per hour. A Clean Clothes Campaign report summed up what this meant on the ground 'There's a saying among girls in the slums of Bangladesh: if you're lucky, you'll be a prostitute – if you're unlucky, you'll be a garment worker.'[61]

When caught out on issues like exploitative wages, corporations will say that it is simply not their business to interfere in local economics. They buy through intermediaries. And this strikes me as being at the heart of the problem. The world today is contracted out. I don't just mean in business. It also applies to hospitals, government, schools, supply chains, investments. What I mean by contracted out is a configuration where *those producing results are separated from those demanding these results*. There is a wall between the two.

David Hieatt, co-founder of ethical clothing company Howies, explained his view on all this to me, by citing an old Tom & Jerry cartoon:

> In this cartoon Tom & Jerry are on a desert island. Jerry (the mouse) is the boss. He sits in a deckchair, under a palm tree and – because this cartoon is made in the 1950s – he naturally wants a cocktail. So he opens a serving hatch in the large wall that divides his side of the island from Tom's and shouts 'Pina Colada!'
>
> Tom rushes around chopping pineapples and what not, and delivers the drink, complete with decorative umbrella.

Jerry downs the drink in one gulp and shouts 'Pina Colada!' again. Tom rushes around. Jerry shouts 'Pina Colada!' again. And again. The cartoon goes faster and faster.

On Jerry's side of the wall we see a succession of drinks being delivered by a flustered looking Tom. But when we pull back and see the whole of Tom's side of the island, we see that it is being devastated, chain sawed, bulldozed and torn up, in order to try to keep delivering Jerry's innocent little Pina Colada's.

Dave told me that he saw this cartoon as a child and had carried it with him since, as a parable of 'what is wrong with the world'. (I've since tried to track this episode down and so far no luck. Perhaps it's an even better story if Dave dreamed it up?)

Anyway I think Dave is right. The problem of a lack of responsibility in the world is often down to the split between those who give orders (or money) and those who execute them to get results. It's the wall. Once you separate the orders and the responsibility, the result is almost inevitable exploitation and destruction. Why? Because people under implacable pressure to produce results at any cost (when the costs are not specified or checked) will do bad things to get these results. And there is a ratchet effect; if you manage to squeeze out the results this year you will be under even more pressure to deliver the next. Here are some real world examples:

Slave labour jeans

In the 1980s Levi Strauss won the Martin Luther King Award for its prosocial employment practices within the USA. Levi's moved manufacturing overseas in search of cheaper and cheaper prices. And it worked. Until an investigative journalist working for the *Washington Post* in 1992 exposed the use of unpaid workers (slave labour) in Chinese prisons to stitch Levi's jeans.

Primary school testing

The National Union of Teachers in the UK voted in 2009 to boycott the primary school SATS tests in the UK for 7 and 11-year-old children. Why? According to the NUT executive 'because they force schools to focus on borderline pupils who can push up their overall score'. The fact that the test affects the school's standing in league tables meant the schools were forced to compete. Studies showed that children learned almost nothing new in the two terms leading up to the test, compared to a big leap forward in the term after the test, when children could get back to learning.

The 'Honorable' East India Company

This wall of irresponsibility goes back to the origins of the transnational corporation: The East India Company. The Company was formed in 1600, under Royal Charter as the Governor and Company of Merchants of London Trading into the East Indies. From 1757 the Company effectively ruled India, taking on administrative and military rule. For several hundred years before this conquest (which started as a trading partnership) India had led the world in manufacture and textiles. And before the East India Company the standard of living of a worker in England and India was about the same.

From 1757 the Company set taxes in the region high enough (and distrained enough valuables, in the case of nonpayment) to pay for their exports, creating a one-way flow of wealth from the region. They plundered India to such an extent it created misery of 'an essentially different and infinitely more intensive kind than all Hindustan had to suffer before' (that description was by a young Karl Marx, then writing for the *New York Tribune*).[62] That was just business as usual. Their real outrages included the practice of cutting the thumbs off weavers who dared to sell their cloth to other traders. They also increased tax levels for farmers to two-thirds of their income. And taxed salt (its high price resulting in heat exhaustion and lowered disease resistance). The last straw was the Company's response to a major famine: raising taxes, allowing them to take grain from starving communities for sale at inflated prices in the cities. Ten million people died as a result. The riots and civil unrest that ensued finally gave the East India Company a taste of their own medicine, as it prompted a ruinous crash in their stock market value. Nehru wrote: 'The corruption, venality, nepotism, violence and greed of money of these early genera-tions of British rule in India is something which passes compre-hension.'[63] Even Adam Smith, the grandfather of free market economics, saw the East India Company as deplorable:

> No other sovereigns ever were, or, from the nature of things, ever could be, so perfectly indifferent about the happiness or misery of their subjects, the improvement or waste of their dominions, the glory or disgrace of their administration, as, from irresistible moral causes, the greater part of the proprietors of such a mercantile company are, and necessarily must be.[64]

Meanwhile England was swelled by new wealth; at its height the East India Company's 'GDP' exceeded that of Britain itself. As economic historian Nick Robins (my source for many of the preceding details) concluded: 'it was the Company's plunder that first de-industrialised their country and then provided the finance that fuelled Britain's own industrial revolution. In essence, the Honourable East India Company found India rich and left it poor.'[65]

Today's descendents of the East India Company have carefully vested many of their responsibilities in subsidiaries, wholesalers, licensing arrangements and so on. Unfortunately for them, if it has their brand on it the media and the public doesn't much care what legal firewalls have been established. Nor apparently do the courts, in the case of local subsidiaries for which the company has seats on the board (this was Coca-Cola's argument over human rights accusations against their bottlers in Columbia – an Alien Tort case now likely to come to trial in the USA). As soon as the wall becomes a window, responsibility and accountability come back into play.

CO-OPERATIVE RESPONSIBILITY: THE POWER OF TRANSPARENCY

The very length and complexity of the modern food chain breeds a culture of ignorance and indifference among eaters. Shortening the food chain is one way to create more conscious consumers, but deploying technology to pierce the veil is another.[66]

Michael Pollan

ACCORDING TO THE CO-OP Bank's 2008 Ethical Consumerism Report, UK ethical spending reached £35.5 billion in 2007, and was up 15% year on year. It has doubled in the last five years.

Within this, ethical food and drink (see Table 8.1) was up by about the same amount (14%) at $5.8 billion. Looking into the details of these increases we can see that Fairtrade was the

Table 8.1

Ethical Food & Drink	2006 £M	2007 £M	% growth 2006–2007
Fairtrade	285	458	61
Freedom foods	18	28	56
Sustainable fish	55	70	27
Vegetarian products	664	826	24
Free range eggs	259	314	21
Free range poultry	116	130	12
Organic	1,737	1,911	10
Dolphin friendly tuna	223	237	6
Farmers' markets	225	220	–2

(Source: Co-operative Bank Ethical Consumer Report, 2008[67])

fastest grower, although organic food remains the number one, accounting for one third of all spending.

The Fairtrade Foundation's own figures show £500 million sales value in 2007 and £700 million in 2008. With brands like Cadbury and Starbucks going Fairtrade in 2009/10 Fairtrade might overtake organic sales in the UK. Cadbury's Dairy Milk alone has £400 million in sales. Meanwhile organic food is known from media reports to be down about 20% in 2008, although analysts mostly blame relative price. That suspicion was confirmed when Tesco reported rising organic sales by mid-2009, after they started price-promoting these.

As the Co-op Report points out ethical goods in the UK are now bigger than alcohol and tobacco combined. Before we celebrate though, let's just reflect on the scale of this ethical consumerism boom. The average British household is spending £200 per year on ethical food and drink. That's £4 per week; one bag of Fairtrade coffee and one pack of organic apples. Now visualise the average British shopping trolley, full to bursting with a week's shopping – plus these two 'ethical' items. What people are buying is ethical treats. When you buy a couple of these ethical items, you assume you are a being good consumer. It's like buying one item of trendy designer clothing and assuming you are fashionable. That's what labels do to our thinking. They accentuate and highlight, rather than dealing with broad sweeps of reality.

Earlier, looking at climate change we followed just one factor – melting ice. To get a handle on sustainability in food, let's follow the sugar ...

I've been asking people to guess how much sugar they consume in a week and the answers tend to be low ('100 grams?'). The truth is the average American consumes 1.1 kg a week!!! When I first saw this figure I thought it had to be exaggerated. So I went and looked at the US Department of Agriculture Economic Research Service's published data[68] just to check, and – sure enough – here are the figures for 2007 (Table 8.2):

Table 8.2

Sugars, dry weight, annual consumption per capita		
Cane & Beet Sugar	62.0 lb	28.1 kg
High Fructose Corn Syrup	56.2 lb	25.5 kg
Other	18.1 lb	8.2 kg
Total	136.3 lb	61.8 kg

How on earth do they (we) manage to eat all that sugar? 1.1 kg is 40 teaspoons per day. Most is hidden as corn syrup and sugar added to manufactured food: bread, mayonnaise, pasta sauce, peanut butter ...

A hundred years ago the average American had only 2 kg of sugar per year in their diet. It has grown by 20%, just in the last 20 years. There is no recommended daily amount for sugar, because many nutritionists feel that we don't need any (refined) sugar at all. The US department of agriculture, in consultation with food experts, has recommended a daily limit of 40 g per day of added sugars – four times lower than the *average* US consumption.

Sugar is a naturally occurring substance (for instance in honey or sweet fruits) but it played little part in the historical human diet as an ingredient, until 100 years ago when industrial food processing took off. Sugar refining is compared by campaigners to refining heroin, resulting in a pure chemical crystal that the human body can be trained to crave but isn't well equipped to deal with. High sugar in the diet can contribute to obesity, heart disease, cancer and diabetes, anxiety and mental illness, hyperactivity in children and of course dental deterioration.

Then there is the effect of sugar production on the environment. According to the WWF one single can of Coca-Cola uses 200 litres of water, nearly all of it for sugar production.[69] A WWF report in 2004 stated that sugar is also responsible for more biodiversity loss than any other crop 'due to habitat loss, intensive use of water for irrigation, heavy use of agro-chemicals, as well as discharge and runoff of polluted effluent associated with the industry'.[70]

That is cane sugar. What about corn (the source of corn syrup)? According to Michael Pollan 'It may be cheap in the supermarket but in environmental terms it could not be more expensive.'[71] It has the same sorts of problems environmentally as sugar; being an intensive monoculture it depletes soil nutrients, requires high chemical and energy inputs while it weakens the topsoil. Organic corn would be different, requiring one third less energy.

Then there are workers' rights. According to NGOs (such as Brazil's Rede Social) little has changed in 200 years – with hard labour, slavery, child labour and appalling levels of fatality. Sugar is hidden from view. Not only would very few people realise it is the most damaging crop, both to the environment and also in terms of human rights – worse even on both counts than cotton. But it is hidden in our diet. What we buy is a pasta sauce from a 'nice' retailer whose eco advertising, community promotions and friendly staff all tell quite a different story. There are ethical alternatives. Tate & Lyle, the British sugar giant, has already moved to 100% Fairtrade for their own retail sugar – i.e. the bags of sugar people buy to put in tea or their own cooking. But retail sugar is a small fraction of what we actually consume.

It would take considerable consumer pressure to change things. It costs $120 more per tonne for organic sugar and $60 more per tonne for Fairtrade. Anyway Fairtrade works well for a single commodity (coffee) or a simple combination (bars of chocolate). But it's a dead loss when it comes to frozen pizza or ice-cream. Here we need greater transparency. In an open letter in the *New York Times* to President Obama, Michael Pollan wrote:

The F.D.A. should require that every packaged-food product include a second calorie count, indicating how many calories of fossil fuel went into its production. Oil is one of the most important ingredients in our food, and people ought to know just how much of it they're eating. The government should also throw its support behind putting a second bar code on all food products that, when scanned either in the store or at home (or with a cell phone), brings up on a screen the whole story and pictures of how that product was produced: in the case of crops, images of the farm and lists of agrochemicals used in its production; in the case of meat and dairy, descriptions of the animals' diet and drug regimen, as well as live video feeds of the CAFO where they live and, yes, the slaughterhouse where they die.[72]

I'm part of a working group called Earth Open Source. Other members include a leading food scientist and one of the originators of the Fairtrade standard. What we are looking at is a combination of a knowledge-sharing network for exciting innovations in sustainable farming, plus imaginative consumer education and engagement campaigns. We want to identify what 'good' food looks like and help people – the customers – adopt it and champion it.

We knew that others like the WWF had been looking at similar issues and solutions. What we never would have predicted was Wal-Mart joining us, with a proposal to make food supply chains transparent.

What Wal-Mart propose to do could revolutionise food sustainability. Their 100 000 suppliers will have to disclose information about the sourcing of their ingredients. Mike Duke, their CEO, says that customers 'want information about the entire lifecycle of a product so they can feel good about buying it. They want to know that the materials in the product are safe, that it was made well and that it was produced in a responsible way.' Wal-Mart have started by asking all of their suppliers to disclose quite basic company-level information on sustainability – the answers to 15 already quite searching questions about energy and climate, materials efficiency, natural resources, people and community.[73]

That's phase one. In the second phase Wal-Mart is partnering with a consortium of universities and advisors to establish a global database of information on product lifecycles. Based on this database the final step will be to provide customers with a simple overall rating (for instance a score out of 100) for every single product. So when you are buying a box of cereal, or a tin of vegetables, or a laundry detergent, you can chose between them based on environmental performance.

The reason this is revolutionary though, is not Wal-Mart's use of the data. That in itself would be like their current practice of telling you how much sugar there is in product after product in aisle upon aisle of processed, unhealthy food. If they all score quite similarly, who would have guessed that they are also responsible for 3100% more sugar than was going into our diets 100 years ago? There could be noticeable differences between local foods and those imported though; the carbon footprint of the latter is huge.

What's revolutionary is Wal-Mart opening up the database for others to use and share. It means (as with carbon calculator platforms like AMEE) independent developers, NGOs, government agencies, even competing supermarket chains can construct their own ratings-based standards and tools. For instance an animal welfare charity might be able to use the same data to highlight the best and worst buys. That's what happened with toxic chemical disclosure and it led to big improvements by the companies.

The difference between this scheme and our plans for Earth Open Source – is that it doesn't have a pioneering point of view on what constitutes 'good food'. The Earth Open Source view would be to challenge some of the norms of industrial farming – GM crops, chemical fertilisers and pesticides, heavy equipment, animals stuffed with antibiotics and crowded in concentration camp conditions ... The cheap oil is running out so intensive farming of that sort is no longer an option. And it is also counterproductive, killing the soil and limiting how much food we can grow. We are looking to support agriculture that is regenerative – working in partnership with nature to grow as much good food with as little external input as possible. Also because there are two billion farmers, this will be a prime force in global equity and tackling poverty. In summary we see 'farming as the new energy' in terms of its central importance to sustainability, resilience and wellbeing. If only people demanded good food, the industry could be transformed overnight and that is why customer education and engagement is key. It could also prove to be as big a revolution in public health as the invention of modern medicines.

We are not starting from scratch. Fairtrade is pretty much the gold standard example of free markets being overturned by co-operation. Fairtrade is basically an agreement between the end consumer and the farms that produce their coffee. We could buy cheaper, but we would rather the price they get paid is fair (double the prevailing coffee market rate), so communities can have a chance to share in the profits of their labour and use this money to develop. A study by researchers at Colorado State University of Fairtrade schemes among coffee growers found that there were additional benefits including lower cost credit, family and community stability, training, new business opportunities, self-esteem, formal education, employment, cultural revival and environmental conservation.[74] On the last point the Fairtrade standard does (unbeknown to most consumers) bind the producers to quite strict environmental standards, covering: buffer zones, conservation areas, protection of virgin forests, prohibited agrochemicals, hazardous waste, maintaining soil health and water quality, water conservation, exclusion of GMOs, including contamination by neighbours. Barring the fact that some agrichemicals are allowed, it's one of the more stringent environmental policies, even before you get onto ethics.

Now that Fairtrade is attracting a sizeable segment of consumers, we are seeing the bigger brands getting on board. Cadbury Dairy Milk, the number one UK chocolate, says they are going Fairtrade for pragmatic commercial reasons. The price of cocoa was so low that they were losing farmers to other crops. The most surprising born-again Fairtrade supporter is Nestlé. Nestlé has for decades been lobbying against Fairtrade. In response to an Oxfam Make Trade Fair campaign this was Nestlé's response:

> In addition, while 'Fair Trade' coffee is useful in benefiting a relatively small percentage of farmers and allowing some consumers to express their views, if (the higher) Fair Trade prices were to be applied on a broad level, it would motivate farmers to grow more coffee, ultimately lowering the price of coffee beans even further. (2002)[75]

And yet in 2005 Nestlé launched its own certified Fairtrade coffee brand called Partners. Nestlé were previously applying a ruthless free market logic. Yet now that the market has proved it does care about other factors than price, Nestlé had to follow suit. I don't mean to sound cynical, I am genuinely pleased to welcome them to the fold.

Nestlé's argument against Fairtrade goes back to Thomas Malthus, who is famous for predicting that the world would run out of food because population expands exponentially, while food productivity does not. Given this legacy you might imagine Malthus to be a humanitarian of some sort. Far from it. Reading accounts from founders of the co-operative movement at the time, it emerges that he was a truly miserable bastard, whose central idea was that the poor should not be supported in any way (even by the miserly poor laws and workhouses) because it would encourage them to breed and also keep them and their children alive. Malthus was also an early advocate of consumerism; arguing that by instilling a desire for better things in the lower classes they could be persuaded to abstain from sex and have fewer children, in order to have more to spend on life's luxuries. Malthus was not an isolated bigot. He was a man of his times. It was illegal in the nineteenth century to look poor and turn up in a new parish looking for work. In a famous test case a magistrate said it was not his role to 'read the minds' of two presumed vagabonds (i.e. starving country workers) who walked into Shoreditch one day and were promptly arrested. If a poor person was found without a means of support they could be sentenced to hard labour in prison, or as a bondsman (an unpaid servant, i.e. slave) in a household.

The argument Malthus put neatly avoided blaming the concentration of wealth and private property, instead pinning the responsibility on its victims. Accordingly poverty became seen not as something terrible that befell workers, nor even an instance of human vulnerability, but the fault of the laborers themselves – as if in being 'idle' they had broken a natural law. Nestlé similarly were neatly avoiding any question that ruthless free market forces, concentrating wealth into corporate profits, have anything to do with the plight of coffee workers receiving starvation prices.

We are all complicit in this view to some extent. Philosopher Peter Singer argues that giving around half our income to Oxfam should be as natural a response to scenes of global poverty as jumping into a pond to save a drowning child. Both are plights any reasonable human being would act to avert. Singer sees no conceptual difference between 'the pond' and TV images from Yemen.

Our lack of connection or concern (in the terms Singer described) is a failure of empathy. That's why I like Kiva.org so much.

Kiva takes the microcredit system explained later in the section on economics and opens it up to private lenders; it is a way of microfinancing microcredit. Using this system I made a loan to a co-operative group in Bolivia called Las Carinosa who retail food and clothes. Note I have not made a charity donation – I have made a loan and as with other microcredit there is every chance of me getting my money back. With Kiva it is an interest free loan. What Kiva does is confront you with people just as proud as you – proud of their businesses, skills and plans. They want working capital not aid.

Kiva is a Swahili word meaning unity or agreement. There are 500 000 Kiva lenders. Together they have loaned $70 million. The current repayment rate is 98.37%. The average Kiva loan to an entrepreneur is $420. This puts it in the micro-enterprise category and it is noticeable that most borrowers have quite developed businesses – shops, factories and farms. As opposed to the client group of Grameen who represent a much poorer sector of the developing world, harder to reach – and with those it is much better perhaps, for all sorts of reasons, to donate straight to a microcredit bank. Kiva works with over 100 field partners – the actual microfinance groups. Kiva is the only organisation in the world for whom PayPal waives its transaction fees. And Kiva also benefits from other help – for instance YouTube has given them free advertising space (next to contested-copyright videos).

There are by now a number of similar services tapping into local (non English language) audiences including Rang De (India) and Veecus (France). And there have been a number of other new models that have followed the Kiva example, not by imitation, but by finding other ways to connect internet users here with microcredit. MYC4 (Denmark) applies interest on loans. MicroPlace.com, a subsidiary of eBay, allows you to invest in microfinance securities, which basically means you are putting your capital at the disposal of microfinance lenders. United Prosperity invites you to guarantee an entrepreneur's loan, allowing them to raise money locally. Another variant, perhaps catering to those who would really prefer to donate some money (seeing it then cycling through a number of loans to parties that you choose) is Wokai, whose client projects are in China.

What I love is the way these systems are connecting audiences here with the lives and stories of people just like us, born in another country. It's an equality that seemed almost impossible 20 years ago, when I worked on advertising for disaster relief appeals. No matter how careful you were with language and imagery, the whole frame perpetuated the idea that the poor were victims. On which basis – whether denigrating, or idealising them – what wasn't often possible was a straightforward empathetic connection.

PUTTING CO-OPERATIVE RESPONSIBILITY INTO ACTION

IN THIS SECTION I WILL outline a variety of ways of replacing the information bottleneck ('the wall') with co-operation. They involve both examples of creating new windows into how the world really works, and also ways of getting people at this end to step in and take responsibility, guiding the behaviour of companies with their purchasing. The point is to provide some inspiration and starting points for the reader's own projects.

CARROT MOBS

Anyone reading this, with a reasonable social network, could organise their own Carrot Mob. Basically what this involves is offering your custom to a company in return for them making improvements in sustainability. The aim is partly to get one business to set an example (hopefully for others to follow). But it's just as much about demonstrating to citizens how powerful we can be when we co-operate to encourage positive change.

Carrot Mob was the brainchild of Brent Schulkin, one of the founders of Virgance, who are building a whole suite of co-operative approaches to sustainability. They call this 'activism 2.0'. Other projects include 1BOG (One Block Off The Grid) and Greenfund – a venture fund for green businesses from microdonations: if 200 million people on Facebook each put in $1000, the fund could compete with the World Bank. Virgance does think big, but then it was co-founded by a Silicon Valley entrepreneur (Steve Newcome).

The output of the Carrot Mob campaign was a global 'look what we did' website and YouTube video. The Carrot Mob organisers visited all the convenience stores within a defined area (South of Market) in San Francisco. Their pitch to each was that they would bring a 'mob' of friends on a Saturday afternoon to one of these stores, to part with lots of cash. They would do this at the store that pledged to spend the highest proportion of these takings on energy efficiency. This would also benefit the store in future energy savings. The winning store was a Korean grocer, who pledged nearly 30% of what turned out to be over $9000 taken on that Saturday afternoon (the video shows a queue stretching for an American sized 'block'). All those who came were then treated to a free music event in the park around the corner; which also gave them something to buy supplies for.

Carrot Mob is an example of joycotting. Where instead of boycotting a bad company you reward a company for good behaviour. In late 2006 Greenpeace had launched a large-scale joycot (with user generated content) called Green My Apple, drawing on the creativity and enthusiasm of green-minded Apple fans, to persuade Apple to make changes. Apple was then at the bottom of Greenpeace's survey of electronics and sustainability. And the campaign seemed to work. The next year Apple declared 'A Greener Apple' and have moved up in the Greenpeace ratings to a more respectable mid position, having answered specific campaign points like setting a date for removing PVC from all products. Whether they were only responding to this campaign we can't know, but it got a lot of attention and can't have hurt.

I think the first time I heard of this kind of joycotting idea was from two activists around 2001 who approached me to discuss a scheme whereby the junk food buying youth of the world would chose to buy from either (only) McDonalds or (only) Burger King for one month, depending which made the best response to a set of sustainability challenges. Their insight was that the real leverage point would be media coverage and relative share price, something the campaign could also highlight and track.

The point about brands is that it often is a marginal choice which one we happen to go with. We truly believe in many categories like banking that 'they are all the same'. Seriously. Think about historical marketing examples like the runaway success of Tetley's Round Tea Bags (which overturned PG Tips' 35-year brand leadership). Small but tangible difference can prove a tipping point. A group of us were thinking about doing a campaign through thenag.net which said '1 million of us will switch our current account to the first bank who ____'. It almost doesn't matter what the sustainability demand would be (we were thinking no junk mail at the time). One million customers would be the biggest account switch since Barclays introduced free banking in the 1980s and stole a march on other UK high street banks. It would almost certainly be worth one of the banks' while.

With joycotting, it has to come from the outside community. Brands have orchestrated consumer power campaigns around the choice of a new flavour, or to bring back a tired old brand by popular demand. But it would never wash for ethics. What we might see in future is the equivalent of 'unions' for positive consumerism, marshalling support for change in a programmatic way. But meanwhile it's quite nice that it is so haphazard – changing a major corporation's policy can just be a Facebook group away.

FROM CONSUMER TO CITIZEN

A few years ago I hosted a 'brainstorming' with Nicky Gavron (then deputy mayor of London) and Amber Nystrom (a Californian entrepreneur working with a company called Lemnis). Here we came up with a variant of joycotting: looking at how a whole city of customers could tip a market towards a disruptive new technology, by being its early adopters. The question for this meeting was: how to get a city to adopt a light bulb?

The light bulb in question was the LED (light emitting diode). LEDs are ultra energy efficient. LEDs also last for 50 years, have low embedded energy in manufacture and raw materials (compared with mercury mining). The problem has been that they have been a bit harsh, and expensive to buy initially. Lemnis had a beautiful soft light LED, at a reasonable price (when you look at the total costs of energy saved) of £10. It was such a promising technology that the Clinton C40 Cities had adopted it – and were looking to start out in London. Google had also signed up for their first ever brand partnership – basically they planned to give two free Lemnis bulbs to every employee.

People are used to buying light bulbs for 30p, and even if they buy CFLs (whose full price is £5) these often are discounted, or given away. I went to my first meeting bristling with scepticism. Could you ever really sell somebody a £10 light bulb, even if you could quite validly argue that it would save you £7–8 worth of electricity in its first year of use compared to a conventional incandescent bulb? It's like asking people to buy a £10 loaf of bread. In conventional mass marketing terms it's a nonstarter.

But there is another whole way of looking at this. What if it wasn't about consumerism? What if it was about taking a stand as a citizen? Why would the citizens adopt a light bulb as if it were 'the next make poverty history' wristband? Perhaps because if a million bought one LED then the light bulb market would have to change. Even if a million bulbs in London didn't make them change, then roll this across C40 cities and the game would be up and then the scramble among manufacturers would be to win (high value, high margin) share of this new market.

GE had committed at the time to 'energy efficient incandescents'. This is like SUVs with hybrid engines (and barely any difference in fuel economy). It would be enough to allow them to keep selling this product after 2013 with the new US regulations. The global lighting market is worth $40 billlion. And GE had already patented a suitable technology.

Philips had taken another line. They invested heavily in marketing CFL (compact fluorescents). These are energy efficient. You also have to suspect that they are great for Philips because the technology is flaky; hence people tend to go for the branded bulbs (whereas incandescents are a commodity). These products often end up in landfill. And this meant a lot of mercury heading for the water table. The product is so toxic that official advice should you break a CFL bulb is to get any children out of the room, fast! If there weren't many bulbs it would hardly be our biggest environmental threat. But once Wal-Mart declared its intention to sell 100 million CFLs it was a worry.

The third option was LED. Low energy use, low manufacturing footprint, long life. It truly is a clean technology. But it would destroy their business model. A \$40 billion market. That's bigger than the global solar industry (just). It was a great opportunity. And we had some great ideas, including:

- Starting a YouTube craze (seeded using London celebrities) to celebrate 'the light bulb joke'. Because the idea of 'changing a light bulb' would barely exist in an LED future.
- Putting a light bulb meter – like a church roof appeal sign but made out of beautiful LED lights – right up the side of City Hall, showing how many of our million we had shifted.
- Creating an adapter for cyclists so they could use their (4 watt) LED as a bike light, demonstrating the extremely low power use, and also creating a catchy visual craze by taking them out on the streets.

For various reasons – one being a change of London city government – this plan never got put into action. Nicky Gavron did get as far as launching LED street lighting to London on International Women's Day. The LED bulb's day will come though. The bigger recognition is this: what if every market could be galvanised this way? Through people power?

FEEDBACK

If you want to improve something, instead of relying on your internal perspectives why not ask around among all those your project or company touches? Especially valuable when it's a case of 'keeping you honest'.

This insight has been put into social network form by Actics – recently rebranded EthicalEconomy.com (in line with a book by the same title by co-founder Nicolai Pietersen). The idea of the community is to rate each other against our own stated values. For instance Clownfish, members of Actics since the early days (2007), state their core value as honesty – 'a disposition to be truthful and not false'. That's a highly relevant attribute for a green marketing agency (it's the opposite of greenwash). And Clownfish score pretty well according to the community, ranking tenth among the 10 best performing members. Obviously this is a very DIY-able approach. You could join EthicalEconomy. Or you could simply invite feedback within your own community in a neutral and confidential format.

Another example was RateMyPrison – the runner up at the first Social Innovation Camp. The idea being that by giving prisons feedback and allowing visitors to share information, the stress of the whole experience for relatives could be reduced.

CO-OPERATIVE STANDARD SETTING

LEED (Leadership in Energy and Environmental Design) – a green buildings standard already covering 14 000 projects – created a co-operative network within the industry: developers, architects, landlords and tenants, all contributing to a joined up standard for green buildings.

Green building is a huge market. And so it should be. Not only is construction one of the biggest sectors for embedded emissions (the CO_2 from manufacture, raw materials, transport). But the ongoing impact of buildings is massive too – energy, water, waste. Buildings use about 40% of all materials and all energy. Plus we live in buildings and they have a big effect on our health. All of which should make a green building a complete no-brainer if commissioning a new office, school or library. The block was this. Developers would get quotes from the builders based upon spec and cost. Tenants would (much later) buy or lease completed buildings from developers based upon spec and cost. Despite the fact that it is in a tenant's interest to have an energy efficient, healthy building – improving business costs and employee wellbeing – the end user wasn't involved with the people in hard hats. The LEED certification process draws in members from right across the industry, from materials sourcing to the tenant.

One learning from early LEED projects is the standard had to be flexible. There is not one way of 'building green'. It depends on the local climate, the type of project and so on. Will a particular sort of grass roof, or lime core work? It depends where and what for. So the LEED standard is points-based. The green criteria group under core objectives. And for achieving any particular one you get a point. The maximum you could score (the number of criteria or objectives in total) is 69 points. To be certified at all, you must achieve 26 points. You can then earn silver status for 33 points or more, gold for 39 or more, platinum for 52 or more. There are very few platinum certified projects (under 100). LEED has just made this standard harder to attain by saying than besides a score of 52+ it has to have high energy efficiency, one of the harder areas to pull off. There are other minimum standards across the categories of energy, water, waste, materials and sustainable siting. An extra category is innovation and design. You can pick up points for combining two functions in one element (plumbing that also provides structure) or building for later reassembly and recycling.

LEED is constantly being improved – it just reached version 3. While the construction industry has already fallen 30% in the recession, green building in the USA thanks to LEED (and now also thanks to Obama) is expected to triple in size over the next four years to $140 billion by 2013.[76]

ETHICAL EXCHANGES

The Carbon Disclosure Project, established in 2000 by Paul Dickinson, holds the largest database of corporate climate change information in the world. The data is obtained from responses to CDP's annual Information Requests, issued on behalf of institutional investors and similar. What this means is visibility on your exposure to climate change regulation (for instance your CO_2 emissions) and also your plans to tackle this. Their latest move, in association with a leading market tracking organisation, is to launch a series of stock market indices relating company financial performance to their carbon management policies. Studies have already shown that there is a strong link between the two. These indices will put pressure on managements via the key thing they are judged on by shareholders. It is like a Carrot Mobbing for corporate financial management.

The principle of getting companies to disclose data and then ranking them on it is a well-established campaigning tool. It's also been used very effectively by Greenpeace (for instance in their Electronics company green ranking) and by Climate Counts. A standard tactic is to give low marks to companies who do not disclose public information, the insight being that once a measure is public and comparable it automatically encourages improvement.

The same principle was applied to the energy banding of UK houses (learning from the experience of the white goods markets). Trials of the new HIPS certificates found that people generally wanted to buy or rent houses in the top two bands (it's that estate agency thing of wanting everything to be near perfect) and hence there was a disproportionate financial return on making improvements to get yourself into these top two bands.

Not everyone reading could start a Carbon Disclosure Project. But any of us could write to every local school and ask them 10 questions about sustainability, then send the resulting league table to a local paper.

LABELS WITH ATTITUDE

One thing that disappoints with most eco labels is their passivity. A test would be if you heard about them would you immediately feel compelled to blog, talk or write about the story? Organic has perhaps the best story of all (soil is the matrix of life on this planet and the treatment of soil may be the key sustainability issue – for climate change too). If only they would tell it.

With the Earth Open Source project we wanted to find a way to certify sustainability in hidden ingredients and complex products, without becoming bland. It's much harder than with a single issue to tap into a powerful story. But it's not impossible. Ideas for labels from the early stages of the Earth Open Source project (i.e. these are interesting cast offs) included:

- **GUARANTEED GREENWASH FREE.** The label would rigorously investigate and assure manufacturer claims. It would consult with companies about what claims they could make and help them develop their business to be more sustainable in a relevant way. And adjudicate in cases where NGOs or individuals raised concerns with claims too. This ought to be the role of advertising standards (or trading standards) authorities, but it is difficult for them to make the right calls based upon context. For instance a poster by Powergen saying 'We're number one for renewables in the UK' neglected to mention they were also rated bottom of the big six for overall sustainability (by WWF/Innovest) and that the UK is near bottom of the European league table for renewables, ahead of only Luxemburg and Malta! I spoke about this at an advertising standards event; it's true – yet arguably misleading.

- **GREENWASH INSURANCE.** What would you be insuring against? The disastrous impact on share price and market share in being found out on sustainability. Corporates pursue sustainability strategies to minimise their exposure to risk. Risks are things to be insured against. Insurance has a business model that is quite different to paying a £50 000 licence fee to use someone's brand (a certifying company). It generates the sorts of profits you could use to develop a large investment programme in sustainable farm research and innovation. Insurers also get to give their customers a really thorough health check. If you took our Greenwash Insurance a condition would be a rigorous inspection not only of your supply chain, but your compliance and ethical decision-making processes, and those of your suppliers.

- **BRAND REHAB.** Say you were in the dog-house. Persil – post Greenpeace attacks over palm oil and deforestation. Starbucks – post Oxfam campaign about Ethiopian trademarks, or, the classic example, Nike – after the child labour scandal of the 1990s. How to regain people's trust? It could take decades. McDonalds for instance won an award in 2006 (from Ethisphere magazine) for being one of the most ethical companies in the world, and are a global Greenpeace partner on reforestation – yet are still seen as one of the bad guys. The idea of Brand Rehab would be to develop a 'Betty Ford Clinic' of ethics where in an open, transparent way, the remedial steps taken by the company are validated and it gets a provisional (probationary) label.

RIGHT DATA IN THE RIGHT PLACE AT THE RIGHT TIME

Today's media make it easy to dial up information on what we buy, and to use expert infomediaries to guide our choice. The Good Consumer Guide was just a start. Great for researched purchases but not something you'd often take shopping.

Now GoodGuide offers independent ethical and environmental information (as well as on product health and safety) on 60 000 consumer products. Within this they have launched a 'comprehensive' food guide and they offer a service on mobile so you can check while you shop. We are only at the starting point with this, but being able to dial up the exact impact of everything I buy and recommend improvements in line with my own values and priorities cannot be too far away. There are various groups looking at ways to build directories of ethical information linked to barcodes (so that you can scan products in store). It could also move beyond simply setting minimum standards; in that there would be a factual basis for brands to compete on their actual programmes rather than minimum standard policies.

Also note that current certification schemes are document submission-based. I was told by one insider that only around 1% of farms are actually inspected currently. It may be that with the prevalence of technologies like mobile phones in the developing world new systems for compliance could be developed. I met Charlie Clutterbuck, an expert on developing world agriculture, recently and he told me there were various moves afoot to use new ways to collect ethical data, because this in itself is such a bottleneck. One reason why the Fairtrade and organic growers tend to be co-operatives is that in areas of low literacy and stretched resources they are realistically the smallest entity that could actually take on the paperwork.

THE WISDOM OF GROUPS

We face a situation in choosing between different types of label and claim, you could describe as 'The Tower of Label'. Should you buy a Fairtrade, organic or local apple? Or maybe support a local, independent shop, whatever apples they happen to sell? It comes down to judgement – but lacking good information, it's more likely to come down to whim.

Myself and several collaborators (Lynne Elvins and Luke Nicholson) developed a scheme four years ago called 'Not Bad'.

The main idea was to help people decide about a much wider range of goods and companies than those covered by eco labels, by differentiating between those who were 'not bad', and those which were: i.e. between the top half and the bottom half. The way we wanted to support it was perhaps the most interesting part of the scheme. Instead of certification (checklists) or experts (juries) or other standard means … we wanted to open the judging of 'not bad' to 14-year-old schoolchildren, as part of the citizenship curriculum. They would be given a range of submissions, including those from the companies, and would rank them based on the evidence. This would be a robust methodology from several points of view. One is that to criticise its findings would be to criticise the kids, a target much harder for corporate PR to go after without looking mean. The other is what I call the wisdom of groups.

The wisdom of crowds is the famous phrase denoting the ability of large samples to converge upon standard answers. But also we know from politics that crowds can be dumb, irrational, prone to manipulation and rule by mood. Whereas small group deliberation is potentially the smartest form of human discourse. That's why juries were invented; to tap into collective debate informing judgement. It's why we hold meetings. A group discussion keeps the debates open, but comes to a combined view; it can show you how the view was arrived at, what issues were weighed. They would be looking at issues from a perspective close to the concerns of other ordinary folk too, informed by questions like what would life for my family be like if I had been born into this community?

PROGRESSIVE STANDARDS

How do you balance wanting as many brands as possible to join a label, with concern about making a significant difference, not a token one? The current thinking seems to be shifting to progressive standards; allowing an accessible entry point but demanding steep improvements over time.

I discussed this trend in my last book under the heading of ethical velocity; it makes sense to buy from those making the fastest improvements, and hence moving us furthest in the right direction. This idea was used in the Carbon Trust label (you are certified for your ambitious two-year targets) and has been applied to GM-free certification of organic programmes in the US, where there is so much contamination of organic farms by neighbouring GM agriculture that it is hard to start from a GM-free base. In consumerist terms it is slightly harder to position 'improving' as virtue. But this probably calls for a more mature engagement with ethics in consumer markets.

CUSTOMISED STANDARDS

Customisation is one of the killer apps of digital media. Nicholas Negroponte in his 1995 classic *Being Digital* pointed out that in the digital universe he was no longer a statistical subset (a target audience) but rather 'I am me'. Your unique preferences, attitudes, habits and beliefs can be now met by companies; for instance, when Amazon recommends something to you based not only on its own normative data but your distinct choices.

If you were a vegan and animal welfare-interested you might weight these aspects differently. Will Watt was looking at doing something with this, using Ethical Consumer data to create a personalised rating system on BBC Green (before the corporation sold it on). The idea would be that you would weight the criteria against which the data was used to judge corporations. You would hence get a reading relative to what matters to you most, whether climate change or human rights.

SEEING IS BELIEVING

Many campaigning breakthroughs in NGO history have been based upon photographic images; Bridget Bardot and the seal cubs, the Pakistani child stitching the football with a Nike logo on it. Several brands (Stone Buhr flour is one) have taken to giving people access to photography and information about the farm your purchase originates from.

A great recent example was the revolution in chicken welfare standards in UK supermarkets brought about by documentaries. In 2007 UK celebrity chef Hugh Fearnley-Whittingstall fronted the TV series 'Hugh's Chicken Run' that exposed (in graphic detail) the appalling conditions used in intensive 'broiler' farming. According to a subsequent RSPCA survey, '73 per cent of people now claim to buy chickens that have had higher living standards'. Sainsbury's reported sales increases of 50% for free-range, organic and chicken adhering to the RSPCA's Freedom Food scheme. Following on from this success Fearnley-Whittingstall launched a second series 'Chickens, Hugh and Tesco Too' putting pressure on Tesco whose '£1.99 chicken offer' right on the heels of the first TV series highlighted the fact that they didn't seem able or willing to respond. So enterprising Hugh organised a shareholder vote on the issue, bringing further publicity and pressure.

RADICAL VISIBILITY

'The whole world is watching' was a popular chant in 1960s demonstrations; not entirely true in those days, but images of police beating up hippy students certainly had an effect. Today we see a much more radical effect of citizen reporting through blogs, phone cameras, Twitter, even in countries with censorship of the media and internet. The important thing is the openness of information.

Heavy coverage was given to progressive Iranian demonstrations and to human rights abuses associated with squashing these; but a discussion of this issue on WorldChanging.org also included comments like the following:

> Watching the protesters in Tehran, many Americans feel a strong sense of empathy, exhilaration and hope. I strongly share those feelings, especially since I know firsthand the danger the protesters face from government thugs on motorcycles, provocateurs and the secret police. But none of this should blind us to the likelihood that our own government is dangerously meddling in Iran's internal affairs and playing with the lives of those protesters.[77]

The #iranelections meme elicited an extraordinary response, many turning their twitpics green, setting up their location as Iran and also offering web proxy and message re-tweeting. That's a display of solidarity, but what's just as exciting may be the way that all those with power are under scrutiny, including our own governments. Academic John Keane sees this as so significant that his 2009 book *Democracy* calls this a third stage (1. Assembly Democracy, 2. Representative Democracy and 3. Monitory Democracy).

The Web has brought monitoring on steroids. Any public stream of data can be commented on, blogged, tweeted, DIGGed and so on. It can also be mashed up and made relevant; for instance the UK government allowed people to enter postcodes to check their flood risk. With over two million homes flooded in the UK an essential guide for anyone buying a new home.

SHARED TEXTS

I think shared texts may be the heart of the media revolution. There are many manifestations of this: Twitter, wikis, blogs with their comments open. These combine the formerly separate processes of writing and conversation.

Tools such as wikis are a huge benefit to those developing and sharing ideas. The Transition network uses theirs as a kind of live, shared 'user manual'. New developments keep spawning in this area. One that's hotly tipped is Friendfeed, pushing real-time conversation (and integrating all the different sources like social networks and newsfeeds) to some sort of logical conclusion.

I think we are just starting to realise what a revolutionary idea this is, or could be. What this points to is a kind of 'group mind'. Or 'conscious market'. Or anyway a big step, just as printing was a big step (and which early on was used to print existing copied texts like the Bible, but later contributed to a whole new way of thinking and organising).

Creative Data is the title of a project by Leonora Oppenheim, a designer (founder of Elio Studio) who writes for Treehugger. Leonora produced the Butterfly Effect – first of a planned series of such events, in Norwich, using climate data and mapping from the Tyndall Centre and working with social scientists from UEA. Here local people could interact with a massive map of the Norfolk Broads on the floor (of the Forum in the town centre).

The key question was 'where are your priorities for this area?' (conservation, agriculture or tourism?). This was something people had to indicate by placing stickers – interacting with other people's choices. For me, this is another kind of shared text; instead of passively receiving plans you are engaging with the real trade offs. This is a different frame to receive scientific information in.

Another initiative in similar vein, and stretching what you might understand as a shared 'text', was A World Without Oil, in which players had to imagine a world hit by a sudden oil shortage and formulate responses. The game aimed both to gather good ideas to be reapplied by policy makers, educators and NGOs and also to map future risks and prevent their worst potential outcomes by planning ahead. The motto of the game (which ended in 2007) was 'Play it before you live it.'

On similar lines was the Energy Crossroads conference in Copenhagen in March 2009. Student delegates from across the world role-played the forthcoming COP15 talks in December; to map out what could come up during these talks and how to tackle blocks and disagreements. More than 45 nationalities took part and the events are being rolled out to other international locations.

USER-CENTRED POLICY DESIGN

Similar processes can be applied within organisations, to open up developing strategy, policy and other forms of planning. One example is at political party conferences. Here any party member can listen and (in theory) debate or even table a motion, or make a speech themselves. These are supposed to be events where parties get ideas from the grassroots. Instead they are stage-managed mass media circuses where at best the parliamentary party tests the mood and bounces ideas off people in fringe meetings and the bar.

In 2007 I came up with an idea for Demos, the think tank, who wanted to demonstrate the power and relevance of social media to the UK Labour Party. My idea was that we divide the entire agenda of the three- day conference into several hundred 'policy chunks' as subject headings, that we register a sample of volunteer delegates and that we continually send out multi-choice text messages asking them to rank three randomly chosen policy chunks in order of importance. Each policy would get a short description, for instance:

036. Reclassify cannabis as a class B, not a class C drug.

121. Seek international agreements on corporate tax evasion.

197. Abolish testing in primary schools for 8-year-olds.

Actually the volunteers could have a handbook giving these descriptions – a useful guide to the policy framework of the conference. Then we could use just the numbers and they could look up the policies. So their text could say:

A. 197: B. 121: C. 036

What you would have to do is reply on which was most important to you. For instance it might be B-A-C if you ranked tax evasion as most important, then schools testing, then reclas-sifying cannabis. By one of those quirks of sampling and statis-tics, you would not need all that many multi-choice answers to rank 200 policies in priority order. You could incentivise answering through prizes, ranging from a pie and a pint in the bar, to appearances on *Newsnight* as the most 'on message' delegate (the one whose answers were closest to the average).

The results would create a shared reflection of what the whole conference was thinking. For instance, you could create a people's manifesto (policies in the priority order chosen by delegates). Also feedback on speeches: you might see climate change moving up the list after Ed Milliband took the stage. You could also highlight what the differences are between local constituency members, trades union delegates and MPs. All of this could be displayed realtime, regurgitated in press releases and used to annotate proceedings.

OPEN SOURCE

Open source started as a software movement: with such communal products as Linux, Wikipedia, Firefox and Apache, built by volunteers working outside the (GDP) economy and usually out of working hours. Although what tended to happen in mature cases like Linux was a foot in both camps: a platform that is free and maintained by volunteers in its core (the kernal) but also businesses making it user friendly able to charge in a conventional way.

The spirit of this movement is as much about quality control and getting it right as it is being free – or open to users with no charges. Eric Raymond's famous paper 'The Cathedral and the Bazaar' (based on his experience of working with Linux development) came to the famous conclusion that 'with enough eyeballs, all bugs are shallow'. I'm certainly a fan of the many eyeballs argument – part of the process of developing this book was exposing the drafts for comment on the PSFK blog which has 300 000 readers.

The open source design idea is a natural approach for sustainable design, given the aims of the pioneers are likely to be about getting to step changes in technology, rather than cornering a part of an existing market for profit.

A typical example is the River Simple car running on hydrogen fuel cells. What open source means in this case is making the designs available so that the car can be produced locally and different teams can contribute to its overall improvement and development. Hugo Spowers says production is due to start in 2013. Also intriguing is their business model; you will lease the car for £200 a month rather than buy/own it. Given the average running costs of a 'normal' car in the UK range from £250–£500 and the sustainability gain from renting this does look like a bit of a win:win.

PART 4

ECONOMIC RESILIENCE

WHY THE ECONOMY WORKS AGAINST SUSTAINABILITY

> Economic growth elevates emissions; what is the point of making a fetish of growth if it in some large part diminishes welfare?
>
> Anthony Giddens, former Director,
> London School of Economics

MY SON'S FRIEND ROCCO is worried about earthquakes. He told me a little uncertainly they 'only last a second' and 'aren't very big' here. He also worries about tornadoes although in this country 'these aren't bigger than a tree'. They'd be safe at school anyway he hoped. Rocco then told us about the floods where his granny lives (Sri Lanka) that 'went up to her neck'.

Rocco is right to be worried. His family experience of natural disasters is shocking but far from atypical. Here (Figure 10.1) is the last century of growth in hydrometeorological (storm, flood, drought, mudslide and so on) disasters worldwide, a

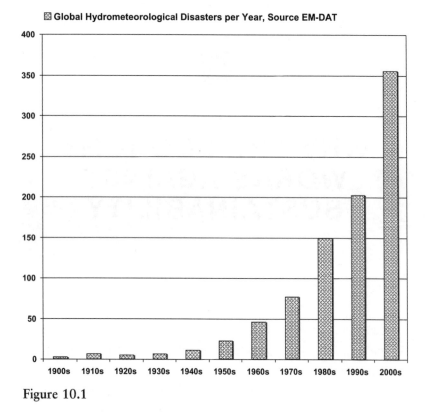

☒ Global Hydrometeorological Disasters per Year, Source EM-DAT

Figure 10.1

'disaster' being defined as 10 or more deaths, 100 or more people affected, a state of emergency, a call for international assistance.

This graph is a familiar shape. Figure 10.2 is another one like this.

These graphs look suspiciously similar. Any statistician will tell you that correlation is not causation. Any meteorologist will tell you that you cannot say any one storm or flood is down to climate change. Nonetheless there is a growing recognition that economic growth has been causing increased risks to human wellbeing, including natural disasters.

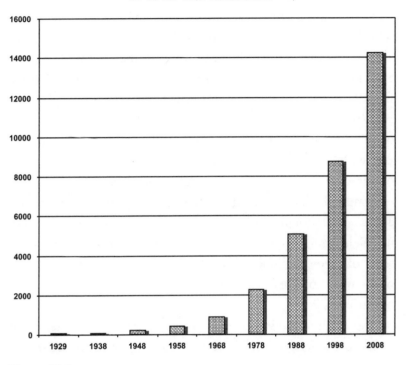

Figure 10.2

- Higher economic activity has led to greater greenhouse gas emissions both directly through increased energy use and indirectly through construction, deforestation and so on.
- Higher greenhouse gas concentrations lead to increased heating which means more energy in the system (which makes it more turbulent and chaotic) and also more water vapour in the air.
- The extremes of global weather, as reflected in hydrometeorological disasters, are driven by how much energy and water vapour there is in the air (as well as being linked to deforestation, disruption of ocean cycles, soil erosion ... also linked to human economic activity).

Growth in itself is not bad. All life is based upon growth. If only we could let our forests grow and support us. If the entire world economy was devoted to delivering more services to ecosystems than human beings took out, then it couldn't grow fast enough. I know of few environmentalists who would argue with those parts of the economy which are expected to play this role (renewables, regenerative farming) having the rocket pack of investment strapped onto their backs, as soon as possible. But with the type of growth we've experienced over the last hundred years we do need to redefine progress.

It may be that human growth is a good analogy. Civilisation could be thought of as like an 18-year-old. Growth in height, weight, power got us here. But to continue the same sort of growth would be deforming and unhealthy. We now need to grow in knowledge, wisdom, capacity, skill, maturity … ?

If economic growth is really driving planet death, then what of the many leaders and experts promising green growth?

What the world needs is a Green New Deal … investment that fights climate change, creates millions of green jobs and spurs green growth.

UN Secretary General Ban Ki Moon (2008)[78]

(The) new energy economy … will reduce dependence on foreign oil, create green-collar jobs and lay a foundation for new economic growth.

Barack Obama (2009)[79]

In the 21st century our new objectives are clear … growth, full employment and environmental care.

Gordon Brown (2006)[80]

The world does not need to choose between averting climate change and promoting growth and development.

Nicholas Stern (2006)[81]

To be fair Nick Stern has moderated his position; he now says the West may need to relinquish GDP growth, he just doesn't think we are quite ready yet. And Ban Ki Moon and Barack Obama are talking about those parts of the economy which must grow to respond to the climate crisis (and letting the audience confuse those with the whole economy). Gordon Brown on the other hand is either calling for a miracle, or simply doesn't get it.

Green growth claims were assessed by a recent UK government report on the issue of economic growth (by Professor Tim Jackson and the Sustainable Development Commission).[82] The report starts by noting that in the last 50 years the global economy has grown to be five times bigger. If this growth continued to 2100 it would be 80 times bigger. Growth so far is associated with degradation of 60% of the world's ecosystems. For instance, in the last 50 years the amount of forest cut down is equivalent in size to North America. That's a lot of trees.

Jackson's report, six years in the making, has troubling news for green growth advocates:

1. We have seen some 'relative decoupling' – with the amount of CO_2 produced per $ of economic activity falling from about 1 kg to 770 g. However emissions are still rising, by 80% since 1970 and 40% since 1990. There is no absolute decoupling; more growth, more emissions.

2. The claims of UK green growth to date were based on not counting those emissions off-shored through increasing imports (e.g. by moving manufacturing, raw material extraction to China, plus the extra shipping from there to here). Studies

by Dieter Helm and the Stockholm Environment Institute confirm the UK had no green growth.

3. Jackson also used the Ehrlich equation $I = P \times A \times T$ (I is Impact, P is Population, A is Affluence, T is Technology efficiency) to calculate that, with the current pattern of economic growth and population growth, then (every single piece of) human technology would have to be on average 17 times more efficient by 2050 than it is today in order to stabilise atmospheric carbon emissions. This is a pipe dream. Even if IT devices could do this, we are talking tractors, toasters and trains too.

So why are policy-makers so fixated with GDP growth?

Economic growth is thought essential to the health of a modern economy. It is so ingrained in the mindset of economists and politicians that few dare even question it. And there is little serious work done on alternatives.

Every society clings to a myth by which it lives. Ours is the myth of economic growth. For the last five decades the pursuit of growth has been the single most important policy goal across the world ... The reasons for this collective blindness are easy enough to find. The modern economy is structurally reliant on economic growth for its stability. When growth falters – as it has done recently – politicians panic. Businesses struggle to survive. People lose their jobs and sometimes their homes. A spiral of recession looms. Questioning growth is deemed to be the act of lunatics, idealists and revolutionaries. (Tim Jackson/ SDC, 2009)[83]

Lunatics, idealists and revolutionaries? In a *New Scientist* issue devoted to economic growth Jackson reported that at the launch of his report 'a UK treasury official stood up and accused

my colleagues and I of 'wanting to go back and live in caves'.'
And that at another of Jackson's recent meetings, a high-rank-
ing official was heard to mutter: 'Well, that is all very interesting, perhaps now we can get back to the real job of growing
the economy.'[84]

One reason why growth is so problematic is compound
growth, an infernal machine. One little rule – go a few % faster
every year – leads in no time to a hurtling, breakneck speed.
It's like the fable of the grain of gold on the first square of the
chess board, two grains on the second ... until soon you need
more gold than exists in the world. Free market supporters will
counter that growth is moderated by 'creative destruction' –
corrections that weed out the weak. This is not an argument to
be 'settled' – it is the subject of ideological conflict. But along
with design faults pointed to by the critics of growth, we do
need to understand why proponents think it so essential.

One of the earliest arguments put for growth (by Adam
Smith) was that only when new jobs were being created would
wages stay high. Otherwise the equivalent of a price war in
wages would set in.

Productivity leading to lost jobs is what modern commentators such as Thomas Homer-Dixon[85] point to as being the
reason why we need to grow. Causes of this include technology,
off-shoring and the end of communist models of full employment (like state factories in China). The result of productivity
gains is that if the (GDP) economy stays static, unemployment
rises. Only by creating new jobs can the economy keep up.
Homer-Dixon reckons this natural wastage of jobs amounts to
2–3% per year in the West and 7% in China.

I have another view, perhaps closer to that of the creative
destruction school. Productivity is not the reason why it hurts
society fast when the economy does not grow. In the USA a

year into a recession unemployment is heading for 10% in 2009. In the 1930s it hit over 30%. This is more than natural wastage. This is about speculative investors running for the hills; or management trying to persuade them not to do so by slashing costs (wages) so they can still pay shareholders from short-termist profits from the savings.

This points to a lack of resilience – systems that collapse just when you most need them to be stable. A 'just in time' world with nothing in reserve is a house built upon sand. But when any shocks hit – being entirely supported today by speculative investment – it turns to quicksand.

But even speculative investment and asset bubbles are not the whole story. The basic sticking point – why we are addicted to GDP growth – may be an innocuous looking factor: the interest rate. This makes competition a matter of survival. That's because for some to pay back interest on their debts, with a fixed overall pool of money to draw upon, others must go bankrupt. Only if the pool of money keeps growing can this be avoided. Here's an illustration:

Imagine an economy consisted of 10 people.

Each borrows £100.

Because of interest rates each has to repay an extra 10% i.e. £10.

There is £1000 in the system.

Each 'player' owes £110.

i.e. only 9 of them can repay their loan.

I adapted this little scenario from the story of The Eleventh Round (a longer parable, involving farmers, chickens and whatnot) in Bernard Lietaer's book *The Future of Money*.

Lietaer is far from being either naïve or academic about economics. He was a prominent banker specialising in currency trading and one of the architects of the single European currency. Lietaer argues that the interest rate has three negative impacts on wellbeing:

1. Encouraging systematic competition, whereby some must lose, for reasons explained in The Eleventh Round.
2. The need for endless economic growth, even when quality of life does not improve as a result (the growth is 'spent' on interest, not wellbeing).
3. A tax on the vast majority to make the few (asset owners to whom net interest is owed) even wealthier.

Lietaer's second point opens up the question of alternative measures than GDP, which do track wellbeing. That was the main thrust of the recent Stiglitz Report commissioned by Nicholas Sarkozy (the full title is Commission on the Measurement of Economic Performance and Social Progress):

Indeed, for a long time there have been concerns about the adequacy of current measures of economic performance, in particular those solely based on GDP. Besides, there are even broader concerns about the relevance of these figures as measures of societal well-being. To focus specifically on the enhancement of inanimate objects of convenience (for example in the GNP or GDP which have been the focus of a myriad of economic studies of progress), could be ultimately justified – to the extent it could be – only through what these objects do to the human lives they can directly or indirectly influence.

Moreover, it has long been clear that GDP is an inade-
quate metric to gauge wellbeing over time particularly in
its economic, environmental, and social dimensions,
some aspects of which are often referred to as sustainability. (2009, p. 8)[86]

One approach taking its lead from the idea of measuring
quality not quantity is the General Progress Indicator (GPI)
proposed by Daly and Cobb in For The Common Good (1989).
The measure has been refined several times but in essence it
adjusts GDP to account for negative wellbeing impacts of inequality, crime, environmental degradation, as well as positive
impact of leisure, home and community work, the quality of
public services. Applying this index to the USA researchers
found that while GDP rose throughout the period 1950–2004,
the GPI had been flat since around 1975.

Another way of assessing wellbeing is to ask people if they
are happy and satisfied with their lives. The famous study comparing subjective wellbeing and GDP by Ronald Ingelhart
(1997) found from the figures from over 60 countries that the
proportion declaring themselves happy and satisfied was lower
for countries below a certain threshold in GDP per capita; but
above this threshold there was little difference. You can see the
data plots for many countries at the worldhappinesstrends.org
website.[87] One caution in leaping to any conclusions though, as
discussed in a subsequent paper from Ingelhart (2000) is that
former communist societies accounted for nearly all of the
'miserable' cluster; the countries with low satisfaction relative
to their GDP. Whereas Bangladesh, India, Nigeria, the Philippines – some of the world's poorer nations – showed similar
levels to Spain, Portugal, Austria and Japan on happiness and
satisfaction. It is not straightforward to say GDP growth or

absolute level 'equals' happiness at any stage of a country's development.

GDP does not correlate well with happiness. However, neither does any other factor. That's why wellbeing which correlates with health, employment, community and environmental quality of life factors seems to many a much more robust thing to aim for than 'the pursuit of happiness'. This was originally already a twist on a famous (at the time) phrase from Adam Smith declaring every person had the right to 'Life, Liberty and Land'. The American constitution, which you can't help noticing was drawn up by landowners, modified this to 'Life, Liberty and the Pursuit of Happiness'. Give up on land rights and we will bring you Coca-Cola, Disney and cable TV?

Let's return to Lietaer's third point; that there are a few at the top of this pyramid scheme who benefit disproportionately. The top 500 wealthiest people account for 7% of the world's GDP. As a country they would rank fifth, just behind Germany.[88]

The growth of the world economy has long been biased towards wealthy countries and individuals. According to a World Bank study (Pritchett 1997) the relative proportions of average income between the world's richest and poorest countries had grown from 9x in 1870 to 45x in 1990. Studies by another World Bank economist, Branko Milanovic, found that, by looking on a household rather than a country basis, the Chinese and Indian 'miracle' disappears: you find that these countries are just replicating the world inequality pattern within their borders with a few billionaires and a continuing majority in abject poverty.

There is also this recurring theme of resilience. While little wealth trickles down in the good times, the effects of recession hit the poorest countries hardest during a slump. Reasons for this in the latest downturn include plummeting remittances (money sent back home to relatives) from migrant workers in rich countries. Also there was the food crisis triggered in 2008 partly by speculative capital fleeing banking into commodities. One UN expert called this 'the silent tsunami' instantly facing 100 million people with hunger and possible starvation. It's also a sign of how loaded the current world economy is; that rich countries benefit from nearly all the energy use, but the developing world faces the worst of the effects of climate change.

Economic growth is one of those issues that people on all sides of the political spectrum argue furiously about. Sharon Astyk is a farmer, author, teacher and blogger: an expert on food, peak oil and climate change – with a huge following (Rob Hopkins for instance is a big fan). George Monbiot is an author, a reknowned anti-corporate activist turned journalist. It's hard to say which one is more 'radical'. However, they take different lines on 'growth':

- Sharon Astyk suggested that given the tipping point model of climate change we had to reduce energy usage by 10% a year; as the enormous 'front load' of fossil fuels required to convert the world to clean tech (to make the wind farms, electric cars, a whole new energy grid ...) could in itself be what pushes us over the brink into runaway climate change.
- George Monbiot replied that a 10% decrease in energy consumption would mean a 10% drop in economic activity meaning 'a deeper depression than the modern world has ever experienced. No political system – even an absolute monarchy – could survive an economic collapse on this scale.'[89]

Once again it depends on your reading of the risks. If you knew there was a good chance of having a heart attack, would you continue your career? It depends what you think would happen if you did, and what if you didn't.

But what is the alternative? Perhaps if society ran on more co-operative lines we could start to manage markets and other systems in a more rounded way. So that we could stop depending on accelerating (compound) growth just to keep the economy afloat. Something of that sort is suggested by Zac Goldsmith's new book *The Constant Economy*, which eschews polarised debates about these extremes in favour of an economy where:

> resources are valued not wasted, where food is grown sustainably and goods are built to last. It is a system whose energy security is based on the use of renewable sources, and communities are valued as a country's strongest hedge against social, economic and environmental instability. The constant economy operates at the human scale, and above all it recognizes nature's limits.[90]

One macroeconomic model covered by Jackson's report did show that it was possible to move a national economy to zero growth (without a crash). This was achieved through less private investment, more public spending and reducing the working week. Jackson explained that this was more than just a theoretical exercise in tinkering with mathematical models:

> Reducing the working week is the simplest and most often cited structural solution to the challenge of maintaining full employment with non-increasing output. And there is some precedent for it, for example, from labour policies in certain European nations.[91]

This is not a new idea. In the prolonged 1930s recession, the idea of a leisure society, with shorter working weeks, gripped the public imagination as offering the potential for improved quality of life. With a third out of work, why not do two-thirds of the hours each? This became such a bandwagon that Congress passed a bill to reduce the American standard working week to 30 hours (although with World War II approaching this was never made law) – five less than even the famous French 35-hour week. It was hailed as being about much more than the prospect of 'less working hours'; it was about a positive enthusiasm for fathers involved in children's upbringing, or lifelong learning as a 'second job', or a life lived simply more for enjoyment and less for toil.

Commentators in the 1930s predicted that by now we would have three-day weeks or similar as the standard arrangement. Thousands of books and articles were published on leisure, including some bestsellers (Currell, 2005).[92] A leisure society with shorter working weeks was seen as a panacea – providing answers to questions about technology, work, economics, social change, democracy and much besides. In today's (indefinite) recession, it looms into view once again as an alternative to mass unemployment. The pivotal thing would be if we agree co-operatively to limit our working hours so that there are plenty to go around. It's a communitarian solution. And that's exactly the discussion that was happening in factories around the world in early 2009. The factories don't want to lose their investment in skilled workers. The workers don't want to lose their jobs, or for friends to do so. So they agree shorter weeks. Business and economics are only blind and dumb if we let them be. And faced with a crisis, we can redraw the boundaries of what is possible.

Another contributor to the Sustainable Development Commission who has been looking at alternatives to the GDP growth for several decades is Professor Herman Daly, former Senior Economist at the World Bank. Daly advocates what he calls Steady State Economics. This would mean a constant population and constant amount of capital, with a low throughput (for instance low rates of production of new goods) within the earth's regenerative capacities. My image of his theory is that of forestry; managing a productive ecosystem for its own benefit and ours, living off its surplus. Whereas at the moment the economy is more like a massive logging operation; productive from the point of view of the sawmill but highly destructive if a broader view is taken of society-wide health and trajectory.

Daly points out that a steady state economy is not at all the same thing as a 'failed growth' economy. A steady state economy would not mean accepting an inevitable collapse. Rather it would mean putting in place structures and policies to support stasis, not boom and bust.

Daly provides a starkly different set of answers to the same questions leading most economists to believe that aggregate growth is the only possible norm:

- Poverty could be tackled through redistribution. A spread of global incomes between the richest and the poorest of less than 100, through a maximum wage as well as a minimum. The current spreads (even within US corporations – of over 500) are after all the result of CEO incentives within high growth economies, not steady state.
- Production of more durable goods to minimise the throughput. I would add upgradeable, repairable, repurposeable. And also looking at models of sharing goods and energy. But the result is the same – that we get the maximum human utility per unit of precious

resources and energy. The easiest way to enforce this in policy terms would be to tax natural resources rather than end products.

- Limiting of bank activities to lending money on behalf of savers and other concrete services; make money a public utility again, not something a bank can 'create' in order to loan and earn interest. Investment would be a smaller part of the steady state economy anyway, and there would be no need for a 'pyramid of debt'.
- The leisure society, as already discussed, where gains in productivity lead to more time being available rather than more goods. We would need to rethink the way that people earn and one of Daly's suggestions is mass participation in business ownership.
- Restriction of intellectual property rights; few patents and much shorter timescales. He discusses this in terms of lifting 'enclosure' (i.e. discoveries and knowledge as public goods, not to be 'owned'). Daly also advocates making knowledge transfer (rather than interest bearing loans) the mainstay of international development aid.

So far we have looked at objections to focusing narrowly on GDP growth, and at proposals for a steady state economic alternative. There is another radical challenge that has been posed recently to GDP. And that is that it does not even properly measure the value of the economy.

Nobel Prize winning economists Stiglitz and Sen state in their recent report that as we live in an 'information age', we should be able to use much better information than crude 'production' measures to assess the progress of national economies. Examples of what's missing from GDP explored in the report include leisure time and nonmarket services. If someone's working hours were cut, but their pay stayed the same, they would experience a big improvement in quality of life that wouldn't be recorded. If you don't assess nonmarket services you can record false growth as these are being steadily brought into the economy; for instance in paying for childcare services that often might in past generations have fallen to a female relative.

What GDP measures is the total value of goods and services exchanged within a year. It is calculated by adding together national figures for the value of:

1. Total household consumer spending.
2. Government spending.
3. Net exports (i.e. exports minus imports).
4. Net investment capital.

70% of GDP in the USA is the first of these, consumer expenditure. This explains why politicians are obsessed with getting us to spend (rather than save, and wait and see) to keep an economy from going into recession. It also makes it clear why consumerism is itself a big issue for sustainability.

The critics of GDP within economics say it is a measure of economic throughput not economic quality or value. Even one of the inventors of GDP, Simon Kuznets, later stated (in his Nobel acceptance speech) 'the welfare of a nation can scarcely be informed from a measure of national income'. GDP was introduced first during World War II to keep track of productivity, since an ever-increasing supply of munitions and equipment were vital for the war effort.

What GDP measures is transactions rather than assets; the sources of wealth in future years. Attention has recently focused on two types of asset which GDP does not measure: social assets and environmental assets. The social side is well captured in this famous speech by Robert Kennedy:

> Yet the gross national product does not allow for the health of our children, the quality of their education, or the joy of their play. It does not include the beauty of our poetry or the strength of our marriages; the intelligence of our public debate or the integrity of our public officials. It measures neither our wit nor our courage; neither our wisdom nor our learning; neither our compassion nor our devotion to our country; it measures everything, in short, except that which makes life worthwhile. And it tells us everything about America except why we are proud that we are Americans. (Robert F. Kennedy 1968)[93]

Apart from Kennedy's appeal to quality, there is also a bias within GDP to immediate earnings, rather than investing time (and lost earnings) in new ventures, changes of career, child-rearing, further education, strong communities – all things that will tangibly determine how the economy and companies and individuals within it do in 10 years' time. In case that sounds soft and insubstantial, consider that 'Web 2.0' was born in a fallow period. During the dotcom slump of 2002, internet developers gave up on chasing whatever investors were looking for next (there was no investment money around) and instead just dreamed up applications 'done right'. These were coded speculatively and partly just to keep their skills fresh. One of these, a nifty app called LastFM (which in the early stages paid its coders in omelettes), ended up as the most valuable internet company in Europe. Exactly as in industrial farming, the notion of any 'fallow period' is anathema to GDP economics, but is a common factor in most stories of creative entrepreneurs.

For valuing environmental assets, one approach that is being evaluated by the EU is TEEB (The Economic Evaluation of Biodiversity). This is a new national accounting system. TEEB's founder, Pavan Sukhdev – who I have seen present a number of times – points out that one third of people in India (where he started developing these systems) live directly on the bounty of nature. Cutting down forest increases GDP, but it devastates natural assets, forcing people to move to city slums because the countryside can no longer support them. TEEB values the natural assets by taking into account the positive contributions and also the onward costs and benefits.

Sukhdev is at pains to point out that he is a capitalist – he works for Deutsche Bank, not an NGO. He just thinks GDP-based economics is (and I quote) 'stupid'. If you ran a company with no regard for valuing and maintaining its key assets you would be fired. Yet this is precisely how countries are governed. The main application of TEEB is to conservation. This can be quantified through valuing ecosystem benefits such as water and air purification, fisheries, timber and nutrient cycling. These are public goods with no prices, so 'their loss often is not detected by our current economic incentive system and can thus continue unabated'.[94] Sukhdev once gave evidence in a court case in Germany, defending a tract of forest against the company (and council) that wanted to cut it down creating many jobs in the process. Sukhdev's argument was that the long-term value of the forest was greater than the value of the commercial opportunity proposed to replace it. Another of Sukhdev's 'for examples' is the Panama Canal. Here nearby deforestation is creating massive silting. Using a TEEB approach it would be possible for insurance companies to finance reforestation in order to avoid the mother of all insurance claims if the canal became impassable. It's a clear example of where a sensible investment in natural ecosystems is justifiable. It would be quite like a 'hedge'; a standard financial manoeuvre to account for.

The pressure is on to include forest protection credits within the next round of carbon talks in Copenhagen later in 2009. According to The Nature Conservancy 24% of global carbon emissions result from deforestation. Greenpeace and Prince Charles have been calling for an emergency investment package for tropical forests. In their scheme it is suggested that rich countries pay the poorer countries to preserve their rainforests. It is estimated – TEEB-style – that halving the deforestation would cost the poor countries $15 billion in lost economic opportunity, so why don't we just pay them that to keep the things? (Compare that with their calculation that the net present value of keeping these forests is $3.7 trillion). Using the remote sensing technology, accurate performance and tracking measures could be put in place. Another suggestion is to create 'rainforest bonds' similar to government bonds, so finance could be raised from the capital markets.

Another proposal for using economics to put the breaks on climate change is Cap & Trade (which is likely to become US legislation by 2010). This means:

- an absolute cap on total national carbon emissions;
- big energy companies have to buy permits (the tax) for cover operations.

They will no doubt pass on the cost of these to customers, but the income from permits will be (85%) passed straight on to tax-payers so that on average (unless you use excessive energy) you'll be better off.

Peter Barnes, one of the proponents of this Cap & Trade scheme, explains this as money recycling; the government passes the additional income from the tax back through income tax rebates. The 15%, which the government is keeping, will be used to finance new energy projects. This is in line with learning from Scandinavia where energy taxes have been levied. The only country that showed a net decrease in energy use was Denmark; because they invested some of the revenue in energy efficiency subsidies.

We saw how effective the energy price rises of 2007/8 were in curbing consumption. America recorded the first serious falls in driving in over 15 years. Anecdotally there were reports of shifts in quite iconic American car behaviour – such as the teenagers the *New York Times* claimed were giving up the 'Friday Night Cruise' in their cars because gas was too pricey.[95]

Jeremy Leggett, speaking at an event I chaired in 2008, believes we are already at or near peak oil production – and that this may have been the underlying cause of the 2008 price spike. Peak oil doesn't mean the end of oil, rather it means the end of affordable oil; in energetic and financial terms it will be increasingly costly to extract from deeper and sparser oil fields. This point was passed in the 1970s within US oil fields. Leggett is a former BP engineer who became so worried by the issue he joined Greenpeace, then later set up the UK's largest solar company (Solar Century). Conservative sources such as Leggett's former employer BP (in their *Statistical Review of World Energy*)[96] estimate that 'the world still has enough 'proven' reserves to provide 40 years of consumption at current rates'. Leggett on the other hand thinks we have a couple of years, at best. It's another epochal risk world leaders do take deadly seriously. The country of Sweden already plans to be oil independent by 2020. Their biofuel plan is based upon wood industry waste (not food crops) – in Sweden there are 6000 trees for every person.

Thinking about peak oil, you have to consider the social and economic impact. This eclipses any discussions of GDP or other measures. If and when we hit peak oil the financial markets would go into total meltdown, as nearly every business model in the world assumes that fuel will be plentiful and cheap. It's the ultimate wake up call that a central task of sustainability is to build a more resilient – and frankly less insane – economy. It also really focuses the mind on issues like local and national food self-sufficiency.

ECONOMIC RESILIENCE: GRAMEEN, CCA AND CO-OPERATIVES

SPECULATIVE INVESTMENT IS something like a wobbly pin in the grenade of economics. It contributes to a lack of resilience because it pulls out every time there is a downturn. It also potentially creates a gap between the goals and ethos of a company and its ownership and financial obligations.

So it's encouraging that other formats are emerging than the company-as-a-vehicle-for-investor-shareholder returns. What I am going to suggest is that in future most ventures could be social ventures. And that employee and community ownership will enjoy a boom. And that speculative investment itself will be eclipsed by more patient, secure and responsible forms – whether ethical funds, local government backed bonds or pensions 2.0.

A social venture is one whose primary aim is to solve a social problem. As a new unit of capitalism, the success of social ventures is a highly significant development. The Said Business

School (in Oxford) pulled together a landmark review of *Social Entrepreneurship* (2006). Their research showed that in 2004 new UK social ventures outnumbered commercial start-ups. Social ventures have been something like another 'dotcom' boom – a talent magnet, with a new entrepreneurial generation being attracted to doing something more worthwhile. And they are quite a media and political 'darling'. What social ventures offer is the best of both worlds; entrepreneurial dynamism and making a worthwhile contribution to society.

Dynamism comes from self-management and innovation. Deng Xiaoping offered a new deal to Chinese farmers in the 1970s. They had to supply the state machine with a fixed quota. Anything over this they could sell (or eat) themselves. This incentivised growing more and it gave them more freedom to grow what they wanted, without a party official dictating from a manual that probably didn't suit their land. And in place of the top-down state farms, self-help village co-operatives emerged to act as safety nets for those hit by misfortune. I'm sure it's still far from perfect, but it achieved what was hoped and successfully halted a long running famine. This may read like a case study in favour of free market liberalisation. But read it carefully. What wasn't introduced was agribusiness, bank loans, exploitative free markets. The people were given more control, not less.

The need for social ventures in my view was created by the narrowness of markets. It's not a glamorous portrayal, but most ecosystems create large niches for those who can use what is left over. In the case of free market capitalism with a narrow ownership and serving a narrow range of needs and audiences, there are huge markets left untapped. A 2001 report in the *British Medical Journal*[97] looked at resources devoted to malaria, tuberculosis, sleeping sickness, Chagas' Disease and leishmaniasis by 11 of the top pharmaceutical corporations. Only two companies reported spending anything on malaria. There are up to 500 million cases of malaria per year worldwide. This is a tragedy – an inevitable outcome of the current system – and it is hardly surprising that alternatives would emerge. Many social ventures have emerged in response to the needs of markets excluded by narrow corporate profit motives, another prime example being banking.

The Grameen Bank's founder, Mohammed Yunus, won the Nobel Peace Prize in recognition of a new way of being a business, which could literally have the potential to save humanity. There are by now also 18 other Grameen businesses, all independent social ventures designed to give employment opportunities and/or services to the poorest people, ranging from telecoms and IT, to health, water and food businesses. But it started with a bank. Well not quite. Yunus says he never set out to create a bank. He started off just loaning some money without collateral. Then one thing led to another.

Microcredit is a system of banking that alleviates poverty by giving small (micro) loans to individuals and small firms to invest in equipment or materials through which they can earn a living. It equips people rather than just making them dependent on aid. Not only is this an investment in improvement rather than alleviation but also it offers dignity and hope. The astonishing thing (compared to conventional banking) is that these are loans without collateral. They are therefore in theory the riskiest sorts of loans going. And they are to poor people living in precarious conditions. And they are distributed into remote regions where debt collection would hardly be an easy task. Microcredit is 'sub-sub prime', and exists in harsh and volatile economies. Yet with microcredit there are astonishingly high repayment rates – 99% is common. That's because it's not dumb exploitation, it is about human beings co-operating with goodwill, respect and trust. It's one of many examples of succeeding by simply refusing to let society be like a machine.

Microcredit is in stark contrast to exploitative sub-prime lending. But it is most often compared to international aid. If you set someone up in business they have the means to support themselves, psychologically and spiritually as well as commercially. Another reason microcredit works is that it is embedded in human networks and real empathic cultural understanding. For a start, the loans are generally to women. Women in the developing world, given a little loan, will not go and gamble it, buy drinks for their friends and so on (like the men will). Women are hence simply a lower credit risk.

Grameen Bank started in the village of Jobra in 1976. It is owned by the community. Borrowers of the Grameen Bank currently own 95% of its equity (the other 5% is owned by the Bangladesh government). Each borrower *must* be a member of a five-borrower group. The group does not guarantee the loans in the formal sense of group liability although you can easily imagine them helping each other out on occasion to keep things on track through illnesses or other setbacks. They function instead to make sure no individual gets into difficulty with repayment and that their circle all behave responsibly. The system is hence backed by real trust, self-esteem, social standing and mutual support. A higher level of repayment than commercial loans reflects this social commitment. Whereas, if you defaulted on a sub-prime mortgage, letting the bank down would be the last of your worries (it could almost be an upside you'd imagine – an act of revenge).

There are 7.8 million borrowers from the Grameen Bank and 97% of them are women. The bank has so far loaned out $7.88 billion, of which $7 billion has been paid back. The bank lends out around $1 billion per year. The bank is entirely funded by its own deposits; it loans out money that it already has and keeps about 50% extra in reserve. Grameen Bank charges different interest rates based on people's ability to repay; the highest at 20% is for income generating loans, 8% for housing loans, 5% for student loans and 0% for 'struggling members'. The interest rates may sound high but they reflect the administrative costs of small loans. And they are tiny compared to the prevalent loan shark alternatives. All borrowers are covered by loan insurance: in the event of their death (or of their husband's death) the loan is paid off in full for them. They also get life insurance funded through their shareholding in the bank. There is also a pension scheme, encouraging borrowers to save a small amount for old age. By saving a little every month over 10 years, they get twice the full amount back.

Community pride is used to drive branch success and performance. Grameen branches are awarded stars for each of zero default levels, profit, becoming self-funding, ensuring education for all Grameen family children, and finally a five star branch is one that has succeeded in raising every one of its members over the poverty line. There are only 57 (out of 2500) 5 star branches. But around 70–80% have collected 3 stars.

Grameen Bank has extended its scheme to 'struggling members' i.e. those reduced to begging. Here the usual rules do not apply, nor do they charge interest. The loans can be as long-term as needed. They are also covered by loan and life insurance. The borrower groups and centres are encouraged to support these struggling members. Grameen Bank has also extended into microenterprise loans of larger amounts. The average for this category is $353. These loans facilitate buying equipment for irrigation, farming and transport. Nearly $1m in sponsorships is given annually to (Grameen member) children with priority given to the girls, who are otherwise less likely to stay at school.

All in all it is a beautiful system. A human system, driving the economics. It is hard to read about what they have done without welling up with tears of joy and pride; about what has been achieved in one of the poorest communities in the world, not just in keeping people alive, but in giving people direction, hope, support, a future. And it is their bank – this is not just a benevolent patron, it is a large successful enterprise owned by its customers.

There is a common experience of entrepreneurs that many others will readily recognise from this account. You start with what you know of human nature, an inkling or initial design, but you are constantly evolving the living system to fit the way that people readily act, relate, think. That's why I see the social venturing sector as significant beyond the bounds of commerce. It is inventing new ways of being human and achieving stuff together. It's truly a kind of 'world building'. That's not to say you have to be a kind of artist-genius. A better guide is to create a system where the community drives the process. Such groups come up with 'whatever works' and are often also freed up by not even knowing what the conventions are that they are breaking.

The social venturing philosophy isn't just for commercial models, it is transforming the not-for-profit sector too. Here what's new is not the social goal (obviously) but this entrepreneurial spirit. Most social ventures I've known and worked with have an early matter of fact discussion about whether to be for-profit or nonprofit. Either way they are not doing it for the money. It's more about the most effective governance structure to meet their goals and gather the right resources, including any funding and projecting the right profile into their community.

In Africa, another inspiring social venture that typifies co-operative principles (in that the community delivers the social services) is Mothers2Mothers or M2M. AIDS in Africa has resulted in 12 million children losing their parent or caregiver. A single busy health clinic in Africa can see more babies born with HIV than the total in the UK, USA and Canada combined. M2M provide education and support for pregnant mothers-to-be living with HIV. Their mission is:

- To prevent babies from contracting HIV through mother-to-child transmission.
- To keep HIV+ mothers and their infants alive and healthy by increasing their access to health-sustaining medical care.
- To empower mothers living with HIV/AIDS, enabling them to fight stigma in their communities and to live positive and productive lives.

M2M was founded by a gynaecologist (Dr Mitchell Besser) as a single support group in Cape Town. But eight years later it is a multinational NGO. The key to its operation is mother-to-mother mentoring. It was founded on the realisation that social and cultural barriers were preventing a more conventional health education approach from being effective. I came across M2M when it won a Skoll Foundation award. It was also picked by the UN as one of the top NGOs that it partners with. The best endorsements though come from the quotes from mothers within the scheme (on M2M.org):

I stepped into a room filled with HIV-positive women ... I was expecting to see sick people, not happy vibrant women, I thought HIV/AIDS was the end of the world, but it is not at all.

Client and mother, M2M

Social ventures are an example of *good growth*. They are generative. They improve human wellbeing and are often expanding into a near vacuum of neglected populations and needs. They cannot grow fast enough, because they simply scale in proportion to the need. And they tend to be conscious organisations, so that for instance even if they focus on human, social issues they will also be mindful of their environmental impacts.

In studies of the effect of growth on the poorest countries the same point – that there are different sorts of growth – has been made.

> Growth can be jobless, rather than job creating; ruthless, rather than poverty reducing; voiceless, rather than participatory; rootless, rather than culturally enshrined; and futureless, rather than environmentally friendly. Growth that is jobless, ruthless, voiceless, rootless and futureless is not conducive to poverty reduction or human development. (David Lukes, UNDP)[98]

For the last 15 years or so corporations have been busy reinventing themselves as looser, mission- (or vision) focused, entrepreneurial human enterprises. Management gurus have lined up around this 'Fast Company' vision of open collar workers, smart IT systems, fluid collaboration and alignment with values. Charles Handy was a lone management voice (that I knew of) urging a humanist, decent approach through the 1980s and 1990s. Other business writers proclaimed speed and money-money-money. Management guru Michael Porter is one who belatedly saw the light: 'I used to see this area of corporate social performance as the last thing on my agenda ten years ago, but now I agree that social and economic issues are intertwined' (2003).[99] A recent development acknowledging this is

B-Corporation. This is a club of serious commercial companies with an equally serious commitment to social good. Here's their definition:

> B Corporations are a new type of corporation, which uses the power of business to solve social and environmental problems. B Corporations are unlike traditional responsible businesses because they:
>> Meet comprehensive and transparent social and environmental performance standards.
>> Institutionalize stakeholder interests.
>> Build collective voice through the power of a unifying brand.[100]

In other words it is a similar hybrid to social ventures, but with a degree of the formality associated with public companies. It is also a sort of 'eco label for companies'. It is attracting well-respected pioneers like Method.

Corporations are the bandits of a growth economy, yet also its hostage. By 'bandits' I mean that they (or rather their shareholders) capture a high proportion of growth. Corporate profits accounted in the US, in 2006, for 12.4% of GDP. Corporate profits were growing at an annual rate of over 20%. National GDP at the time was growing at an annual rate of 2.2%. In other words *roughly 100% of the growth in the GDP was corporate profits*. That was an exceptional year for corporate profits, but in a typical year GDP growth is more than 50% corporate profit growth. This starts to explain why America, with the strongest economy in the world, also has the third highest rate of infant mortality, the third lowest level of black male life expectancy. Not only the poor, but the middle classes in America are losing out.

The question a prolonged slump will pose is whether corporations can prove resilient in conditions where growth isn't an option. Would they implode – or indeed morph into some hybrid (like the now publicly owned banks)? It is a question no one wants to face; like asking the 1985 Politburo whether Soviet communism had a future. But it will be asked by events, sooner or later.

Corporate finance is far from the only way to build sizeable, efficient organisations; for example look at Linux, Grameen, Craigslist and Wikipedia.

The other question for corporations is whether they can compete with structures that can meet the same need without huge inputs of resources and energy. Increasingly these inputs will be expensive, not cheap. Imagine that the main determinant of the price was how many miles a product travelled. And how that would tilt almost every market into local alternatives.

It may also be that we see a new line being drawn, not between public and private – but between corporate and commons. The commons is a part of the economy, often rooted in both natural and human rights, which it would be both immoral (short term) and incautious (long term) to exploit on a maximum shareholder return basis. It is already being argued that food should have this status. A surprising addition to the commons may be banking. And if they aren't careful, the motor industry. The BBC is a longstanding example of a commons winning over the more commercial shareholder model.

An example of the commons approach being deployed against sustainability goals is Community Choice Aggregation (CCA) schemes. How these work is that a community (for instance a city) aggregates its energy buying. It then demands an aggressive renewables strategy and uses its buying clout to get this energy at no price increase or even more cheaply. The first – highly successful – CCAs were put in place in Cape Cod and Ohio. San Francisco and 40 other Californian local governments are in the process of setting them up. The key difference with CCAs is that they are set up to serve customers and green plans (a 2–4x increase in the proportion of renewables is typical), whereas the deregulated energy utilities serve shareholder interests. San Francisco is pushing ahead with a CCA plan that will allow the city to procure its own power in bulk, for citizens to buy. It is opening for electricity providers to bid in October 2009. The city will not own the transmission or generation but will rather buy from existing providers and sell to businesses and residents. The CCA's promise to San Francisco (against PG&E) is to:

> Use 51% local and/or renewable energy, tripling San Francisco's green energy to 360 megawatts by 2017!
>
> Place the risks of the energy market on the new Energy Service Provider as opposed to the City, County, and its ratepayers!
>
> Establish stable and reasonable rates, unlike PG&E's rates that spike along with the global gas markets!
>
> Meet or beat PG&E's rates![101]

The function of buying decent (in this case green) goods and reselling them at decent prices was the founding principle of nineteenth century co-operatives.

Robert Owen originally put forward a plan (which harked back to the Diggers) to set up 'villages of co-operation' where workers grew their own food, made their own clothes and were self-governing. Owen, a wealthy industrialist, drew up meticulous plans for these communities: they would be based upon 1200-person communes, with communal child rearing (past the age of 3) and housed in a single, large, square building (looking like a Victorian take on an oversized Oxford college).

The several experiments in this utopian arrangement failed. But Owen's attempts fired up the imagination of others. One of these, Dr William King, scaled down the ideas and made them workable. His key modifications were:

- co-operatives set up and run by the working classes themselves (rather than founded and owned by a rich patron);
- forming a 'co-operative' society within existing society, rather than cutting themselves off in new build colonies;
- basing these societies on shops, addressing daily needs;
- sensible governance design such as having trustees and audits; and 'no meetings in pubs';
- a monthly periodical, *The Co-operator*, spreading the philosophy, the latest news and ongoing practical advice.

The best known Co-operative Society was founded in Rochdale in 1844. The Rochdale Equitable Pioneers Society were a group of weavers and other artisans who, like many skilled workers, were being forced into poverty. They were not the first co-operative (*The Co-operator* had launched in 1828) but they have gone down in history as such, thanks partly to an 1858 book about their story, *Self Help By The People*, that became an international bestseller.

By the 1870s 300 independent co-operatives formed a wholesale society, giving them access to bulk buying and greater stability. The key throughout these booming times was that they worked with and for their community (rather than against them to maximise profits for the owners). Accord-

ing to the Rochdale rules, the objectives of the society were as
follows:

The establishment of a store for the sale of provision and
clothing.

The building, purchasing or erecting a number of houses,
in which those members desiring to assist each other in
improving their domestic and social condition may reside.

To commence the manufacture of such articles as the
society may determine upon, for the employment of such
members as may be without employment, or who may
be suffering in consequence of repeated reductions in
their wages.

As a further benefit and security to the members of this
society, the society shall purchase or rent an estate or
estates of land, which shall be cultivated by the members
who may be out of employment, or whose labour may
be badly remunerated.

That as soon as practicable, this society shall proceed to
arrange the powers of production, distribution, education, and government, or in other words to establish a
self-supporting home-colony or united interests, or assist
other societies in establishing such colonies.[102]

We are entering an era when the charter of a company might
once again reasonably offer to create a self-supporting home-
colony, or in other ways provide lifelong security for its members
as a primary aim and function.

That's not just because of climate change, peak oil, food
security, economic instability and so on. It's also because the
corporate model has lost its ability to provide this. The pressure

on corporates to slash costs in downturns spelled the end of the job for life. It has been known since the 1980s that pensions will not be able to meet their commitments by the time my generation retires (the so-called 'pensions bomb'). A key factor in any future collapse of the corporate model may be that it will look like a risky employment model, compared with the 'all in this together' alternatives?

PUTTING ECONOMIC RESILIENCE INTO ACTION

THE WAY THAT YOU FINANCE A PROJECT, and also the way its benefits and ownership are distributed, could have a bigger knock-on effect than the actual social mission that you set out to tackle.

For instance if you started a hugely successful recycling 2.0 business, funded by venture capital, selling credits to a carbon market, creating a substantial cash float which you bank ... these secondary issues could unintentionally be providing funding and support to models you would oppose.

A case in point was a recent report from Harvard Medical School showing that US health insurance groups also held between them $4.5 billion in tobacco stock. The report's authors described this wittily as 'the combined taxidermist and veterinarian approach: either way you get your dog back'![103]

That's perhaps an example of a lack of joined up thinking. But similar points could be made about all the idealistic projects using Facebook groups and inadvertently contributing to its success. The *Guardian* carried a piece in 2008, by Tom Hodg-kinson, about the main early Facebook investors: Peter Thiel, well-known for supporting ultra rightwing activism, and Jim Breyer, who also sits on the board of a group identifying and developing cutting edge technology for use by the CIA. Face-book has demonstrably helped mobilising people on human rights issues – for instance for Burma in 2007. So it's a shame to think it might actually also be funding stuff in the opposite direction. I'm not saying you need to be purist – I've used Face-book groups – but maybe there is a case for all of us to start asking these questions.

STARTING A SOCIAL VENTURE

A social venture starts with an itch that humanity can't scratch. It's some sort of unmet social need. Usually it would be some-thing that really bothers, fascinates or otherwise has its hooks into the life story of the founders. Dave Stewart got involved (with Paul Allen) in starting music training facilities for disad-vantaged youth because of his own lucky break, in being taken under the wing of two musicians when he was a young guitarist. Quite a number of ethical fashion businesses have started as the result of a founder visiting areas like Nepal and wanting to create better employment and chances for these communities. Enabled by Design was started by a disabled woman who was frustrated by the poor design of much of the home equipment on offer.

The great thing about a social venture though is that it isn't about you. It is about a need or cause that is bigger than you. One of the subtle differences you tend to notice between social entrepreneurs and the other sort is a distinct humility. There are hugely likeable commercial entrepreneurs mind you; but more often because they are misfits, dreamers and rebels. They can also tend to be a bit ego-driven and self-important, in my experience.

If you know what your issue is, then the entrepreneurial part is working out a way to meet the need, with almost no resources. If you had a government department, meeting the need might be more a case of throwing money at the problem. Studies show that social ventures generate jobs at one third of the cost of the public sector. Starting a social venture is always something of an Indian rope trick. It's quite usual to spend several years toying with alternative ideas, false starts, tests. Having said which, if you can set something up 'in your garage' it's well worth trying. Not only is trial and error often more valuable than theorising, but satisfying that itch even at the smallest scale is rewarding and sustaining.

What I have also found working with social ventures is that a key thing to get right at the outset is the structure (or in legalese, the governance). How can a social business be designed so that it is compelled forever to act in accordance with its founding vision and values? It is all very well having good intentions. But how do you know your successors will stay true to these?

For profit or not for profit? There are some technical differences, for instance with a charity the (paid) management cannot be on the (unpaid) board. Financially charities do well with tax breaks. For-profit social ventures appeal to investors, although it depends how strict you are about not being 'built to flip' (i.e. for their exit, when they won't be too concerned about 'selling out'). Some for-profit companies transition to employee or customer ownership. Riverford Farms, a high growth UK organic food business, plans to transition from family to employee ownership long term. A good readymade hybrid structure comes with the recent (2005) Community Interest

Company structure in the UK. The CIC governance rules say that you must:

- have a purpose which the regulator recognises as a social good;
- never sell off the assets of the company (for instance sell the company) – you can only pass it on to the community or a charity;
- limit the dividends paid to investors;
- reinvest the majority of profits in the community goals;
- produce a public report accounting for meeting your community goals.

It may look strange to choose a structure that is limited compared to both commercial (e.g. investor return) and charitable (e.g. tax relief freedoms) models. But it does take out any room for doubt, pressure, cutting corners. It gives you a simple discipline, something that will be stuck to. I wouldn't underestimate the value of simple. At my old company, St Luke's, we had equal shares (based only on length of service). Which took making a life-changing amount of money out of the equation and that was liberating. All that was left was to create a life-changing company instead.

RETHINKING OWNERSHIP

The modern corporate model is based upon applying ownership and property rights (i.e. things formerly associated with land) to production. Some of the most exciting businesses of the last 20 years (like Grameen or Linux) have been born out of challenging this. Ownership doesn't have to be separated – the alternative is co-operative ventures owned by their workers and/or customers. Social production (like Wikipedia) is another alternative; like a commons, the land (the website) belongs to Jerry Wales & co, but the maintenance and benefits of use are free to a much broader public. That's really good of them because you could make a case that about 1% of the value of this book was down to the research and references they provide. Imagine Wikipedia's content was music; how much (thanks to music biz lawyers) even short samples would cost to sample and re-use!

Intellectual property helps someone corner a market, but it also puts the market into a corner. That's why even the music biz allows users to experience their music for free on the radio. It isn't going to be worth anything until it becomes popular – and it can't do that unless large numbers can hear it for free. They charge the radio stations mind you.

ALTERNATIVE MODELS OF GROWTH

The growth of a start-up can create bigger jobs for young, ambitious and talented individuals to grow into. It can also create a critical mass and hence some stability. But many start-ups are not happy human stories. It seems to be a recipe for stress and symptoms like scapegoating. And it can estrange the founders, and the early joiners, from the company that it later becomes. Many founders are talked into a position within a few years in where they are not the right person for the job, now that a 'professional CEO' is needed.

One route is to think about alternative models of growth. A good one is the 'copy me' model. Eric Ryan, founder of Method, told me that one of the things he is proud of is establishing the concentrated detergent category in the USA. This saves a fortune in shipping energy and costs. The success though was not that Method cornered this market, but rather that they created a compelling case for Unilever to get into it and do it much bigger with Small and Mighty. If you mainly cared about growth, profit and narrow company measures of success you would think it a disaster. But if you are motivated by climate change, health, water ... then imitation is a great result.

INVESTMENT AND DECENT RETURNS

Let's assume you have an idea that really should grow, to achieve a big global impact; because for instance it reduces carbon emissions, tackles poverty or makes people happy. Let's assume it's the sort of idea that while in the long term could support itself (it has incomes as well as costs) in the short to medium term will cost quite a bit of money to set up. There isn't really a problem with your model growing per se. Ideally you will be regenerative, i.e. you provide more services to the human and natural world than you take out.

But you might still want to think about the implications of the type of growth that you engage in. If you use 'hot' venture capital then you are part of a speculative economy that in other ways is not resilient, nor for the common good. Many have told themselves they will make their millions and put it to good use and this is exactly what the founders of eBay (Jeff Skoll and Pierre Omidyar) have done – they are both prominent support-ers of the social venture scene. Plus in eBay they invented a system that keeps used goods valued and in circulation. It's hard to fault and I'm not saying capitalism is wrong, just that it *can* have unintended side consequences. And these matter more when you have a social mission – as they can work against it.

Consider how Craig Newmark (of Craigslist) chose to stay independent making a decent income from a few (charging) IT recruitment ads, in order to keep the whole rest of the service free. They originally charged for these ads in three cities, now it's 11. The service is not exactly a charity and now also has eBay and the current CEO Jim Buckmaster as investors. Silicon Alley Insider estimates that their operating profits are in the region of $25 million a year.[104] But Craig has avoided selling for billions. And in so doing has avoided inevitable pressure to monetise the service more heavily. Which means they are still pretty true to Craig's old adage of being 'free as in free speech'. The true value of Craigslist is in its culture and its following. How many newer dotcom stars have basically failed as a result of selling out on these? Whereas Craigslist, which has been running for 15 years, shows every sign of just carrying on growing. It takes 30 million ad listings a year and was estimated to have grown in revenue by nearly 50% last year (2008) alone. Described by some as a giant flea market online, it's hard to see Craigslist being anything but helped by the new mood of thrift and a recessionary squeeze (although job recruitment might dip, it sounds like they have plenty of income to run the service; worst case they could add some more cities.)

PATIENT AND PRINCIPLED CAPITAL

If you can't start your social venture by writing your own code, or through grants, fees or other revenues, you will need capital. What people developing social ventures generally want is something a lot like a long-term interest free loan. That's exactly what Mohammed Yunus secured for Grameen.

The technical term for this is patient capital. This is a good thing for businesses which have low pricing to serve poor communities, or are otherwise not just for profit. It's also a pretty essential condition if the investment is to be mixed with philanthropic grants. Just as investors loathe the thought of putting in money then used to pay existing debts, donors are not keen on seeing grants turned into investor dividends. If you are to mix those forms of funding you need a clear structure; having a charity and a trading arm under the same banner, but with clearly separate finances.

To those of a traditional capitalist investment persuasion, patient capital sounds like wishful thinking. But actually there are quite a few funds these days that have social mission charters too. NESTA exists to support early green inventions and sector development using government money; £50 million for now, but lobbying for a further £1 billion, which would put them into the range of some of the biggest and most serious ethical funds, such as Generation (founded by David Blood and Al Gore). Other weighty London-based ethical funds include Edge (£70 million focusing on vocational education) and 4IP (£20 million focusing on social media for social good). For those just starting out UnLtd provides some handy early-stage no strings grants.

Before you decide that if you need half a million then it must mean big, rich investors – remember to check into the possibility of big, rich philanthropists. Coutts Bank did a survey in 2008 and found that the number one issue for such donors today is climate change. I've met and heard of a number who gained significant funding from this sort of source.

Big Issue Invest (BII) recently announced[105] that it is launching a £10 million fund to support social enterprises. BII is offering a way of investing money where you are locked in for 10 years, don't get any dividends for the first four years and then earn sensible returns (just to offset inflation and ensure you aren't actually losing money) of 3–5%. This is exactly what you would actually want, if you were a foundation or philanthropist much more interested in social and community results than financial results. But it still gives you somewhere to put money in a safe, well-managed way, rather than directly trying to select and support social entrepreneurs.

The other advantage is that the same team who made the *Big Issue* a success can bring experience, support and advice. They are still dabbling themselves too. One innovative service they are launching is an alternative credit-scoring index, to enable reliable payers of rent and bills from the poorer sections of the population to have this taken into account by banks and high street lenders (so that they are not left to the mercy of loan sharks, dodgy sub-prime and 'consolidator' loans with high interest). While this is a new fund, Big Issue Invest had already been operating for over four years, helping social ventures, the most famous being Fifteen – catering training for the unemployed set up by TV chef Jamie Oliver.

The pivotal question for your investors, if you want to run an ethical business, is this; do they want to make a reasonable return? Or an unreasonable one? The CIC legislation in the UK is very helpful in flushing investors out on this. If they are supporting you for the social mission (which is ideal) then why would they want to bleed the business with excessive dividends?

I once interviewed Sir Mark Moody-Stuart, the former Chairman of Shell and Anglo American. He told me that Shell has in its longstanding investor statutes that it should make a 'reasonable return'. Moody-Stuart told me that this gave him the latitude needed to justify the right decisions including turning away short cuts to big profits that you just knew would turn out to have substantial catches, in ethical or environmental terms. Moody-Stuart is an unusual sort of company chairman, mind you. A leading figure in debates on business ethics, and one of the leading figures of the Rio Summit, he hit the headlines in 2008 with a call for a ban on 'gas guzzlers'. Arguably this might be the sort of leader we need going forward though.

CROWD FUNDING

Big Issue are also looking for ways to do microcredit in reverse: microfunding. They even considered doing this by putting a few pence on the price of the magazine, and then making each copy a de facto share certificate.

Microfunding is a way to raise investment from the public, for instance from your customer base. The Obama campaign raised a lot of its donations online in $10 amounts and in the process also demonstrated a broad base of support and a new kind of political savvy. Community Supported Agriculture is another longstanding version of this approach. It brings customer and producer into a co-operative relationship that goes beyond just the money.

If you need to raise quite a small amount and have a good network of likeminded friends and contacts then Fundable.com gives you an easy tool to organise collection. The Dark Mountain Project (a manifesto and journal supporting writers to engage with climate change) succeeded in getting £1500 in a few weeks. On a slightly larger scale Causes.com from one of the Facebook founders has also proved popular, although more with NGO causes than social venture start-ups. BetterPlace.org connects individual donors with projects raising money (you browse their listings, with a similar interface to Kiva.org).

Numerous commercial ventures have used a fan base who want to follow the project they fund: A Swarm of Angels (digital movie), BeerBankroll (microbrewing), Cameesa (fashion), IAmVerity and Sellaband (music production). These and many other initiatives such as the hilarious GreedyOrNeedy (anybody posts any wish and the community decide what to fund) can be found in the directory at http://crowdfunding. pbworks.com/.

Crowd funding is often either a donation, or a loan or associated with a reward (like a free advance copy of the album) rather than some sort of investment for profit. It attracts enthusiasts who want to see a project fly, rather than people looking to make a living (or a killing) out of investing. A recent addition to the list is Kickstarter, which raises money for artists and creative entrepreneurs. Kickstarter see the role of the community not just as providing funding but also providing encouragement. They have a well worked out model (for instance if the project doesn't make its target in pledges then no money is collected) and judging by the amount of theatre, art, film and community projects already getting substantial backing on there, seems to be gathering critical mass. Why does it work? The idea of funding a creative project through donations actually does seem to have a broad public appeal. Why should we leave it to the Vanderbilts after all? Plus the way the projects are listed is catchy and appealing. I was slightly tempted to join the $9 already backing a project called 'Fund Nothing'. At the other end of the scale was Scott Thomas' book showcasing the design art used in the Obama campaign – both the official designs (which Thomas led) but also the volunteer creativity. It has $30 000 in pledges so far; these are basically pre-orders, as at different levels of pledge you get an electronic or hard copy. If I ever self-publish a book this could be a good way to go.

RESILIENCE AS GOING OFF-GRID

The easiest way to explain this is in energy terms. If you are on grid you are vulnerable to energy prices fluctuating. With oil and natural gas shortages (when demand exceeds supply or there is disruption due to conflicts, embargoes, tough positions taken by Russia or OPEC ...) then the countries that have energy hoard it. That's why you could also get instant full-blown 1970s-style energy crises, as opposed to just higher prices.

Going off-grid is a way to avoid these domino effects. Companies like BT and Timberland are building their own wind farms, so that their businesses become independent not only of energy shocks, but also energy price shocks. It's better to pay slightly more, price it in and be able to plan around this.

Communities are being encouraged to follow suit by 1BOG from Virgance (1 Block Off the Grid). Here using community group buys and the efficiencies from a group of fitters doing a street rather than isolated roofs (plus the handsome public rebates) whole communities are being encouraged to fit solar panels. In economic terms this is a different paradigm than having an umbilical relationship with a (shareholder profit motivated and global energy market indexed) utility. You are investing in something that will harvest the free energy arriving from the sun every day. This is like a different form of savings account, and I know several groups who are looking at ways to finance home energy and home energy efficiency as an asset or investment. One version of this is Pay-as-you-save put forward by the Sustainable Development Commission as one of 19 promising innovations they are supporting.

Think about all the ways our personal and/or business finances are on- or off-grid. Anticipating risks is always easy in hindsight but a resilience review – what are we dependent on which could change? – could spot such risks, at least in theory. It may make neglected ideas like local manufacturing look a much better option. The same goes for your personal finances. On what assumptions are your long-term savings or sources of income based?

Another sort of off-grid idea that came up in my workshop on sustainable alternatives to banking was to create a land bank. The alternative to interest rates (deriving from financial assets) would be the return on the food, or wood being grown on it. It would possibly be a more secure long-term store of value than most, the only problem being that you might need the last wave of finance and developer speculators who bought land to go bust first.

LOYALTY

Nearly everybody in marketing is hooked on acquisition, i.e. attracting new customers. When you read marketing textbooks you encounter models like the 'leaky bucket'. This says because you are losing customers all the time, you have to keep topping up your customer base. I think it might be better to call it 'the leaky boat'. That makes it clearer how elegant it would be to approach marketing as hole plugging: focusing on loyalty rather than acquisition. The resistance in marketing (that sustainability means having to sell less) is easily countered when you look at the financial benefits of retaining customers longer.

Eco consumerism is a 'fashion' view of marketing (the churn of 'latest' ideas to grab people, and just as soon 'so last year'). But there are plenty of ways to work with loyalty instead. If it's a consumer durable then make parts of it *really* durable. Sell a laptop for life, then live on parts and upgrades.

Long-term contracts are another way of cementing loyalty. I once tried to get a mobile phone operator to do three- or four-year phone contracts (along with a green handset) as their 'Prius' equivalent. Howies have brought out their HandMe-Down range where customers buying a jacket promise to keep it in use or hand it on to someone else; and Howies in turn promise to keep the zips and buttons in stock.

Of course loyalty doesn't have to be contractual, it can be habitual. Once you are used to getting your weekly vegetable box, for instance, it becomes part of your household routine.

VALUES AND VALUE

If a market is driven by price, it's a sure sign that really there is nothing much to choose between the options. One insurance quote, supermarket, cheap flight or delivery pizza is pretty much the same as the next. It's hard to make this sort of business sustainable, partly because you don't have the margins to invest, partly because you have to screw your suppliers or move to lower cost minimum wage production in sweatshop conditions. It's a vicious cycle (and often vicious in environmental and ethical terms too).

If craft and regional variety apply (like in cheese) then people value the product and will pay more for it. And employers value their skilled employees. If they don't (like processed cheese) it's a race for the bottom.

Values and value business means going a different way. Making something unique. Nobody compares the price of each dish in independent restaurants; it's a matter of ambience, skill, location, ingredients.

Take a sector that has low trust, differentiation and huge price dependence – financial services. Just imagine there was a bank that was also an exciting global cause (like Body Shop used to be within toiletries). That your money was put to meaningful good use. That the products were conscious. That the branches doubled as community education centres. That the bank was mutually owned and democratically run by its customers. Not only would you bank with them, but you would buy on need and value, not price. Partly because the products wouldn't be directly comparable. Perhaps instead of insurance the bank could allow its customers to put some of their saving money into a 'shared risk' pool. Chances are (because of a totally different fee structure) you could get more cover for less money. If you think this is fanciful, check out ZOPA, a community-driven borrowing and lending model.

DIRECT TO CONSUMER

Howies originally sold their fashionable clothes through fashion wholesale. But when they switched to organic cotton and had to put the prices up accordingly, they lost large parts of this distribution. This forced them to develop a catalogue and this is now one of the mainstays of their success. It works because they have an enthusiastic loyal following and also the catalogue is much more than a list of garments, it's a creative publication.

The way that supermarkets sit between fork and farmer has a crucial effect on how food is grown, who gets paid what, how far it is shipped, the open refrigeration and car journeys to store, and even how healthy it is. Not only is this chain a major block on sustainability but also it is fragile and lacks resilience. A month-long oil crisis would lead most cities to the point of starvation. As an alternative consider Localfoodshop.co.uk which facilitates ordering from local farms and suppliers. This is good for the producer because they get 93% of what you pay rather than about 9% if they sell through supermarkets. It's good for you because you get fresh seasonal local produce at decent prices. And it's convenient too for buyers and sellers as they bundle your order so neither have to juggle separate deliveries. This means it is good for the environment too, reducing the carbon footprint.

CO-INNOVATION

Amazon doesn't pay for the reader reviews. Neither do customers pay for this amazing resource to browse for inspiration, or to make idle wish lists. Social production (where the customers make the product) is a way of escaping the old 'make it then try to sell it' model.

If I had to explain social media in one word I'd say 'enthusiasm'. And the natural corollary of this is valuing the enthusiasts. One million people queue up to beta test a new Nintendo console. Why not develop a product testbed club for the green consumer vanguards, who are always looking for the latest thing to green their home? I got as far with this idea as registering the URL bedshare.org, before the cities innovation group I was talking to moved onto another model (the kind where you fit a whole city for electric cars). Developing pioneering products in partnership with pioneering green or ethical consumers would mean that you can change the economics; whether it is through advance orders, higher margins or selling direct. You will also get better ideas, because they will come from people enthusiastic and knowledgeable about green innovations in use.

SOCIAL FINANCES

There are some simple decisions about the ethics of who you bank with. I've opened an account for a social venture with Triodos for those reasons.

What interests me more than just the provider is the financial products that we buy. That's something we can all take fairly easy decisions on. It's also possibly an area ripe for innovation. I did some innovation work with the Co-operative Bank in 2006, looking into how their ethics could apply to product innovation. It was around the time ZOPA launched – where the bank simply acts as an intermediary between lenders and borrowers. That's something Virgin Money in the USA have done since with facilitating lending between friends and family. I explored something similar in the work I did with Co-op; my idea was to create a joint savings bond across family members, sharing benefits and also acting as a kind of group safety net that anyone in the circle could use as a lender of first resort in case of illness or setback.

I've just run a workshop as part of Greengaged (the sustainability part of the London Design Festival) where we set ourselves the task of reinventing banking for the common good. Ideas we came up with on the day included

- community owned local banks (taking over disused shops, providing jobs and peer-to-peer coaching, for instance on starting a business);
- mobile banking serving street market communities, offering microcredit, shared card payment facilities, cashing up;
- a 'balance bank' that helped people manage all of their life priorities including but far from only limited to cash.

Another green savings route would be to build renewable energy or other green infrastructure (e.g. green office spaces) then draw a reasonable income from this asset. It's actually how Islamic banking works; for instance you could buy a building and live on the rental income (that's called Sukuk). This is something I have pitched to senior bank execs and also the Cabinet Office. No takers so far, but I like the name I came up with: The Rainy Day Account.

Another idea which came up in a recent discussion involving several bank marketing execs was what if you could apply higher credit ratings to those who do more for the environment? They are likely to be more 'responsible' (and also older, more affluent). Pricing in financial services is based on risk profiling. If green customers are better credit risks then you could see not only 'green products' but 'green segments' – being targeted with relevant offers but also far better pricing. Banco Real (in Brazil) only lends to companies with good environmental standards and policies. They argue that this is good business because – actuarial figures show – they are better managed and lower risk overall. The Carbon Disclosure Project has claimed that much the same is true of corporations, a fact they use to help persuade investors to put pressure on companies in their portfolio.

The UK government is investigating new ways that people can invest in local businesses and services. Individual schemes to set up your own village shop or community supported agriculture have already proved popular and successful. The project – called community shares – is currently in a two-year evaluation research stage. The move to a social, committed, embedded investor base is one with multiple benefits, including that the local people are putting money into something that benefits their own local quality of life. Philip Blond, a key figure in Conservative Party policy, has the idea of taking community investment much further, giving the poor investment vouchers which they spend on the community businesses they select and support – and having a share in the returns. Rather like Grameen, in a way.

BARTER – ALTERNATIVE ECONOMICS

We are going to look at systems for sharing assets in the next section. But just to mention one alternative economic system, which is barter.

When people hear 'barter' they think of primitive societies and pre-money systems of exchange. But actually during the Cold War large barter deals were done between East and West – for instance Russian grain for Rolls Royce jet engines. And in recent years B2B (business to business) barter has boomed. One such system called BarterCard from Australia enables small businesses with tight cash flow to supply their business needs, and to sell surplus of their own products and services to repay this. A printing shop could get extra business this way, and then pay for redecorating the shop front or other needs with other suppliers who are members. BarterCard is 18 years old, has 75 000 members in nine countries and has enabled members to trade goods and services interest-free to a total value of £3.5 billion.

Bernard Lietaer (author of *The Future of Money*) takes the view that because of financial instability, unemployment, climate change and an ageing population (with a ticking pension bomb) we face a decade ahead of 'an unprecedented rough ride' for business and that lack of credit will be key. Without credit, businesses will fold, unemployment will increase, consumer spending will fall – a vicious spiral seen in the 1930s. Because of the pivotal role of credit in this, Lietaer has been advocating business-to-business mutual credit (using a complementary currency to keep track of barter transactions), as a key means to avoid any 'domino effect' in the economy. Lietaer points to a scheme in Switzerland called Wir, meaning 'we' and being short for Wirtschaftsring or economic circle. This is an independent bank using book-keeping for mutual credit (not its own printed money) to serve 62 000 small and medium businesses, which traded goods and services worth around a billion pounds in 2005. Wir was started in 1934, as a way of getting the economy moving during the Great Depression.

THE SOCIAL ECONOMY

I have a theory that most social networks are based upon some sort of currency, and these often act in a way to complement or even counterbalance the cold cash economy. Think of the hard earned feedback stars and ratings in eBay – providing a money-can't-buy reputation. Authority (number of followers) acts as a measure of kudos and tends to add weight, interest and further followers in a cumulative way; which partly explains why some end up with a million followers on Twitter while others struggle to make 10. Other currencies include YahooAnswer ratings, Myspace friends, Digg ratings – and in some ways all the content that people exchange, like links to funny videos, key stories, downloaded music and movies, Facebook gifts.

Whuffie Bank recently launched with the promise to rank users of social networks in terms of reputational trust (based on who interacts with or supports them and their trust ratings in turn). Apparently I am worth 113 Whuffie per day, whereas Deepak Chopra ranks 11th in the world with 110 000 Whuffie per day. Deepak ranks nearly 500th in terms of his numbers of Twitter followers, but his interactions and following show a much higher level of trust than most of the celebrities in the top 500 – much as you would expect. Let's see how it develops, but I suspect that in future something that is a kind of hybrid between the CouchSurfing Vouch For trust rating and the traditional credit rating could make a killer social media application. The value would not come just from having lots of friends who vouch for each other, but involvement in values-based activity (like the hospitality and decency of most CouchSurfing community members) that says a lot about you.

PART 5

ABUNDANCE

THE DIFFERENCE BETWEEN ABUNDANCE AND (FINANCIAL) PRODUCTIVITY

In the early 1970s, it dawned on me that no one had ever applied design to agriculture. When I realized it, the hairs went up on the back of my neck. We'd had agriculture for 7,000 years, and we'd been losing for 7,000 years: everything was turning into desert. Ecologists never apply good ecology to their gardens. Architects never understand the transmission of heat in buildings. It's curious we never apply what we know to how we actually live.[106]

Bill Mollison, co-founder of Permaculture

IN MALAWI, SINCE THE 1960s, the government had been pushing maize as a cash crop, requiring heavy use of machinery and agrichemicals. This was the time of the 'green revolution' when high tech farming methods were thought to hold the key to feeding the world's hungry and fast growing populations.

The shift to mass maize cultivation meant a less varied diet and also a more seasonal output. The time of year leading up to maize harvests became known as 'the hungry season'; something that had been unknown before the switch to modernised farming. Then in 2002 the maize crop failed and this caused a nationwide famine. Malawi had no other food being produced in significant quantities for the population to fall back upon.

The IMF is heavily implicated in this shift and the resulting food insecurity; telling countries like Malawi to grow cash crops to repay their loans. There was a scandal in when the IMF (local officials claimed)[107] even advised them to sell off the maize reserves ... just before the 2002 famine struck, affecting 76% of the population. But the problem goes deeper than the reserves – to why the population was so dependent on a single crop in the first place.

Permaculturalists in Malawi have been training people to grow a wide variety of indigenous plants (over 500 varieties, including food and medicinal herbs) without relying on agrichemicals that are expensive and damaging to the soil.

Maize had quickly become an African staple, rather like rice in South East Asia. Through classes, demonstrations and patient work on the ground, the permaculture revolution in Malawi has really started to take hold. It's been as much about cultural change as farming change; maize had become the high status crop in Africa – the diverse diets (millet, sorghum, green bananas, cassava and many varieties of fruit, nut and vegetable, including wild varieties) of their grandparents' era, becoming seen by modern Africans as uncivilised. The permaculturists have been helping people return to 150 local varieties that will grow all year. This style of agriculture is better for the soil, is self-fertilising and self-weeding, and avoids the need for any hungry periods. But it required a lot of persuading, to help people see the benefits over what seemed a more 'scientific' modern approach.

The 'Life of Aesop' (a book from the 2nd century) tells the story of Aesop and his master Xanthus' conversation with a gardener. The gardener asks Xanthus why it is that the weeds always grow up faster and stronger and threaten to overwhelm his fruit and vegetables. Xanthus can't think of an answer and says it must just be divine providence. Aesop however has an explanation. The weeds are like Mother Earth's children and they thrive on her love and attention. Whereas the fruit and vegetables are like stepchildren which her husband burdened her with from a previous marriage. The gardener is delighted with the answer and gives Aesop a box of vegetables in reward.

Permaculture is based upon a similar insight: a forest produces 1000 times more energy than a wheat field. A wheat field is productive in a narrow sense because wheat is a marketable commodity and can also be harvested in large quantities using (high energy) machinery. That's the financial logic but it involves turning the countryside into a factory, complete with oil-based agrichemicals. It is ultimately a flawed model since intensive agriculture depletes the soil, leading to a need for yet more fertilisers. Ultimately as Mollison says it can lead to desertification. Add a global transport system to bring these commodities to market, plus change of land use (forest and grasslands brought into agriculture as soils erode and/or fail) and you also have agriculture as the biggest single contributor to climate change.

Permaculture was the brainchild of Australians Bill Mollison and his then research assistant David Holmgren. Mollison had spent the previous 15 years studying forest ecosystems. Based on the insights gleaned from these observations, Mollison realised there was an alternative to mechanised industrialised agriculture. Instead of piling energy (oil) into growing a single, fragile crop (e.g. wheat) and waging war on nature with pesticides and chainsaws, his vision was of a forest garden approach, where an abundance of edible and otherwise humanly (or mutually) useful plants and animals would grow themselves. In this way we could stop destroying the earth's remaining resources – the forests, soil, biodiversity – and live in harmony with nature.

The way that permaculturalists go about designing is that they think carefully about the needs of each element of the system, and what services they can provide to other parts of the system. Even fast-growing weeds can play a role in these systems (as fuel or fodder), or can be managed into the periphery by other elements like shady trees. The key principle is to minimise the amount of energy, waste and ongoing human input required. As permaculture has evolved it is increasingly designed. A permaculture forest garden may look unkempt, but actually it is purposefully arranged. A simple permaculture solution is the use of straw overlaying potato beds. This means you don't have to dig, the potatoes will do this for you while protected by the straw from birds and the elements. Other typical innovations include earth bank-based water-harvesting methods to trap water in the ground in arid areas with occasional heavy rain (like Australia). There are plenty of videos, and short courses online, showing permaculture design in action.

Permaculture is about managing a diverse system for abundance rather than a narrow (mean and lean) monoculture approach. It's about problem solving by reasoning and experimenting in interaction with nature. The design process is slow, because you need to observe nature working at its own pace. It is common to observe a site for a year, so you can see it through all the seasons, before even starting to make human interventions. The 'just in time' and 'hurry-hurry' approach of quarterly-returns capitalism rule out this way of working. But how costly are the mistakes we rush into instead?

Permaculturalists think in terms of functional zones, but also place a high value on understanding the creative interactions that often occur at the boundaries. Again this is simply – empirically – how nature works. The most thriving action is at the edges, on the coastlines, in the hedgerows. It's partly because of the creativity that happens as different systems interact. We can certainly see many parallels in human systems.

The recent agricultural revolution in Cuba – prompted by an energy crisis, post the endless supply of Soviet oil – has consisted of moving to more diverse seed stocks, organic methods (to heal the soil) and smaller farms. It has also been heavily influenced by permaculture thinking. And a move to co-operative independent farms rather than centrally state controlled ones. The development of Cuban agriculture blends traditional techniques with entirely new and innovative solutions. For instance nets over growing areas have been used to keep insects out – rather like mosquito nets over beds. Of course the agriculture now is more labour intensive but still only 200 000 out of 11 million Cubans are full-time farmers. In an article in *Successful Farming* magazine (2003)[108] Hal Hamilton described how, initially cynical about the stories from Cuba, he returned convinced 'from a research trip that challenged all conventional assumptions about progress and feeding the world'. Not only had the system successfully overcome the lack of oil, chemical fertiliser and pesticide, but also food yields had actually increased.

90% of Havana's food is now grown within the city limits, most of it by citizens working with ingenious permaculture methods, making full use of roofs and vacant lots. Urban farming is a hot topic in the West now too. Not least because growing food near to markets is itself less energy intensive. Havana has been redesigned as a city too, the layout rethought. For instance, the university has been split into local campuses, so that students don't have to travel from all over town just to get to one central point.

Nature is seldom 'lean and mean' – it is abundant. That's because only abundance is resilient. Los Angeles has two days' supply of food and the rest arrives across the desert on trucks. If there were an energy crisis, there is no fallback. And given the global dependence on oil to ship food around the world, we all live in a kind of global LA. In nature there will always be crises, and hence structures like Los Angeles would be selected out by evolutionary pressure. Given we've only had cities for 15 000 years or so and oil-dependent ones for 100 years, it's a moot point whether manmade cities as currently designed are exempt. Natural systems are resilient because they produce a cornucopia of excess. We have 10 000 times more energy than humanity uses arriving every day from the sun.[109] And the rest of nature capitalises on this, always storing away for a rainy day.

Leanness is the result of 'profitivity', not true productivity. It depends what you want to maximise. Long-term positive contribution to wellbeing, or short-term financial profit? Large farm yields are often reported by agribusiness in yield per farm worker. Know why? Profit per worker stats hide a troubling truth: large-scale industrial agriculture is less productive of food per hectare than small farms. That's partly because small farms raise a variety of crops, making more efficient use of space and the whole growing year. It is also because of small farm initiative and care, with healthier farming for the soil. George Monbiot reports:

... an unexpected discovery. It was first made in 1962 by the Nobel economist Amartya Sen, and has since been confirmed by dozens of further studies. There is an inverse relationship between the size of farms and the amount of crops they produce per hectare. The smaller they are, the greater the yield. In some cases, the difference is enormous. A recent study of farming in Turkey, for example, found that farms of less than one hectare are twenty times as productive as farms of over ten hectares. Sen's observation has been tested in India, Pakistan, Nepal, Malaysia, Thailand, Java, the Philippines, Brazil, Colombia and Paraguay. It appears to hold almost everywhere.[110]

Food yields matter because how we are going to feed nine billion people is in question. The world has, according to Professor Beddington (UK chief scientist), food reserves (of 16%) equal only to the amount of food currently in transit. There is no room for setbacks. And we face many of those ahead. But we should be able to grow or source enough food, enough water and enough energy if we can find new ways to organise agriculture. We are going to have to radically rethink global food anyway, because the 'LA' model of imported food will run up against future energy shocks and the end of affordable oil.

The large intensive farms are modelled on factories. And these are descended conceptually from Adam Smith's pin factory, with each operator confined to one simple action. The whole system is run purely to optimise money out vs. money in. And yet even in these terms what Smith didn't spot is that it can fail because it destroys value too. It is an economic anorexia. Under the force of its own logic, it makes pins into an almost worthless commodity. That's the scourge of farming too; being screwed by free market price fluctuations and rapacious agents representing retail and wholesale. But the real risk to wellbeing is in focusing on monocrop (i.e. single crop) farming. This is much less resilient – the crops and soil become weak and have to be supplemented with increasing quantities of chemicals. It requires huge inputs of water and energy. It also has disruptive effects on the nature around it – for instance the dead zone in the Gulf of Mexico caused by low oxygen levels, caused by algal blooms, caused in turn by fertiliser run-off. The dead zone in the Black Sea disappeared between 1991 and 2001, because fertilisers at that time had become too expensive for farmers in the region to buy.[111] Michael Pollan, who blames monoculture agriculture for current problems both with the environment and health, explains in his book *The Omnivore's Dilemma* how all this came about:

> The farm could now be managed on industrial principles, as a factory transforming inputs of raw material – chemical fertilizer – into outputs of corn. Since the farm no longer needs to generate and conserve its own fertility by maintaining a diversity of species, synthetic fertilizer opens the way to monoculture, allowing the farmer to bring the factory's economies of scale and mechanical efficiency to nature. If, as sometimes has been said, the discovery of agriculture represented the first fall of man from the state of nature, then the discovery of synthetic fertility is surely a second and precipitous fall. Fixing nitrogen allowed the food chain to turn from the logic of biology and embrace the logic of industry. Instead of eating exclusively from the sun, humanity now began to sip petroleum. (2007)[112]

The rationale for agrichemical agriculture was that it was believed to generate higher yields than organic. As with Sen's small farms finding, this has been refuted by recent studies. A report by UNEP and the UN Conference on Trade and Development surveyed 114 small-scale farms in 24 African countries (2008).[113] Yields had more than doubled where organic, or near-organic practices had been used. Studies in southern Brazil showed that maize and wheat yields doubled on farms that changed to green manures and nitrogen-fixing leguminous vegetables instead of chemical fertilisers. In Mexico, coffee-growers who chose to move to fully organic production methods saw increases of 50% in the weight of beans they harvested. In an analysis of more than 286 organic conversions in 57 countries, the average yield increase was found to be 64% (according to Leu and Pretty, quoted in *The Ecologist*).[114] The UNEP study found that organic practices outperformed traditional methods and chemical-intensive conventional farming and also confirmed the environmental benefits such as improved soil fertility, better retention of water and resistance to drought.

Industrialised agriculture is supposed to be good for one thing at least – return on investment. Yet even investors had largely abandoned farming for the last 20 years as the free market prices were so low it was failing even in these terms. This all changed after the food crisis of 2008, prompting the movement of the investment sector (venture capital, hedge funds and similar) back into this space. With little apparent knowledge of farming, these say they will bring 'industrial efficiency' to the developing world. Given everything we know about the impact on soil, climate change and food security this is a big step back – especially as investor enthusiasm was also justified by the new markets for biofuels. Since the collapse of the banking sector billions flowed into investment funds buying up farmland in areas like South America and sub-Saharan

Africa. An article in the *Financial Times* trumpeted the marvellous investment opportunities arising from a new era of higher food prices.[115] Two months earlier Martin Wolf's column in the same newspaper had pointed out how serious the humanitarian and social impacts of this shift were:

> Of the two crises disturbing the world economy – financial disarray and soaring food prices – the latter is the more disturbing. In many developing countries, the poorest quartile of consumers spends close to three-quarters of its income on food. Inevitably, high prices threaten unrest at best and mass starvation at worst.[116]

This crisis intensified the debate about whether food security really should be protected from the speculators. Organisations like Via Campesina are calling for Food Sovereignty. They say local people should be able to define their food and farming, rather than having it dictated by international market forces. They call for the recognition that food is firstly a source of nutrition and only secondarily a source of trade; and that cheap imports should not be allowed to undermine local farms, tipping them into commodity production too.

Of course speculative investment, directing operations to maximise financial return, is the essence of modern capitalism. Large companies are fronts. They may look like they are making cars, or tinned cat food, but you could argue they exist as legitimate outlets for making money out of money.

Leverage is one way of doing this – borrowing money from the bank to supplement what your investor put in. If the business grows fast, and the bank only wants a 5% return, then the shareholders or investors absolutely coin it. Here's an illustration of the algebra of leverage:

As an investor you put in enough money to cover 20% of a company.

The other 80% is bank debt or 'leverage'.

The company doubles in size.

The bank is paid back its 80%, plus interest let's say a further 20%.

The company is now worth 200%.

You pocket 100% for your initial stake of 20%.

100/20 = 500% return.[117]

I've just described Private Equity by the way. It's not a resilient strategy because if the company value doesn't grow – for instance in a recession – the bank debt is crippling. You win some, you lose some. Capitalism today is run for return on investment. Not for the overall benefits for human wellbeing.

Some corporations take a firm line with investors and hold to the principle of doing the right thing being best for all involved. Others remind me of the Vichy regime in France during World War II. Between the investors and the workforce there is a senior management whose job is to translate the needs of the one into the actions of the other; maintaining a pretence of having the company's best interests at heart, of the company having a culture, values and a trajectory all of its own – but really working to make the quarterly numbers that matter to investors. In some corporations it is made explicit throughout the organisation that nothing matters except making your budget, to keep shareholders or private equity owners happy. In others it is hidden from employees, making (cost saving) 'restructurings' and constant changes of 'strategy' a mystery. Charles Handy used to quiz board directors about why shareholders had to come first; 'It's awfully nice of you,' he'd say, 'but do you actually know any of these shareholders you are working so hard for?'

That fact that business is run for investors explains the modern obsession with intellectual property. Ownership of intellectual property (patents, copyright) allows a company to corner a market and keep profits high. GMO (genetically modified organisms) brought the same principles to farming. Why else would someone produce these Frankenstein Foods, strongly opposed by the public and environmental NGOs, with all of the concerns about human health, biodiversity and their own effectiveness? I'm not taking an extremist position – the whole EU region has banned GM crops. Typically a GM crop like cotton with inbuilt resistance to one pest, by disrupting the ecosystem (taking out a food source or predator controlling other populations) can end up promoting the growth of other pests that prove even worse. So that after several years pesticides have to be used heavily as well. But GM crops are a money-making machine. They brought food under intellectual property rights. Instead of farmers storing and sharing seeds (to use indefinitely) you could now license them to farmers like software. And they would have to buy the matching agrichemicals, such as Monsanto's 'Roundup'.

Pharmaceutical patents last 10 years. The entire marketing and distribution machine of pharma is about maximising returns during the patent period. They also exploit loopholes; for instance if they can prove that an existing drug is effective against a new condition, then the patent is reset. One of the more (perversely) inventive areas of pharma marketing is the discovery and branding of new 'conditions', like 'social anxiety disorder' – which serve the dual role of persuading patients (and doctors) to take (or prescribe) drugs, and also justifying patent extensions. Speaking of discovery there is a more basic objection to the patents which pharma make money from – in many cases these were not their ideas in the first place:

> The pharmaceutical corporations and others claim they need this protection via patents and intellectual property rights so they can recoup the costs of research and development. But have a close look. A very substantial part of the research and development is paid for by the public anyway. In a narrow sense, it's of the order of 40–50%. But that's an underestimate, because it doesn't count the basic biology and the basic science, which is all publicly funded. (Noam Chomsky, 2000)[118]

Business from an investor point of view has to do with why your model will reliably provide financial returns on investment, through patents, know-how, access to markets and so on. That's their skill – spotting a good return. Investment is a gamble and they want to stack the odds. If you work in this area you know that this is the 'game'. And also in most cases you are investing other people's money. The suggestion there might be anything wrong with this whole process can draw derision – clearly critics just don't understand how the world really works. But from a whole society perspective this is wasteful and perverse. It resembles Borges' story about The Babylonian Lottery – a numbers game that takes over a society. The need to own and to protect intellectual property means there is needless duplication and reinventing wheels to get around incumbents' patents. It also leads to a limited access to the end product – reducing the wellbeing benefits of discoveries – a scandal in the case of pharma companies keeping life saving drugs from countries that could not afford them. Until countries like India and Brazil risked the wrath of World Trade

Organization-type sanctions and produced their own cheap generic copied drugs anyway.

The free software movement grew out of opposition to intellectual property rights and enclosure. The basic demand is that computer programmers should be able to access and modify computer software. Operating systems had been free and freely shared during the 'hacker culture' early years of computing. The application of restrictive licences by companies like Microsoft was compared by Neil Stephenson to 'charging people for the washing instructions that come with the clothes'.

The open source software movement, which grew out of the free software movement, takes a different position. The view is not that it is unethical to ever charge for software. Rather that the method of developing software in a public collaborative manner is simply superior; as argued in the famous white paper by Eric Raymond 'The Cathedral and the Bazaar'.

The new networks explode bottlenecks previously used to corner markets: for example P2P systems exploded music (Napster) and telecoms (Skype). The internet has been an exciting story partly because the Robin Hood models which undermine corporate profit streams have had such a good run. Many of the models work because instead of relying on a central bottleneck, they draw upon resources as distributed as the users. This could mean where the files are stored, how information gets relayed, or in many models that the users generate most of the content. Either a dedicated core of developers or contributors/editors, in the cases of Linux and Wikipedia. Or a greater mass of users as in blogging, YouTube, Facebook pages and so on.

These systems are abundant because they work with the natural productivity and enthusiasms of people using the media. As with software bug checking, a million heads are better than one. And the self-organising architecture of such systems mean that ranking (or votes, social bookmarks, links, Diggs) allow the user base to evaluate and quality control content for each other. It's very much like permaculture working with how things 'want to grow'.

'Social Production' is the way that Yochai Benkler explains this trend. I like his analysis because it goes beyond the surface of who does what – into what this means for economics and intellectual property (Benkler is a Yale law professor). In *The Wealth of Networks* Benkler describes the emergence of a 'system of production, distribution, and consumption of information goods characterized by decentralized individual action carried out through widely distributed, non market means that do not depend on market strategies'.[119]

That's creates a new middle layer. Between corporations and consumers. Benkler argues that an open system is more efficient and innovative. That patents, private interests and closed processes are largely impeding progress. To quote one of Benkler's favourite sites (Wikipedia): 'Benkler argues that blogs and other modes of participatory communication can lead to a more critical and self-reflective culture, where citizens are empowered by the ability to publicize their own opinions on a range of issues.'

Benkler also describes this as peer production and outside the market production. The key features of this movement, pointed to in an essay on Benkler's book by Hassan Masum are:

- acting for more than material gain;
- using networked information technology;
- orienting and organising collaborative actions;
- creating new knowledge on an open source basis;
- promoting general wellbeing and seeking to reduce inequality.[120]

Today newsrooms are working alongside millions of bloggers and witnesses to events with camera phones. In 2008 a video blog (Kings Cross News) scooped the *Guardian* newspaper (based in King's Cross) on the story of a fire in the *Guardian*'s own office!

The media have by now incorporated this trend within their own processes, for instance in the *Guardian*'s CommentIsFree site, where world-class thinkers write, but the comments are open to all. Similarly newsrooms have learned to benefit from video footage shot on the scene by amateurs.

We are often seeing such hybrids emerge – part corporate (although seldom able to charge for access) – and part social production. Amazon.com is highly abundant in some respects: the way it isn't a monoculture (only selling bestsellers), the contribution that 10 million Amazon reviews freely make to the site, the network of partnerships that underpins 'new and used'. The reason for this is that Jeff Bezos, the visionary Amazon founder, set out to create the most customer focused company in the world. Not another company whose sole focus was on investor returns.

The organisational and operational forms that have emerged in the internet are inclined to be distributed, democractic and abundant because they draw on the productivity and energy of all. They are the complete opposite of 'do it all for you' broadcast media, convenience meals and so on. They are also much more efficient in connecting up markets, processing transactions and so on. They have opened up an awareness that there are not only alternatives to the corporate model but improvements.

Corporations have been moving to incorporate these gains: through open innovation competitions, presence in social media, customer utilities like parcel tracking. But it's not just a different way of being efficient it's a different set of ideas about the right way humans should organise and whose interests everything should centre on. Kevin Kelly, the editor of *Wired*, wrote about this recently under the heading 'The New Socialism: Global Collectivist Society Is Coming Online':

> Rather than viewing technological socialism as one side of a zero-sum trade-off between free-market individualism and centralized authority, it can be seen as a cultural OS that elevates both the individual and the group at once. The largely unarticulated but intuitively understood goal of communitarian technology is this: to maximize both individual autonomy and the power of people working together. Thus, digital socialism can be viewed as a third way that renders irrelevant the old debates. (Kevin Kelly, *Wired* (May, 2009))[121]

These communitarian principles continue to present quite a challenge to conventional business models. Partly because they are so much more productive, having cut their ties with narrow ways to make money. And because they are able to rally so much public enthusiasm and effort. These are new developments in internet and commerce, but they are far from being new forms of human organisation. They represent in many ways a return to pre-industrial modes of organisation, such as the craft guild.

ABUNDANT SYSTEMS; CRAFT GUILDS AND COMMUNITY CURRENCIES

SOME OF THE EXAMPLES in this section happen to be historical although they connect with cutting edge trends. The first – craft guilds – could just as easily have been written about the open source software movement. And the second – community currencies – first established during the 1930s is a hot topic again today. Seeing these co-operative structures in historical context is a valuable counter to the idea that there is no alternative to today's 'realistic' view of society. And to the 'scrapheap' mentality that leads us to devalue other ages than our own.

The other thing to note about this section is that, despite the subject being abundant systems of productivity, these are essentially human stories. They are not born from a modernist worldview where 'productivity' is a separate technical discipline, divorced from human values. 'Care' – to name one such value – had all but been eradicated from productive human systems by the 1970s, replaced with 'quality control'. Since then even big business has realised that human systems are fundamentally *human* systems. That the true success of companies and nations lay with the human spirit and a shared cause. So by the 1990s we saw a dramatic swing towards human factors – the war for talent, mission statements, self-managed teams, armies of organisational change consultants. Taking people out of the picture was the scourge of management science and technocratic policy. It created a divorce between practice (what it's like being a leader or entrepreneur) and theory. Or even worse, the mechanical theories were put into practice, as with monetarism and re-engineering (aka making workers redundant to maximise financial returns). People developing tomorrow's systems for the common good need a kind of stereoscopic vision; seeing both material flows and human engagement. The linking principle is one of self-organisation, which is both more effective (open source software tends to be much more rigorously tested and challenged) and liberates human energy, passion, care and also ethical concern.

The justification often given for the hierarchical status quo is that people are incapable of self-management. We need private owners, authoritarian governments or some such elite to protect us from the fact that, left to our own devices, we would not look after our collective best interests. This is an old argument. The British said India was incapable of self-rule. Gandhi's response was the idea of Swaraj, meaning self-rule not by a new hierarchical central power but through self- and community rule.

The Tragedy of the commons is another way of suggesting that human communities are incapable of self-management. This concept is widely accepted, even within the green movement. Originally the title of a 1968 essay by an ecologist named Hardin, it traced the environmental problems we face (the essay was particularly concerned with overpopulation) back to Adam

Smith and the concept of the invisible hand: the idea that an individual who 'intends only his own gain,' is, as it were, 'led by an invisible hand to promote ... the public interest'. Hardin's answer to Adam Smith was to suggest that, led only by self-interest, a population would overshoot its resources:

> The tragedy of the commons develops in this way. Picture a pasture open to all. It is to be expected that each herdsman will try to keep as many cattle as possible on the commons. Such an arrangement may work reasonably satisfactorily for centuries because tribal wars, poaching, and disease keep the numbers of both man and beast well below the carrying capacity of the land. Finally, however, comes the day of reckoning, that is, the day when the long-desired goal of social stability becomes a reality. At this point, the inherent logic of the commons remorselessly generates tragedy.

Hardin started from a critique of Smith, but ended up advocating private landlordism to protect the environment from common use: whereas real instances of giving back land to the people (for instance, on the Isle of Eigg in the Hebrides) has led to sustainable communities. Hardin assumed the primacy of individual selfish interests and the absence of self-rule. He came to the same conclusion – that we need masters to stop us descending to a mode of life that is 'nasty, brutish and short' – that Hobbes came to when making a case for monarchy in Leviathan.

The real history of commons shows that for over 500 years they suffered no notable tragedies of over-use. The organisation of the commons bound individual users to mutual responsibilities. And it wasn't, as Hardin suggested, that there simply weren't enough people to put a strain on the land. In the UK, lacking commons organisation for woodlands, we'd already proved capable of almost total deforestation (tree cover being reduced to 15% of its original extent) by 1066.[122] Medieval commons (common meadows for grazing) operated as self-regulating communities – active, moral, intentional communities, capable of agreeing and managing their limits and bringing members into line.

It was only after these commons were enclosed (i.e. the land taken away from common use by private landowners) and the self-organised responsibility that went with them was smashed, that Hardin's modern tragedy began in earnest. Mechanised fisheries, turf wars on American ranges ... these were products of the free market being let loose, without community self-management.

Alan Greenspan writes that 'it was left to Adam Smith to identify the more-general set of principles that brought conceptual clarity to the seeming chaos of market transactions'. But arguably what Smith put forward as common sense was actually a radical departure into speculative thinking. It depended on a smashing of the prior steady state system, whereby guilds in the towns (like the commons in the countryside) had regulated supply and demand, keeping the number of bakers and the amount of bread and the quality just right, and keeping prices and wages stable in the process.

Adam Smith was writing near the end of the time of the craft guilds; with skilled work's replacement by the mechanical looms. In the Middle Ages and Renaissance, modern-style capitalism had existed but was limited to the merchants, speculating in import/export-type businesses. The means of production, the trade secrets, the number of workers in a town and their competition were all controlled by the guilds. It was the guilds that prevented workers competing destructively over prices. It was the guilds that prevented too many workers entering a trade and depressing prices. It was the guilds that also stood in the way of self-interest ruling in the way Smith described. It was with the introduction of mechanical factories, where unskilled workers could be hired for minimum wages, that the world Smith described became a possibility. What this move did was to give the merchant speculators access to production, rather than just its output.

The craft guilds were a (highly religious) moral, benevolent and democratic order. They were self-regulating co-operative networks; with instructive parallels with guild-like movements today, like the open source movement. Both display self-organisation, self-government, peer-to-peer quality control, a common store of knowledge, a duty to future generations and the whole community, protection against autocrats. It's a different position from later versions of organised labour – the unions – who operated from a position of protest, because they were otherwise powerless. The guilds enjoyed considerable power and autonomy because they were the expert artisans of their day. A medieval town simply was a network of guilds. Taking on the guilds by authorities would not be done lightly, even in an age of despotic Feudalism. In many cases the guilds actually ran the towns anyway.

The commons were being enclosed at the time Smith wrote (this trend started earlier, but peaked between 1760 and 1820) as landowners appropriated public land for private benefit. At the same time in the textile trades, mechanical looms began to displace skilled artisans; the Guild of Stockingers were the group behind the famous Luddites who rebelled against this. Being out of work, starving and desperate, what else could they do? The two trends – enclosure in the countryside and the mechanical factory in the town – were connected, displaced and starving country peasants being forced to move to the new industrial cities, and take any work at any pay.

The Luddite uprising of 1811 is stereotyped today as a protest against progress. It was actually about a more complex set of grievances. The country was close to starvation due to the Napoleonic wars. The Luddites targeted magistrates and food merchants (profiting from near famine by pushing up prices) as much as industrialists. From 1799 collective bargaining had been forbidden by: 'An Act to prevent Unlawful Combinations of Workmen'. Historian Kevin Binfield points out that Stockingers had been organising industrial actions since the 1670s. But only now was the legal framework in place to make this illegal. Lord Byron, the romantic poet, was a passionate supporter of the Luddite cause. Speaking in the House of Lords on the poverty – which appeared to be the true cause of the uprising – he said that 'never under the most despotic of infidel governments did I observe such squalid wretchedness' and he described the out-of-work Stockingers as 'meager with famine, sullen with despair, careless of a life'.

The Stockingers' complaint was not only that the new machines needed fewer workers, but that they did not need skilled workers. In deskilling the work industrialists were able to 'race for the bottom' as we would say today, hiring purely on the cheapest wages. And Byron complained, 'it is to be observed that the work thus being done is inferior in quality, hardly marketable at home and hurried over with a view to exportation'. It was also at this precise moment in history that modern capitalism was born. Not a natural order, but a mechanised society with a deliberate banning of co-operation. Much attention has been paid to the productivity of the new factory machines, the wealth and advancement brought by the industrial revolution. But less to the beautifully self-regulating and sustainable system it replaced, where people were engaged in spiritual and professional careers based on skills, community and their 'masterpiece' (a piece of work presented to your peers, as a condition of acceptance as a full guild member).

What about the thought system that replaced the guilds? Reading *The Wealth of Nations* there is much to like about it – Adam Smith was a beautiful writer, a philosopher, a humanist, and he believed in social moderation of markets. Nonetheless he put forward a radical experiment, masquerading as a description of the natural order. He was part of the enlightenment project. In crude terms the hope was that society might run on more scientific lines. Smith put forward 10 key propositions (he didn't frame these as 10 points, this is my own précis):

1. Society is based on self-interest. 'The butcher, the brewer, the baker' do not work from a philanthropic concern. They do it for their own gain, and this promotes the interests of society more effectively than if they had welfarist intentions.
2. The counterpart of self-interest is healthy competition. A monopoly will not serve society, it will scheme against it. But vigorous competition will – leading to the best bread at the best prices.
3. The division of labour is the wellspring of productivity – creating the most efficient returns on capital.
4. The ultimate value of any object is measured in the amount of labour required to purchase it. The price of any labour depends on whether supply or demand for workers are greater.
5. Monopolists always use either their control of overall production or trade secrets to distort prices and cheat the public by limiting supply.

6. The 'market' should be allowed to set prices and wages. (But don't worry, it will not set wages too low because, below a living wage, tradesmen would starve or find another trade).

7. Profits tend to be highest where competition among workers is greater than competition among employers.

8. Any society is only able to increase the amount of employment and hence hold high wages, and also a general mood of enthusiasm, when it grows in economic output. Growth (rather than size) is the key.

9. A free market will act as a wise 'invisible hand' leading society to produce the right amount of goods at the right prices.

10. Subsidies should be avoided because these will draw more workers to a trade, suppressing prices and wages in the long run.

What Smith's propositions emerged as a challenge to – although he glossed over any historical context unless it suited his arguments for a rational economy – was the system of crafts guilds. Smith barely even mentioned guilds, but when he did it was in negative terms:

> People of the same trade seldom meet together, even for merriment and diversion, but the conversation ends in a conspiracy against the public, or in some contrivance to raise prices. It is impossible indeed to prevent such meetings, by any law, which either could be executed, or would be consistent with liberty and justice. But though the law cannot hinder people of the same trade from sometimes assembling together, it ought to do nothing to facilitate such assemblies; much less to render them necessary.

The Wealth of Nations was one of the most influential books of its time. It's hard to read these words and not read the intellectual justification for the Combinations Act of 1799, which actually did ban any such meetings.

In the popular historical view today, what came before industrialism was dirty, squalid, diseased – a mass of labouring peasants dominated by a few feudal nobles. We conveniently forget that the Renaissance dates from the fourteenth to the seventeenth centuries; that Isaac Newton, Galileo, Leonardo De Vinci, Francis Bacon, William Shakespeare and so on were children of this age. I doubt the twentieth century will go down as so culturally productive. What if our industrial age is seen as barbarous; complete with its mechanised world wars?

Another myth is that 'leisure' is a new invention. That's true if your reference point is sweatshop industrial cities. But the Middle Ages are misremembered as a time of unrelenting toil, which somehow technology has saved us from. Their true cultural history is one of festivity; innumerable feast days. We forget that those (now) sterile Norman churches were in their own day not whitewashed, but as colourful as a Brazilian carnival. Farming can be hard work, but it's not like working in a call centre, let alone a pin factory. Large periods of time are spent watching the herd or crops – and mucking around with your mates. Factually, peasant farmers and labourers in the Middle Ages had much shorter working hours than today's averages (see Table 14.1):[123]

Table 14.1

YEAR	TYPE OF WORKER	ANNUAL HOURS
13th century	Adult male peasant, UK	1620 hours
14th century	Casual laborer, UK	1440 hours
Middle Ages	English artisan worker	2309 hours
1400–1600	Farmer-miner, UK	1980 hours
1840	Average worker, UK	3350 hours
1988	Manufacturing workers, UK	1855 hours

Take careful note. The success of the last century has been in undoing (or more accurately exporting) the ruinous working hours for low pay of the industrial century before. Before that people lived more balanced lives.

The medieval craft guilds emerged some time around the eleventh century. The central idea was that of a fraternity of artisans in a given trade. They co-operated in training, avoiding destructive competition, mutual support in hard times and so on. The place of production was a household not a factory. A master baker would have all his workers living on site, apprentices working for their food and lodging, plus training.

So how did medieval guilds work? Firstly – at least originally – every guild corresponded to a distinct craft. That is not to say that the workers only had one trade; it was common to practice a number, giving you some flexibility in turbulent social, political and economic times. There were also household synergies. For instance baking families often also made beer (both using yeast), butchers often also grazed flocks and herds. Ferrell (1999)[124] lists over 76 trades in a typical medieval town which each had their own guild. Contrary to Smith's claims about not working in the public interest, these were heavily regulated by the town authorities too. There were harsh penalties for instance if bakers made too little bread, or bread of insufficient quality.

Guilds were based on rules and agreements. These were as powerful in their own way as the church or legal system, although their sanctions gentler (fines rather than floggings). In general the guilds operated through a set of positive group norms and codes of practice which benefited all, and which seldom needed enforcing in the way criminal law might. The central principle was co-operation; acting for the common good instead of only self-interest. Guilds relied on mutual obligation and responsibility. Members would swear an oath and share out administrative duties. Importantly they were swearing allegiance to the guild – rather than simply joining a club or union devoted to their own self-interests, they were signing up to the good of the group.

The artisans had their own businesses and these were not subsumed within the guild. Guilds were learning organisations. Their primary aim was the protection (through trade secrets) and transmission of craft skills. While you could argue this was restrictive IP in modern terms, the restriction was to prevent exploitation by merchants or there being too many workers. It's how law or London black cabs still work today. The organisation to achieve this aim consisted of apprenticeships; journeymen free to work for various masters, for a salary; and masters – the brewers, bakers and so on in town.

Guilds were self-help support networks, helping members who fell on hard times or widowers. They provided a type of insurance role inherited by the modern welfare state. They also played a vital role in dispute resolution and had many benevolent activities within the broader community. They were high minded, religious and spiritual – pursuing both piety and profits.

Guilds controlled the numbers who entered professions. That's not to say you had to be in a guild to practise those trades. Guilds were quite flexible in allowing nonmembers to practice, usually in return for a fee. But they regulated the numbers in a trade to match demand. This is a key theme of co-operative systems: it is possible for groups to consciously and morally control their group activities.

Guilds played a prominent role in civic society. In many areas the guilds effectively were the town councils (although the rich merchant guilds were often more prominent in that role than the humbler artisans). Being in a guild made you a 'freeman', bestowing the full rights of citizenship too. Guilds fundamentally existed to moderate the market, make life less risky. All of their restrictions against 'free runners' meant that from one year to the next work, pay and prices remained more constant. Guilds proved remarkably resilient. They survived invasions, plagues, revolution, the Reformation, civil wars, abuses of currency by the monarchy, financial crisis after financial crisis. They offered safety in numbers. And were quite powerful enough to act as a channel for dissent; guilds staged annual 'Miracle Plays' often featuring banned characters and storylines such as Robin Hood and (a wicked parody of the venal church) Abbott Unreason. Why could they get away with it? Despite the historical image of a feudal society being run by the local nobility and church, the truth is that the guilds had a lot of power and autonomy. They were in a sense the trades unions of their day, providing safety in numbers. Guilds seldom armed or got involved in violent conflicts, but why would they need to? They were the town.

Fundamentally guilds did provide an alternative – and an answer – to all of Adam Smith's 10 propositions. If Smith had been truer to his professed empiricism he would perhaps have troubled to test his propositions against the social systems that had pertained for 500 years. But you have to see *The Wealth of Nations* as something of a break with the past book. Questioning our inheritance today – an infernal growth machine set to self-destruct – we would do well to hear the guilds' side of the story too:

1. *Society is based on self-interest.* Actually no, it isn't. In civil society a bit of 'give and take' is the norm. Society and especially trading is founded in community and trust. Competition divides people and you need compensating co-operative systems to ensure that positive relationships prevail.

2. *Competition is in society's best interest.* Guilds regulated the core of the market and prevented members from destroying each other through price competition. They acted for morality and wellbeing, with community good works, mutual support and other duties being central obligations. They actually did act out of altruistic concern and higher values. And quality of production was a very high value; craft itself was a kind of 'worship'.

3. *Productivity – creating the most efficient returns on capital.* It's a false economy. The reduction of labour to mechanical actions leads to deskilling, reducing the working population to tedium. It opens you to competition from those who can make the same cheap crap even cheaper. Most modern brands of any value have a 'craft' basis – compare the design of Apple computers to a cheap generic PC.

4. *The ultimate value is the amount of labour required to purchase it.* On the guild view it's the opposite. The value of a product depends on the labour, knowledge and resources that went into producing it. Guilds didn't make things that weren't needed, otherwise they wouldn't sell. But they cost what they cost to make.

5. *Monopolists using control or trades secrets will seek to distort prices.* What if you substitute the word 'maintain' for 'distort'? Plus if they were trying to overprice key goods like bread they would face the magistrate. Being in a collective made them more accountable too.

6. *The market will not set wages below a living wage.* If we have learned anything since Smith it is that regrettably this is not true. Smith himself criticised the East India Company for exploitation of 'the Hindi'.

Corporates can and do destroy communities by economic means and they will justify themselves in economic terms. It doesn't make it right or even 'natural' though, any more than slavery.

7. *Profits are highest where competition among workers is greater.* True. The question is what good to society are those excessive profits? Making the richest richer? How's that an ultimate good? If these excessive profits come from workers being underpaid.

8. *Economies need to grow for employment and other structural reasons.* This is also absolutely true. It is the result of several features of the free market capitalist system, notably speculative capital. It's hence a circular argument: if you create a pyramid scheme it will need to grow.

9. *A free market will act as a wise 'invisible hand'.* The bailout of UK banking has saddled my six-year-old with so much debt that it will not be paid off until he is 30. Banking on the other has recovered sufficiently in 12 months to be paying big bonuses. Under-regulated self-interest is not always aligned with the common good.

10. *Subsidies should be avoided – they draw more workers to a trade.* It is not valid in the case of guilds because they also regulated the numbers entering, through restricting the intake of apprentices. Also skilled work is not exactly easy to chop and change.

Would the industrial revolution have taken off in the same way had guilds been allowed to regulate and moderate it? Possibly not. Would we be better off today if the guilds had impeded the industrial revolution? Given every indicator of crisis in the book, including the fact that we are close to having

burned all the affordable oil reserves in under 100 years ...
you've got to admit it's a possibility?

The co-operative networks emerging today are not trades
guilds. They are new forms with some guild-like qualities, but
also some notable advances. In place of village-style localness,
they have global village extensiveness – especially in the ability
to share ideas, innovations and informational resources. Instead
of secrecy they have greater transparency. But it's important
not to lose sight of the living traditions behind our modern
guilds. And many of the key features of these antique abundant
systems: learning, craft, ethic, democracy, loyalty, narrative and
(judging by the mystery plays) a certain amount of joyous mis-
chief ... are still pretty valid.

Our next historical parallel will be to look at the self-organising co-operative systems that emerged in the 1930s Great
Depression.

What is a recession? There are technical answers: more than
two quarters of negative economic growth; a cyclical business
slowdown or contraction; a period of falling employment; falling
investment; under utilisation of capacity. In summary: a big
decline in economic activity, lasting a fair while. But these are
symptoms; like describing smallpox as a fever and skin spots.

Bernard Lietaer, in *The Future of Money*, offered another
analysis: a recession is a time of restricted money supply.
According to a monetarist view, an economy is an inanimate
machine, controlled by government. What Lietaer realised is
that an economy is something different than that. It is a human
consensus. The reason money goes into short supply in a recession is not a lack of spending or borrowing by government. It
is that people are acting out of fear and panic. In these circumstances they hoard money. If they have it they hold onto it, just
in case.

That looks like a prudent policy. Just wait and see. The trouble is that everyone else waits and sees too. And the economy goes into seizure. That's because anyone who has cash isn't spending it. And that freezes everyone's income. A recession, if you look at it this way, is an economic heart attack – a circulation failure. With money not in circulation there is no money to pay workers or debts, firms close and unemployment rises.

In the 1930s they discovered a new solution to this problem. One so scandalous to the establishment it was stamped out, a move Lietaer felt led indirectly to Hitler and World War II: *communities started printing their own money.*

What to do in the 1930s if you were the mayor of a little town in Austria, where the entire economy had ground to a standstill? The mayor in the town in question had read a book by a radical Austrian economist called Gessell who was opposed to usury and interest rates and argued for issuing new currencies, which avoided these. In 1932, Herr Unterguggenberger, mayor of Worgl facing 35% unemployment, issued 14 000 Austrian schillings' worth of 'stamp scrip'. In other words he printed his own currency. These were covered by exactly the same amount of ordinary schillings being deposited in a local bank. He then paid people to do public works, using stamp scrip, fixing school roofs and roads. And then they paid each other. Within two years, Worgl had returned to full employment. Not only that but the town was in tip-top shape, with new roads, houses repaired, forests replanted. Why the economic miracle? Because the Worgl managed what the real money Austrian schilling did not. It circulated, from buyer, to seller, from employer to worker, from worker to tax payment and then back out again in public works. On average the Worgl circulated 14 times faster than the schilling, which means (Lietaer points out) that it created 14 times more jobs.[125] Two hundred other towns in Austria and Germany followed suit at which point the regulator in Bonn panicked and blocked community currencies. A legal appeal was made and lost.

What was it that made issuing a new currency so successful? A key factor was the 'stamp scrip' system recommended by Gessell. You have to pay every month to keep a note in this currency current (and it then gets stamped). This policy – called 'demurrage' – ensures that no one is tempted to hoard the replacement currency. You could even pay local taxes in stamp scrip, which led to one of the few cases in history where people have wanted to pay their taxes early (to avoid paying the scrip as well). Another way of saying 'demurrage' is 'negative interest rate'. What the clever economist and canny mayor had found was the economy's missing reverse gear! Just as interest rates impel people to hoard (at the first sign of negative growth) negative interest rates impel people to spend now, before their savings decrease. In real currencies this could prompt a spiral of inflation, but in the well-controlled stamp scrip it just got the whole town ticking over nicely.

We face a difficult and unreliable economic future. Transition periods are usually choppy. There will be opportunities, but also probably long recessionary slumps, when flooded world cities, a collapse of confidence in oil supplies and similar could trigger collapses in the conventional economy. Along with schemes like microcredit, complementary currencies offer a safety net. For a couple of years we can at least trade and share what we have while the economic storms blow over. And invest (hopefully in our education, energy efficiency and suchlike) when times are fatter. Because they act like a safety net in recession-hit communities, these schemes have in modern times been given a regulatory break; Timebanks were even made tax exempt by the IRS. The green dollars prevalent in New Zealand received a different ruling. If you were a plumber and you were paid for plumbing then you should ensure at least part payment is in real currency so that you can account for it and pay tax. But if you were a plumber and went fruit picking, or sold some old records that was fine, just take the green dollars.

The reason I got into considering alternative currencies was musing about how to meet people's needs while substantially reducing their carbon emissions. The obvious target was all the duplication between households – lawn mowers, drills, books ... If we could get people to turn a whole community into a library then substantial carbon savings would be possible. Especially if the same platform also encouraged them to share lifts and so on.

There have been many attempts to create such sharing platforms:

Public services. We all pay taxes then use them on a needs basis.

LETS. Mutual credit schemes; earn green dollars by lending or selling goods (and services); spend green dollars when there are things I need.

Libraries. Not just for books, e.g. the power tool library in Oakland.

Rental. A hot area of innovation. For instance city car clubs. And Bag Borrow Or Steal (works like Netflix or LoveFilm, but for handbags).

Pooling. A Heidelberg community scheme, whereby each person bought and maintained one item from an inventory list; when anyone needed something on the list they'd phone the holder of that item.

Peer-to-peer rental. Rentmineonline and Zilok are two recent attempts at this, whereby people hire goods off each other for real money.

Freecycle. If you are about to throw something away, see if someone else wants it first.

Swapping. Find someone who does want to barter. For instance readitandswapit.com. Or clothes swapping parties (like Swishing).

Liftshare. A 'dating site' for sharing lifts to your given destination.

Landshare. The idea of turning spare land into allotments.

The opportunity I could see was to do something similar to the LETS schemes. But with three differences:

1. We would pay people to reduce their carbon emissions.
2. The way people traded would use an innovative new system.
3. We'd make it an abundant model that could scale to large volumes.

My business partner (Robert Colwell) and I have spent a great deal of time trying to find the model that could break through and both provide community support and carbon reduction.

We looked at a number of variants. All had the same problem, a central processing bottleneck (they had to pass the goods through us). We needed to find a more abundant framework that would sit more effortlessly in a community. So we went back to my original idea (covered in my last book), which was an internet 'Barter Bank' (i.e. similar to a LETS scheme). Except with one difference: what if we could do it through messaging media like mobile phones and email? Then we would have a scheme that could work in any country. And we would have something with no central administration, just a contact service. The result is a system called Coin, which stands for community involvement (and also refers to the currency).

At the moment we are developing the system working with an experienced coder (Michael) from the financial markets. And will be testing it soon in a number of pilot communities. It will probably evolve. But through exploring the 'market' we have become aware of hundreds of other complementary schemes starting: mobile-based encrypted currencies; actual coins called S.Coop which you can redeem in Petticoat Lane market for ice-cream (a promotional thank you from the store owners); the Transition Towns' Totnes pounds and Brixton pounds are encouraging use of local independent shops. HubCulture, a managed office and professional network, has its own currency, the Ven. By far the most interesting parallel though is the MPesa.

Critics of microcredit point to the high (by Western standards) interest rates. In Bangladesh these are limited by the government to 20%. And Grameen only charge those rates when the income is more than sufficient to cover the loans. There are microcredit schemes charging much higher rates than 20%, e.g. in Africa where the populations can be harder to reach and costs are quite high. That was the reason why Vodafone and the DFID (the UK Department for International Development) created a scheme in Kenya, to support microcredit using a mobile phone currency instead. The result is MPesa, which means mobile-pay.

I went to a talk by one of the technical developers, Dave Birch, recently. How can people afford mobile phones in the developing world when so many (97% – see Chapter 7) earn less per day in equivalent local spending power than the price of this book? The answer is they can't. What they can afford is SIM cards. There will generally be one phone handset shared around a friendship group or enterprise. Also, given high illiteracy rates among some rural segments, there is co-operation in the use of these phones (people dialling or entering security PIN numbers for you). The phone is a lifeline given the number of families whose father is working in the city most of the time, while the mother tends the farm, and raises the children. In sub-Saharan Africa women do up to 80% of the farming.[126] When I visited Nairobi in the 1990s, there were reckoned to be about 500 mobile phones in the country, nearly all of them reckoned to be used by multinational employees. There were 11.7 million mobile phone subscribers by 2007. This is more than half the number of adults in Kenya.

The idea behind MPesa was to reduce the costs (and hence interest charges) of microcredit schemes. The MPesa system is SIM-based. When you unlock your SIM, if you have credits on the phone you can text them to another user just by using the keyword 'pay' and their number. You get credits on the SIM by paying in cash at the many Safaricom (Vodafone) outlets; the exact same place people get their SIMs and phone minutes. There are over 100 000 outlets nationwide. If someone has sent you MPesa currency you can cash this at an outlet too, just by texting the person in the kiosk. The service is free to use, as Safaricom makes its revenue from the text messaging. If someone sends you MPesa and you don't have a Safaricom SIM you can still cash the text at an outlet. You just can't pay others.

How does this help with microcredit? Firstly the microcredit agent does not have to bring cash with them when they assess you for the loan. Or to return a second time with the cash, or to collect all the regular payments. Or – more likely – get you to travel to a town for both transactions, They can just text you the money. And you can repay by text. Thus the transaction costs are dramatically reduced.

Birch explained that microcredit proved an excellent way to get the currency into circulation and accepted by a critical mass of people. But by now people are using the MPesa outside microcredit as a full blown currency. There are 5.5 million users (defined as people who have sent MPesa) i.e. about half of all mobile phone subscribers. They make around 160 000 transactions a day. They are also still joining the scheme at a rate of 300 000 new users per month. A second main use is sending remittances back from a husband working in the city. This saves a long regular bus trip, or paying a driver, so is a massive convenience and saving. Another common usage is for safe storage. Not in a long-term savings manner, but depositing an amount before travelling, and then withdrawing it at the other end. A SIM if stolen is useless to anyone without pass numbers. Robbers tend therefore to be after cash.

MPesa is also planning to support the government welfare social service payments. And new mobile phone-based services have sprung up around the currency, for instance a translation service where you can text in a message in one of the many tribal dialects and get it translated into your own.

The wide adoption of mobile phones is bringing openings for many such abundant systems to the developing world. Another one is Tradenet which helps farmers to check where the best prices can be found for their produce, and contact buyers there.

PUTTING ABUNDANT SYSTEMS DESIGN INTO ACTION

WHAT EXACTLY ARE ABUNDANT SYSTEMS? How are they different? Let's get into the details. What follows are some of the key principles that differentiate abundant systems from lean and mean 'mechanistic' systems. We'll see from the examples that these can apply to almost every area of collective human activity, from town planning to social media.

SYSTEMS THINKING

I think of abundant systems being as like sailing. It's about catching abundant resources from your surroundings, rather than chugging away with a motor (i.e. high energy inputs). And because of this you need a sailor's eye for patterns in the systems around you: weather, tide and so on.

A good example of systems thinking for sustainability is industrial symbiosis. Symbiosis is when several organisms in an ecosystem co-operate for mutual benefit. Industrial symbiosis applies this to business clusters. An initiative that Nicola at theGINlady.com (GIN = Green Independent Natural) is championing is the development of farmer co-operatives enabling organic meat farmers to find decent markets for secondary products like wool – for instance, supplying these materials to UK eco-fashion brands, or for use as loft insulation. The rates they would get as individual farmers for these material streams are piffling (for instance 30p a kilo for wool). And also the quantities they could supply would be too small to be significant. But it could be a prime material if co-ops aggregated and found direct buyers for sustainable materials rather than them shipping wool in from New Zealand.

Similarly WornAgain are making fashionable clothes and bags out of materials like old plane seats, staff uniforms and hot air balloons; doubly fashionable because they are reclaimed materials and hence sustainable in a 'street' way.

Systems design nearly always involves looking 'one level out' at the larger context. So if your task is a community centre, look at its total interactions with the community, literally everything that flows in and out (deliveries, staff, flows of air or materials …). I worked on a local government sustainability innovation project ('i-Team') and one of the councils, Kirklees, decided to do just this. One of their ideas was training midwives who worked from the centre to act as carbon/energy saving coaches.

The way to look at a human system is as a 'panorama', according to Patrick Geddes, an inspiring chap from the nineteenth century when it comes to town planning, sociology and much besides. Geddes' advice looking at his native Edinburgh – don't get lost in the details of the (then worst slums in Europe) just yet. But look at the big picture. What are all the influences from places and times that make it exactly how it is now? The agricultural supplies that start in the glen? The remains of the medieval market? The economics of landlordism which accounts for the appalling lack of both public and private space? That's a better way of saying what systems thinking is really about. You could just as easily call it narrative thinking, to avoid confusion with the institutional 'systems' associated with men in lab coats with clipboards.

MAXIMISE LAZINESS

I've watched and worked with quite a number of social ventures, and seen some flourish, while others really struggle. Paradoxically it is often the ones with fewest resources that seem to thrive. I've come to believe that one key is to find an effortless model. Finance is a bit like oil, you can pump a business with that and see results (lots of this went on in the dotcom years) but often those ideas don't really take root or become self-sustaining. Rather, as with oil fuelled intensive agriculture the system becomes less resilient and addicted to constant input of further resources to keep it going.

The effortless model is born out of having almost nothing – except a good idea and the potential for people in some way to help themselves or each other. Freecycle for instance was just a 'service idea' if you could call it that. It didn't need to build a million pound website – it used Yahoo Groups. It didn't need to market itself because people recruited their friends. And after a while the media and writers like me picked up the story. The key to their success is the volunteers, not only the actual organisers but also everyone involved at every level doing their bit. Freecycle has six million users and counting.

Laziness is actually another key idea from permaculture. That's because systems thrive when nature does most of the work. Permaculture farms look more like forests, with interacting crops, animals and other elements at different levels all providing services. They look like they 'just grew' but don't be fooled. In common with internet systems like 'open source' they are carefully planned and constructed using experience-based rules. It's a matter of things being in the right place to thrive together. The effort goes into design, rather than constant struggle.

When it comes to social production (internet or community) systems, another key to this kind of abundant effortlessness is the proverb 'many hands make light work'. Fordhall Farm, the Obama election fundraising … there are numerous examples in this book of people who have raised a lot of money by asking for a small amount each from a lot of people. One of the key things open source software developers say about their approach is that the quality control is much higher because many more coders are checking each other's work and challenging it from new angles.

Bottlenecks – the common feature of many lean and mean systems – are places that become hard work. From high volume internet systems (Twitter hit a crisis of this sort) to children's party arrangements (it's a long story!) bottlenecks are also the place where systems most often fail. Bottlenecks are often deliberate; for instance SMS allows operators heavy charges for moving light amounts of data.

Lazy doesn't mean low quality. Or 'lazy' in moral or artistic terms. It means designing something so elegant that it supports itself without the need for constant input. Like the idea we will meet later for desert greenhouses below sea level (so that the sea water they will evaporate to use for moisture can run downhill, rather than having to be pumped). The old technology tries too hard. Twenty-first century society will be more Taoist.

Laziness extends to needing minimal inputs. Abundant systems are often self-supporting. Grameen Bank for instance hasn't taken in a penny in funding since the early 1980s. It gets what it needs from its customers and also, because they are also the owners, shares any excess (profit) with them too.

In technical terms what maximising laziness means is an optimal position on the curve describing the relationship between energy/input and work/output. It doesn't mean putting no energy into the system. It means designing things so that you put in a wise amount of work to ensure abundance. Howard Odum described all this through 'power curves'. If you drive at a steady 50–60 mph in a car you cover the distance with the lowest fuel use. Go faster or slower and you use more fuel. Many modern systems are not optimal simply because they are so impatient – revving for short-term results.

DISTRIBUTEDNESS

While many of the examples in this book are social ventures, social networks and social change campaigns, it must be pointed out that not everything 'social' is a co-operative network. Many apparently 'social' systems actually lack distributedness. For instance NGOs run 'campaigns' which get each person to do something far from engaging their full human potential or giving them an active and free part in creating the campaign. I am happy to sign worthy petitions mind, but there is a slight feeling of 'is that all you want?'

Human beings struggle to operate something like an airport or a logistics (delivery) business using lean and mean systems.

Bees on the other hand, with no central control, but rather a beautifully choreographed series of evolved micro (bee-to-bee) behaviours, manage to visit several million flowers (the right flowers for the season, for the maximum yield of nectar and pollen) every single day in the right order. One elegant little move in this schema is that a bee – when a flower is empty of nectar – will mark it so with a pheromone. This scent fades at roughly the rate that the flower replenishes itself. So that other bees don't waste time checking until it's full again. Bees also follow established learning trails, for instance returning to the same location a number of times. The colony also has large reserves of foraging bees dormant at any one time, so that upon an exciting new find (the bees not only 'direct' the other bees to these, they 'sell' their discovery with varying degrees of enthusiasm), up to a third of the whole colony can be mobilised fast. Bees also maximise the yield for the flowers – a trans-species act in favour of common wellbeing – as a single bee while foraging will stick to a single type of flower, even if there are others around in the same location. That's because the bees are gardening; there will be more flowers next year if they help flowering plants thrive. And rose pollen isn't much use to mari-golds. Bees do all of this not through central control but simple rules and distributed brilliance, each bee working like a little miracle at simple tasks.

Distributedness is in some ways a special case of lazy (low energy and complexity) design. Hierarchies are bottlenecks. If you want a nimble organisation on any scale, make the decision as close as possible to the ground. Anything else is a recipe for massive bureaucracy.

This brings us back again to the revolutionary idea of social production – of many hands making lighter work than a cen-trally organised corporation. It's the success story behind such internet giants as Craigslist, YouTube, Wikipedia, blogging, Flickr, Facebook. All of these are made out of small contributions by each member; but smart contributions, not menial tasks. They are also organised by members. By tagging content, you get the ability to search in the terms that people would use to describe them. Distributed tagging in internet systems leads to what's called a folksonomy (as opposed to a rigid centralised taxonomy). Instead of centrally defining what someone might be looking for when searching for something, you employ the natural (and often diverse) ways that people classify things themselves. Looking for a particular song one might search by era, another by artist, another by a lyric and so on. It's a branch of a bigger shift in culture, from official culture to a folk system, based on consensus.

A lovely little example of distributedness and abundance in action is ReCaptcha. Captchas are those annoying little boxes where you have to type in the fuzzy words and letters to get access to some result or site online, for instance to post a comment on a blog. It's intended to create a trap for nonhuman agents (little parcels of code, called 'bots', spreading spam by posting links across millions of sites). It works because recognising indistinct and distorted type is a hard task that only humans can perform reliably.

Recaptcha uses this process to help with digitising old books, one word at a time. These display words that computers did not recognise in the process of scanning books. How do they know that they are dealing with a human who will get it right, not a bot who might enter something wrong? Because they give you two words to transcribe, one that is already known, and one which has been thrown up – as not recognised – by scanning a book. If you get the first one right, they assume you probably got the second one right too. It's just one example of how tiny tasks in large-scale interactions can become productive by drawing on human talents; rather like in a bee colony.

MULTI-CELLULAR ORGANISATION DESIGN

When I say multi-cellular, I mean structured like multi-cellular organisms.

Why did (biological) multi-cellular organisms evolve? Why didn't amoebae and bacteria just get bigger? The answer is that the multi-cellular design is evolutionary genius at work. One reason is that cells can die and be replaced all the time. In 'amoebae the size of a beanbag' self-repair or upgrade might be trickier! In a superorganism (like an ant or bee colony) the bees themselves take on this cell-like role, within a larger whole.

In a social system a 'cell' would usually mean about 20–140 people. The size of a small village or tribe, or a large extended family, a small business, or an independent working unit in a big business. On that scale you can have smart interactions – relate your ideas and spark off others and be bound by strong relationships. Which – note – doesn't mean it is all peace and love, by the way. This is the scale of optimal collaboration; a sports squad, a science park outfit. On this scale there is passion, autonomy, identity, a real sense of belonging. Whereas within larger groups, unless there is this cell-like structure, individual contribution and identity gets lost. Decisions through longer chains of double guessing and patchy understanding can turn into lowest common denominators.

A multi-cellular design allows smart cells to act in a beautifully choreographed and interrelated way. A multi-cellular organisation can work on any scale, but avoids the bureaucracy and the alienation that happens in any larger crowd.

One of the functions of multi-cellular organisations is distributed learning. How to benefit from learning in one cell, across the whole community of cells? A new social network called Ivili.com is seeking to spread great grassroots sustainability solutions across a whole network of those facing similar challenges in geographically remote locations. The idea was born out of research the founder Jeremy Smith was doing into a book (called Clean Breaks) on sustainable holiday hotels and hostels. Smith saw similar solutions emerging in locations across the world; often variants or different solutions to the same problems, such as harvesting rainwater. Smith's idea is to use video clips to demonstrate ideas so that others can pick up the whole recipe in an accessible format. It's a new idea and time will tell if this community reaches a tipping point, but the concept seems well founded. It relies on the fact that the participants are generous sustainability-minded types who do want good ideas to be adopted by others to have a bigger impact. They don't want to be in a Starbucks-style chain, but they do potentially want the shared learning effects of a larger scale association.

Another current example of multi-cellular learning is creating a format, which abstracts the learning from one setting into a 'recipe' ready to be applied in other settings, without going through all the trial and error. SPIN (Small-Plot-INtensive) farming is a programme designed for people new to farming. It is organic (and hence produces high value crops to sell locally) and they claim it is easy to learn, nontechnical and inexpensive to apply. SPIN Farming is designed for half-acre plots and is equally suitable for city or rural farming. You can buy the instruction guides online for $12 each (you buy a set of these depending on what you are planning, but it's likely to cost you less than $100 in total) and you also get free email support as part of the deal. The guides are a complete how-to guide to running a tiny farm, with titles like: Tools and Investments, and Work Flow Practices. There are also specific farm operation model guides, for instance the snappily titled: 'GARLIC. Part-time, Multi-site Operation (6000 square feet, \$23250 in gross annual sales)'. Which if you were planning to buy a small plot of land and grow garlic on it would probably be priceless!

DESIGNING OUT WASTE

We already saw examples of this (as industrial symbiosis) under systems thinking but it is an enormous subject. Broadly speaking, living ecosystems are like reservoirs, collecting energy and using as much as possible for their own work. Waste in the extravagant human sense is a big hole in the dam.

Cradle to Cradle is a seminal design book. The authors, McDonough and Braungard, hate the vision of sustainability as just leading to restriction and rationing. They think we simply need to design smarter material flows. In nature, they argue, there is no waste, it is always food for another process. Actually there is always some waste escaping from a system, for instance in heat energy and my only minor criticism of their book would be that (compared to the work in a similar vein by Howard Odum) they focus too much on material rather than energy. It would still be possible to invent harmless onward uses of existing materials which because of their energy requirements (including transport and processing) created huge CO_2 emissions.

Landfill sites are full of valuable materials that have been used for a while then 'thrown away'. In the Cradle to Cradle view, every component of an artifact should be designed to be a technical or biological nutrient in its next phase of life. In the 1950s Alfred Heineken had the idea (when on holiday in Jamaica, and seeing so many discarded bottles) of designing square beer bottles that could subsequently be used as bricks to build houses with. It was called the World Bottle and the story goes that he got as far as getting a test house built from this material – to prove the concept – and pitching it to his board of directors (who voted it down for reasons unknown).[127]

Many sustainable systems today simply find a waste stream they can sit in and create value out of. One such initiative is REiY, from Bioregional (their most famous project being BedZed, an affordable and zero carbon housing community in South London). REiY takes in building waste and either resells it as is, or reworks it into new products (for instance furniture) to sell in shop outlets. It hence creates opportunities for employment and training. A similar (but simpler version of this) idea has been operating in the USA for some years, under the name RE stores or the less snappy title Building Material Reuse Centres. The first three REiY centres, funded by the UK government, are planned to open in the UK in 2009. There are also a number of specialist wood recyclers out there, making new products (from furniture to equestrian flooring) out of old wood.

A similar idea for electrical waste called RUSZ (Repair and Service Centre) has been successful in Austria, training the unemployed to repair electrical goods – otherwise on their way to landfill – for resale. RUSZ also provides an affordable repair service for households. In the last 10 years RUSZ claim to have repaired two million kilos of electrical goods, and have also won awards for employment creation (they only employ long-term unemployed).

Kept, from Luke and the team at More Associates, is a brand that celebrates keeping things you decide not to replace, like a mobile phone getting a second life. The idea is to use stencils or other such devices to help users proudly display the KEPT logo and hence make keeping old stuff iconic. They are currently putting together a shoot celebrating how cool second hand goods are (compared to new). I see it as a kind of 'anti-matter' – making a brand out of not consuming.

Glove Love. This from the folks at DoTheGreenThing. The idea came to Naresh, one of the founders, when he found an odd glove at home. He threw it away. He then found another glove in the park. So he retrieved the first from the bin. Cleaned them both and made a nice bold LEFT/RIGHT label for each, uniting them as a pair. Green Thing will be collecting in gloves that people find stranded at home, and then creating new pairs, complete with a little story about the previous life of each glove.

Another way to design out waste would be to produce things which are easy to repair and upgrade. If you think about it this is the ultimate loyalty scheme; people will keep buying your parts, software, re-skins and so on. I am amazed no one has cottoned on to this yet, but I am sure they will. Imagine Sony selling you the last home entertainment system you will ever buy on this basis, and then signing you up to a lifetime of upgrades. In a green utopia we may reconnect with community and need TV soap operas less. But assuming people do still want mass media this would be a good stepping stone. It would also open up Sony's business model to external developers; in the same way as Facebook Apps; independents could design cool upgrades.

Also needed are products designed for long life, not for built in obsolescence. I've been predicting for 10 years that Moore's Law[128] will come to an end (I call this Moore's Ceiling). If you think five-blade razors are daft what about eight-processor Macs (expensive to fabricate and costly in power and cooling)? Most markets reach a point where what the engineers can produce exceeds what people need. Unless you are rendering your own video films or processing huge quantities of scientific survey data, very few things you do with your computer today would even tax the machines of five years ago. The answer may come with cloud computing anyway, when users pay for processing power remotely and their local computing device is just a thin client. This extends what the internet already offers with virtual storage (imagine if all those websites had to live on every local computer).

Companies offer choice because they say that is what people want. The evidence is that largely people really don't want choice. Check out psychologist Barry Schwartz's 2005 video on the TED site. There is empirical evidence that offering people more choice makes them less happy, for instance in the gift they are offered as a reward for participating in a (dummy) experiment. They become anxious about what they are missing, rather than rejoicing in what they have. Or consider that Apple only makes four models of computer. I'm all for localised diversity. But not when it comes to global products like mobile phones. The future is design along the lines of the old VW Bug (or Beetle): iconic, economical, easy to repair, fun and customised by the owners in vivid ways that exceed any 'customer styling' options today.

CO-OPERATIVE MARKETS

Markets are literally co-operative in cases where user needs are incorporated into service delivery. A service in Germany (GTO) allows pedestrians to turn on street lighting late at night as needed, reducing energy costs and light pollution when there is no one out walking that street.

A new scheme from super geek Mark Gorton, aligns public transport routes with clusters of realtime demand. Gorton, the founder of P2P file sharing site Limewire, calls his proposal Smart Para Transit:

> Currently on the road networks of big cities, you have lots of people making similar trips in private automobiles. And now, thanks to the advent of cell phone technology, computer technology, and other information technology, it's possible to build a system that dynamically gathers information about where people want to go, and routes a fleet of vehicles to make those same trips much more efficiently.[129]

The system is used in Portland Oregon and is being trialled in San Francisco. The platform is open source and based upon a platform called Geo-Server with many further applications to smart city planning.

Another approach to co-operative markets is to think about distributing resources more equitably. There have been a number of products marketed on a 'one for me one for the developing world' basis. The One Laptop Per Child project used a buy one give one (or more) free mechanic.[130] 'Tom's shoes' gives an identical pair to a needy kid in an impoverished country. BoGo (buy one give one) light is a solar power charged torch, bought on a buy one give one basis, distributed to refugee camps and other areas where a handy night light can make a real difference.

The same model is being applied to large-scale infrastructure and markets. Smart City Grids will manage the relationship between demand and capacity within the grid, something which is currently done manually and is wasteful. The intermittent nature of renewable energy generation (it depends on wind, sun and tides, which all can vary) means that smart systems in transmission can pose challenges, as could much larger distances (for instance connecting Europe to solar power from the Sahara). But the best-known application of smart grids is creating a co-operative relationship between producers and consumers. Dynamic demand and variable pricing mean that people (or automatic devices in their fridges and water heaters) can use power when it is cheaper, and hence reduce the need to keep spare capacity 'spinning' in case needed. It's an abundant system, managing the whole of its capacity through a network of interactions rather than the old 'use it or lose it' top-down (or centralised) 'grid'. A cute version of the same principle is the Tea Light, another idea by More Associates – a traffic light on your computer to tell you when is and is not a good time to put the kettle on in your office.

JOY

Grameen founder Mohammed Yunus describes 'joy' as one of his key business principles. Abundance releases a kind of 'joy' to do with creativity and the human energy involved in doing something out of shared enthusiasm and ethos. It also relates to craft work, something that draws on your full human capacities, and develops you as you develop the work.

ABUNDANCY AS AN ETHIC

If there is no central command and control, how can a community work well together? The answer is that they need a shared ethic. Without this all you have is a set of individuals.

With it you have an aligned group working towards something they believe in.

Examples in this book are often born out of a sustainability purpose; for instance Transition Towns out of the need to tackle climate change and peak oil. But the idea of an ethic goes beyond just the idea of a purpose or agenda, or target, or mission. Many central government and big business actions also target reductions in emissions or increases in resilience or energy security. But they do so within an ongoing central command and control structure. They do not share the passion for grass-roots involvement. Conversely the genius of Web 2.0-style social production systems, highly relevant to sustainability, came out of a belief in a more democratic, distributed arrangement of society.

Co-operative systems have a shared human idea, rather than just being 'logistical' systems. It is a holistic, human realisation – often experienced by the members of a group as a kind of epiphany. The core idea varies greatly across the examples in this book, for instance Wangari Matthai's Green Belt movement or Mohammed Yunus' Grameen both took the empowerment of women as a core component. Others such as Freecycle or DoTheGreenThing have an overt environmental root. Others such as the P2P transport systems or Carrot Mob take delight in the liberating potential of technology. And all of them are specific ideas and it is often the creative idea itself which burns in people's minds, inspires and motivates them.

Some common themes do emerge in these ideas – a list may help us to sketch what I mean by having an ethic;

The play ethic

The lean and mean society makes for monotonous heavy work. This was the core idea of The Protestant (or Puritan) Work Ethic; an absence of enjoyment or delight in work. Instead work was subsumed into renouncement of earthly pleasures. Co-operative systems of the sort discussed in this book tend to be playful and joyous rather than heavy. This is a cause that has been promoted by UK magazine *The Idler*. Working from a profound rejection of work as suffering, the clever chaps at *The Idler* have set out to critique modern society, their Crap Jobs, Crap Towns and Crap Holidays revelling in exposing the aspirations and values most toil under. When I say 'play' I don't really mean a kind of ironic 'playing at'. I have in mind something far more committed. Another word for it would be creativity, but again that facility has been debased by the 'brainstorming' mechanical view.

The grassroots ethic

There is a profound split between grassroots, democratic processes and the top-down approach; often what goes in the name of 'green' is actually the latter, and what goes in the name of advanced capitalism (such as eBay) proves through its community rule to be thoroughly co-operative.

The partnership with nature ethic

There is no split between human beings and nature. There never was. That was always an illusion. Our science, plastics, shopping malls are all natural products. What has been lacking is the ethic of partnership with nature. We have been denying the umbilical cord that links us with our ecosystems. We've been sawing the branch that we sit on. It's taken a looming global crisis of sustainability to point out the perversity of that position.

The lifelong learning ethic

Human nature is defined by our plastic ability to learn and form ideas. Lifelong learning is not some newfangled trend. It's actually, I'd argue, our default state. What we have today in our opportunities to experience other cultures, to access information and to share insights is still arguably unprecedented. We are, if we want, able to learn for our whole lives. And it appears we do want this, as the explosion of interest in blogging, craft hobbies, the interests in history and popular science and so on suggest.

The acceptance ethic

This again is hardly news. Most world religions have turned on the need to accept suffering and sacrifice the ego. Modern culture is something like a flight from this realisation: to addictions, consumerism, Prozac or anything to dull the pain, which of course is all the stronger for being held at bay.

The transcendent ethic

We've been in a quite uniquely materialist phase. Any hint of the metaphysical is seen as hocus-pocus. Any notion of 'God Delusion' is still to this day treated with disdain. Yet we are manifestly a religious species. We are genetically disposed to believe in an implicate deeper order and reality. Otherwise religion and the associated rituals, myths and archetypal images would not be a proven (in anthropological studies) human universal. What you find anyway is that behind quite diverse stories and characters there was often a 'spiritual' dimension to their quest, some sort of 'epiphany' at least.

The ownership ethic

I don't mean ownership as in 'it's mine' (exclusively, all mine). I mean the other sense of emotionally having a common stake in something and feeling responsible for it. Within a distributed system this becomes a mutual or reciprocal matter – like the way you might watch out for other kids than your own in a school setting, or raise the alarm in a workplace if someone was trying to steal from somebody else's desk.

DIVISION OF BRILLIANCE

The abundant potential of the human world is apparent when we imagine a large proportion of the population being challenged to work to the limit of their talents, learning and creativity. We don't have that system now because we need to support an order where an elite few gain all the rewards.

THE EARTH RACE

Maybe the new 'space race' – i.e. a cultural enthusiasm big and broad enough to define a generation and an epoch – will be about climate, biodiversity and poverty rescue: the Earth Race?

One exciting Earth Race example is biochar, the so-called 'black gold' from traditional Amazonian agriculture. What you do traditionally is take smouldering organic matter and cover it with soil. The resulting charcoal is a stable way to lock carbon in the soil and also promotes soil fertility. Modern versions use anaerobic kilns. Craig Sams, the founder of Green & Blacks chocolate, is one enthusiastic convert. Sams estimates that if 2.5% of the world's productive land were used for biochar CO_2 levels could be returned to pre-industrial levels.[131] Sams has serious Silicon Valley venture capital backing and is starting trials this year both in the UK and Belize.

Another school of thought which makes particular use of this idea of partnering with nature is biomimicry. Not because of a romantic drive to go back to nature (which often means copying or incorporating inert natural materials). But because nature's designs, given aeons of evolution, are often better than ours (for instance photosynthesis is pretty much the most efficient solar power system imaginable).

Complex living systems usually do not work like machines. They are more interesting than that, with qualities of complexity like resilience and emergence. To compare human society – how our world works – with a machine is like comparing a human infant with a doll. Our machine thinking has got us so far. But it has also been creating problems, notably in the natural world, where our mechanised farming, logging and building have worked against other natural systems. The alternative is learning from other living systems. To pay close attention to how complex living systems really work. And reapply this to our human designs, and to understanding the rich, emergent processes of our societies. This is in itself an intellectual revolution, one at least as big as the industrial revolution and scientific age.

Michael Pawlyn, the British architect who designed the massive biomes of the Eden Project, is a leading biomimicry practitioner. The inspiration for the biomes came from dragonfly wings, using hexagonal frames and membranes made from a polymer called ETFE. The result was that when the structures were finished Pawlyn calculated that the weight of the domes was less than the weight of the air they contained.

Pawlyn is now working on a future project called 'The Sahara Forest'. The idea is to make large greenhouse structures kept moist by evaporated sea water. The evaporation and flow of moist air also keeps the greenhouses 15 degrees cooler than the outside air. It could be integrated with concentrated solar power (CSP) generation too. Providing ample food, energy and fresh water from the most unlikely place on earth. The solar farm also evaporates the sea water, and the damp air keeps the greenhouses cool enough for plants to thrive. The system is based upon the way that a particular desert beetle (the Namibian Fog-Basking Beetle if you must know) manages to manufacture its own fresh drinking water in desert conditions by capturing condensation. A prototype was built in an arid region of Tenerife. The full-scale projects will be built in deserts of North Africa below sea level (so that no energy is needed to pipe sea water to the site). It is a beautifully elegant idea, self-sustaining and supportive of life.

The Sahara Forest Project is probably as good an example as any of the sort of 'technology' which we really need going forward. It is not just a clever trick which has been copied from nature either. It is a system designed to work in partnership with nature. These greenhouses create about five times as much water as is needed for the crops and much of this seeps into the surrounding land, creating a microclimate. Compare this with conventional greenhouses that, according to Pawlyn, take water from the ground, resulting in a drop in the water table, resulting in salination of the remaining water, which ultimately makes the land barren. Pawlyn's greenhouses would reverse that effect. It is not just 'carbon neutral' (whatever that means) it is a restorative technology. And that is the heart of the vision which is so exciting about where technology and human systems could go next; a step change which would make industrial, mechanistic models look crude, compared to the elegance of partnering with nature to meet our needs, with a fraction of the effort (and the damage).

If you ever want a pep talk, to pull yourself out of doom and gloom, check out Pawlyn presenting these ideas on YouTube – and also making the case that we should positively seize the opportunities to innovate thrown up by recession, climate change and peak oil.[132]

POSTSCRIPT:
A CHECKLIST FOR
WORLD BUILDERS

HERE'S A CHECKLIST for any stage of reviewing a world improving co-operative idea in progress. These are some very common features of the examples featured in this book of co-operative networks for the common good. If one of these doesn't apply, maybe it should?

☑ DIRECTED

The difference between a social network and a co-operative network is that co-operation assumes some group goal or ethic, a shared task. In the case of examples in this book the goal will generally be to increase the common wellbeing; but obviously in a specific way, like local food self-sufficiency.

☑ DISTRIBUTED

There is no centre, no chain of command (although there may be central functions, for instance of distributing, editing or monitoring). The network is led by local interactions from which large-scale properties emerge. The examples often have a 'multi-cellular' structure where local circuits of links, towns or interests give structure to prevent getting lost in a mass crowd.

☑ DEMOCRATIC

Not just in the sense of getting a vote, but rather in the full sense of being an empowered equal partner; and having systems whereby the group can shape as well as choose outcomes, i.e. democracy is more than just 'a vote'.

☑ DELIBERATIVE

Creating forums where citizens or members can learn, share ideas, form agreements and commitments. As opposed to communications from a centre. Although good ideas may circulate between cells of conversation.

☑ DESIGNED

These are like pieces of a future tradition; they have a 'way things are done' quality encoded in rituals, rules and formats. They are also carefully designed for abundance, low energy input and waste responsibility. They often have specific innovations, for instance in ownership models, or tools.

☑ DEVELOPING

These are learning organisations, both for the people involved and for the collective (and changing) genius of the central design. They work on an open source principle of continuous review and improvement, like living systems.

☑ DIVISION OF BRILLIANCE

Instead of the stupefying division of labour described by Adam Smith, co-operative networks draw upon full human capacities or individual contributors. This in itself releases reserves of wasted talent, enthusiasm and human energy.

☑ DETOXIFIED

The networks are careful in sifting and rejecting toxic thinking, such as the wrong kind of investment ... that work against the common good. In the words of Craig from Craigslist they are 'free as in free speech'.

☑ DECENT

While few are outright moral crusades, all have some basic values locked in, that any reasonable human being would recognise as being decent. The arbiter of all decent values being 'is this for the common good of humanity?'

☑ DISARMING

These are not (or very few are) activist challenges, mini revolutions against the status quo. Rather they are a peaceful, flourishing development of today's systems. They tend to meet other parts of society in a spirit of co-operation not criticism.

☑ DECELERATING

Against all the urgency and sense of panic felt by those who have realised the dire straits we are in, the co-operative networks are about relaxing and having a longer view, taking the speed out of society. They aren't about slamming on the brakes, they are about getting off the bus.

☑ DURABLE

There is a different mindset involved in seeking solutions that are built to last. One of caution and observation – being determined to make the right move because it needs to stand the test of time.

☑ DEVOLVED OWNERSHIP

It may be a distant goal, but I tend to think that the legacy of any decent system would ultimately include it belonging to the people who build, work in or buy from it. That seems only fair.

ACKNOWLEDGEMENTS

A SPECIAL THANK YOU to all those who helped with comments and suggestions at various stages of this book: Aladin, Dan Burgess, Robert Colwell, Tom Crompton, Gavin Crouch, Kath Dewar, Dale Dickins, Ed Gillespie, Tamara Giltsoff, Vinod Khosla, Peter Korchnak, Paul Macfarlane, Jamie Mitchell, Jules Peck, Harry Ram, Lucy Starbuck, Ian Tennant, Matt Ward.

Thanks too to all the people who have been in the stream of conversations which led to this book and are as much its authors as I am. Thanks too to the many sources, resources, blogs and tweeple who have kept me informed.

Thanks to Piers Fawkes and Dan Gould at PSFK for having the vision and the patience to host our online 'crowdsourced' collaborative editing experiment.

Thanks to Claire Plimmer, my ceaselessly amazing editor. And to Nick Mannion, Melissa Cox, Michaela Fay, Jo Golesworthy, Julia Lampam, Viv Wickham and the rest of the team at Wiley for all their ideas, support and enthusiasm.

Thanks to Laura, Charlotte and Sophie of Thomas.Matthews for the design.

And finally huge thanks, gratitude and respect to all those whose inspiring examples, thoughts and insights I have featured in this book and to all the people who are out there co-operating and changing the world for the common good. Including my collaborators in Tweehive, EOS, Coin, We20.

REFERENCES

[1] http://en.wikipedia.org/wiki/Three_Monks

[2] http://climateprogress.org/2009/09/12/
nicholas-stern-china-co2-ghg-emissions-per-capita/

[3] http://www.stanforddaily.com/cgi-bin/?p=1386

[4] http://www.timesonline.co.uk/tol/news/world/us_and_americas/
article6725588.ece

[5] http://www.un-documents.net/wced-ocf.htm

[6] http://www.amazon.co.uk/Social-Entrepreneurship-Models-
Sustainable-Change/dp/0199283885/ref=sr_1_1?ie=UTF8&s=boo
ks&qid=1254303936&sr=1-1

[7] http://www.tomorrowscompany.com/global%5Cdefault.aspx

[8] http://www.hm-treasury.gov.uk/sternreview_index.htm

[9] http://faculty.babson.edu/krollag/org_site/soc_psych/latane_
bystand.html

[10] http://www.youtube.com/watch?v=KE5YwN4NW5o&feature=pl
ayer_embedded#t=118

[11] http://www.independent.co.uk/news/uk/politics/climate-change-
how-green-is-your-mp-424377.html

[12] http://tigger.uic.edu/∼pdoran/012009_Doran_final.pdf

[13] http://www.kooperation-international.de/en/usa/themes/info/
detail/data/39197/?PHPSESSID=c33269fafb89cb7622d0c5cb8
c6a7

[14] http://www.amazon.co.uk/Last-Generation-Nature-Revenge-
Climate/dp/product-description/1903919886

[15] http://www.amazon.co.uk/Vanishing-Face-Gaia-Final-Warning/
dp/1846141850/ref=sr_1_1?ie=UTF8&s=books&qid=124376917
8&sr=1-1

[16] US National Oceanic and Atmospheric Administration (NOAA)
and the University of Washington in Seattle using the six most
sensitive computer models of the Arctic region. http://www.
independent.co.uk/environment/climate-change/arctic-summer-
may-be-icefree-in-30-years-1662240.html

[17] http://www.scientificblogging.com/news_releases/
researchers_warn_of_a_methane_clathrate_destabilization_time_
bomb_due_to_global_warming

[18] http://people-press.org/report/485/economy-top-policy-priority

[19] http://www.greenbiz.com/stateofgreenbusiness/html

[20] http://www.guardian.co.uk/environment/2009/sep/11/
stern-economic-growth-emissions

[21] http://www.independent.co.uk/environment/climate-change/
big-business-says-addressing-climate-change-rates-very-low-on-
agenda-774648.html

[22] http://www.mentalhealth.org.uk/EasySiteWeb/GatewayLink.
aspx?alId=71270

[23] http://www.ippr.org.uk/pressreleases/?id=2240

[24] http://www.ecoamerica.net/sites/default/files/press/ecoAm_
Climate_Energy_Truths.pdf

[25] http://www.mentalhealth.org.uk/EasySiteWeb/GatewayLink.
aspx?alId=71270

[26] http://www.fastcompany.com/magazine/134/boy-wonder.html

[27] http://www.transitiontowns.org/

[28] http://www.localplanet.ie/index.php?option=com_content&task=v
iew&id=191&Itemid=49

[29] http://www.alternet.org/story/140138/?page=2

[30] http://www.dark-mountain.net/

[31] http://www.telegraph.co.uk/earth/3322329/Philip-Pullman-new-
brand-of-environmentalism.html

[32] http://www.capefarewell.com/diskobay/
artistic-response-to-global-warming/

[33] http://www.wwf.org.uk/filelibrary/pdf/weathercocks_report2.pdf

[34] http://transitionculture.
org/2008/03/21/12-tools-for-transition-no10-how-to-run-an-open-
space-event/

[35] http://climateactioncafe.wordpress.com/

[36] http://eab.sagepub.com/cgi/content/abstract/39/3/416

[37] http://www.channel4.com/news/articles/arts_entertainment/art/sta
rck+challenge+to+fashion+fans/3258882

[38] http://www.ifm.eng.cam.ac.uk/sustainability/projects/mass/
UK_textiles.pdf

[39] http://brandstrategy.wordpress.com/2008/03/06/
exclusive-blog-article-martin-sorrell-calls-for-end-of-super-
consumption-era/

[40] http://www.guardian.co.uk/environment/2009/mar/17/
climate-change-china

[41] http://www.planetark.org/dailynewsstory.cfm/newsid/18176/story.
htm

[42] http://www.theecologist.org/blogs_and_comments/commentators/
other_comments/269633/the_end_of_consumerism.html

[43] http://www.faulkingtruth.com/Articles/GlobalWarning/1024.
html

[44] http://news.bbc.co.uk/1/hi/programmes/breakfast/5163976.stm

[45] http://www.amazon.co.uk/Bowling-Alone-Collapse-American-
Community/dp/0743203046/ref=sr_1_1?ie=UTF8&s=books&qid
=1242902487&sr=1-1

[46] http://www.amazon.co.uk/Sociology-Anthony-Giddens/
dp/074563379X/ref=sr_1_1?ie=UTF8&s=books&qid=124290225
5&sr=1-1

[47] http://www.newscientist.com/article/dn14100-did-hyperactivity-
evolve-as-a-survival-aid-for-nomads.html

[48] https://www.express.co.uk/posts/view/42050

[49] http://www.telegraph.co.uk/finance/newsbysector/
retailandconsumer/3723510/Recession-will-create-a-new-breed-
of-consumer-says-Asda-boss-Andy-Bond.html

[50] http://www.scientificamerican.com/article.
cfm?id=organic-farms-say-wwoof

[51] http://geographyfieldwork.blogspot.com/2005/02/malawi-permaculture-network.html

[52] http://www.liebertpub.com/products/product.aspx?pid=300

[53] http://www.theschooloflife.com/what-the-press-say/independent-on-sunday.aspx

[54] http://www.brc.org.uk/details04.asp?id=1047&kCat=&kData=

[55] http://www.timesonline.co.uk/tol/news/uk/article691423.ece

[56] http://en.wikipedia.org/wiki/Louis_Brandeis

[57] http://www.vanderbilt.edu/vcems/papers/tri.pdf

[58] http://www.theatlantic.com/issues/2000/04/graham.htm

[59] http://en.wikipedia.org/wiki/Poverty

[60] http://www.guardian.co.uk/business/2007/sep/14/fashion.retail

[61] http://www.marxist.com/fashion-victims-textile-workers150399.htm

[62] http://www.opendemocracy.net/theme_7-corporations/article_904.jsp

[63] http://www.newstatesman.com/200412130016.htm

[64] http://www.adamsmith.org/smith/won-b5-c1-article-1-ss3.htm

[65] http://www.opendemocracy.net/theme_7-corporations/article_904.jsp

[66] http://www.nytimes.com/2008/10/12/magazine/12policy-t.html?_r=1&pagewanted=print

[67] http://www.goodwithmoney.co.uk/corp/pdf/ECR_2008_Web.pdf

[68] http://www.ers.usda.gov/Data/FoodConsumption/FoodAvailQueriable.aspx#midForm

[69] http://www.forumforthefuture.org/greenfutures/articles/BigWetFootprints

[70] http://assets.panda.org/downloads/sugarandtheenvironment_fidq.pdf

[71] http://www.washingtonpost.com/wp-dyn/content/article/2008/03/06/AR2008030603294.html

[72] http://www.nytimes.com/2008/10/12/magazine/12policy-t.html?_r=1&pagewanted=print

[73] http://walmartstores.com/Sustainability/9264.aspx?p=9191&sourceid=milestone&ref=

[74] http://www.colostate.edu/depts/sociology/FairTradeResearchGroup/doc/fairtrade.pdf

[75] http://www.maketradefair.com/en/index.
php?file=20092002150848.htm

[76] Source: McGraw Hill Construction (2009). *Green Outlook 2009: Trends Driving Change)* from http://www.usgbc.org/ShowFile.aspx?DocumentID=3340

[77] http://www.worldchanging.com/archives/010013.html

[78] http://www.usgbc.org/ShowFile.aspx?DocumentID=3340.

[79] http://www.cbsnews.com/blogs/2009/04/22/politics/politicalhotsheet/entry4962412.shtml

[80] http://news.bbc.co.uk/1/hi/business/6096084.stm

[81] http://www.chinadialogue.net/article/show/single/en/528

[82] http://www.sd-commission.org.uk/publications/downloads/prosperity_without_growth_report.pdf

[83] http://www.sd-commission.org.uk/publications/downloads/prosperity_without_growth_report.pdf

[84] http://www.newscientist.com/article/mg20026786.100-special-report-why-politicians-dare-not-limit-economic-growth.html

[85] http://www.amazon.co.uk/Upside-Down-Catastrophe-Creativity-Civilisation/dp/0285637940/ref=sr_1_1?ie=UTF8&s=books&qid=1246442243&sr=1-1

[86] http://www.stiglitz-sen-fitoussi.fr/documents/rapport_anglais.pdf

[87] http://www.worldvaluessurvey.org/happinesstrends/

[88] http://www.globalissues.org/article/26/poverty-facts-and-stats

[89] http://www.guardian.co.uk/commentisfree/2008/nov/25/climate-change-carbon-emissions

[90] http://www.amazon.co.uk/Constant-Economy-Build-Stable-Society/dp/1848870671/ref=sr_1_1?ie=UTF8&s=books&qid=1254172391&sr=1-1-spell

[91] http://www.sd-commission.org.uk/publications/downloads/prosperity_without_growth_report.pdf

[92] http://www.business.uts.edu.au/lst/downloads/wp9veal.pdf

[93] http://www.mccombs.utexas.edu/faculty/michael.brandl/main%20page%20items/Kennedy%20on%20GNP.htm

[94] http://ec.europa.eu/environment/nature/biodiversity/economics/index_en.htm

[95] http://www.treehugger.com/files/2008/06/gas-prices-curtail-teenage-cruising.php

[96] http://www.scribd.com/doc/16304689/
BPs-Statistical-Review-of-World-Energy-Full-Report-2009

[97] http://www.bmj.com/cgi/content/extract/323/7317/827

[98] http://www.wto.org/english/news_e/events_e/symp05_e/luke10_e.
ppt

[99] European Business Forum (2003). Interview with Michael Porter,
Copenhagen Business School

[100] http://www.bcorporation.net/about

[101] http://communitychoiceenergy.org/a-whatis.htm

[102] http://archive.co-op.ac.uk/downloadFiles/rochdale_Pioneers_
Rules_1844.pdf

[103] http://www.scientificamerican.com/blog/60-second-science/post.
cfm?id=health-insurers-want-you-to-keep-sm-2009-06-03

[104] http://www.businessinsider.com/companies/craigslist

[105] http://www.philanthropyuk.org/NewsandEvents/Latestnews/
ABigIssuefornewsocialinvestmentfund

[106] http://www.scottlondon.com/interviews/mollison.html

[107] http://news.bbc.co.uk/1/hi/business/2014396.stm

[108] http://www.sustainabilityinstitute.org/pubs/
columns/03.24.03Hamilton.html

[109] http://www.greenpeace.org/international/photosvideos/photos/
close-up-of-the-sun-globally

[110] http://www.monbiot.com/archives/2008/06/10/small-is-bountiful/

[111] http://en.wikipedia.org/wiki/Dead_zone_(ecology)

[112] http://www.amazon.co.uk/Omnivores-Dilemma-Natural-History-
Meals/dp/1594132054/ref=sr_1_2?ie=UTF8&s=books&qid=1254
220246&sr=1-2

[113] http://www.twnside.org.sg/title2/susagri/susagri072.htm

[114] Andre Leu, Organic Farming, Winter 2007, citing Jules Pretty,
2001 Pretty, 2006. http://www.rimisp.org/getdoc.
php?docid=6440

[115] http://us.ft.com/ftgateway/superpage.
ft?news_id=fto042520081750240858

[116] http://www.ft.com/cms/s/0/2e5b2f36-1608-11dd-880a-
0000779fd2ac.html?nclick_check=1

[117] All percentages relate to the original value of the company=100%

[118] http://www.zmag.org/ZSustainers/ZDaily/2000-05/30chomsky. htm

[119] Benkler, Yochai (2006). *The Wealth of Networks: How Social Production Transforms Markets and Freedom.* New Haven, Conn: Yale University Press

[120] http://web.archive.org/web/20070623192027/outsidethemarket. info/intro.htm

[121] http://www.wired.com/culture/culturereviews/magazine/17-06/ nep_newsocialism?currentPage=all

[122] http://www.stewardwood.org/woodland/tree_loss.htm

[123] http://en.wikipedia.org/wiki/ Working_time#Annual_hours_over_eight_centuries

[124] http://www.antithetical.org/restlesswind/plinth/wimguild2.html

[125] http://www.transaction.net/money/cc/cc01.html

[126] http://www.un.org/ecosocdev/geninfo/afrec/vol11no2/women.htm

[127] http://www.vestaldesign.com/blog/2006/07/heineken-beer-bricks/

[128] Moore's Law (named after the Intel co-founder Gordon Moore) predicted that the number of transistors on an inexpensive integrated circuit would roughly double every two years

[129] http://www.planetizen.com/node/35009

[130] http://laptop.org.en/

[131] http://www.independent.co.uk/environment/climate-change/ ancient-skills-could-reverse-global-warming-1055700.html

[132] http://www.youtube.com/watch?v=w_c5g6tXvK8

INDEX